About This Book

As you can probably guess by the title, this book is about developing Wi
Visual C++. The Visual C++ development system is the most sophisticat
for developing applications for Microsoft Windows. The MFC cla
development tools provided by Microsoft are a great collection of tools for Windows programming.

Who Should Read This Book?

This book assumes that you have some knowledge of C++ and Windows programming, and it
also assumes that you are familiar with using the compiler and basic tools that are packaged with
it. However, there's more to producing a robust, well-designed application than knowing the
language syntax. Issues such as good architectural design, code reusability, and class library
design are all important parts of real application design.

Conventions Used in This Book

The examples used in this book follow the development of a Personal Information Manager
called InfoMan. Along the way, steps that might be done differently for other projects are
presented also. You can follow along with a project of your own, or develop InfoMan using the
examples and documents found on the CD.

The following typographic conventions are used in this book:

- ☐ Code lines, commands, statements, variables, and any text you type or see on the
  screen appears in a computer typeface.

- ☐ Placeholders in syntax descriptions appear in an *italic computer* typeface. Replace the
  placeholder with the actual filename, parameter, or whatever element it represents.

- ☐ *Italics* highlight technical terms when they first appear in the text and are sometimes
  used to emphasize important points.

Within each chapter you will encounter several icon boxes:

Note: Here you can find supplementary information that doesn't fit within the
structure of the current chapter.

Textbook Tip: Here you can find formal methods and guidance. For example:

The syntax of the InStr function is

InStr(*start,search_string,find_string*)

Developer's Tip: Here you will find hints, descriptions, and rules of thumb that
are gleaned from experience rather than formal learning. For example:

Punching out your customers will have a detrimental effect on your future income.

Showstopper: Look here for warnings and cautions about things to watch out for
or avoid. For example:

If you stick the CD-ROM in the floppy-disk drive, you will probably break the
disk drive.

At the end of each chapter are two special sections. "Modification Notes" describes the
differences you would expect to apply to the process if you were modifying an existing
application instead of creating one from scratch. "Debugging the Process" describes possible
problems to avoid at this stage of the design, and it also indicates some solutions.

Develop
a Professional
Visual C++™
Application

in 21 Days

Develop a Professional Visual C++™ Application in 21 Days

Mickey Williams

SAMS
PUBLISHING

201 West 103rd Street
Indianapolis, Indiana 46290

For my wife René, my favorite skiing partner and book reviewer.

Copyright © 1995 by Sams Publishing

FIRST EDITION

International Standard Book Number: 0-672-30593-3

Library of Congress Catalog Card Number: 94-69272

98 97 96 95   4 3 2 1

Interpretation of the printing code: the rightmost double-digit number is the year of the book's printing; the rightmost single-digit, the number of the book's printing. For example, a printing code of 95-1 shows that the first printing of the book occurred in 1995.

Composed in AGaramond and MCPdigital by Macmillan Computer Publishing

Printed in the United States of America

Trademarks

Overview

Contents

Acknowledgments

It's difficult to know where to start thanking people for the help and support I've received over the past few months.

Great thanks go to everyone at SAMS, including Chris Denny, who convinced me to take on the project in the beginning, and my development editors, Todd Bumbalough and Brad Jones, who gave me great advice and guidance on the book's content. Kim Spilker helped me put together all of the sample code and documents on the accompanying CD. Technical reviewer Jeff Perkins helped the book along greatly by identifying some key areas that needed improvement. Tonya Simpson did a fantastic job of editing my initial manuscript into the book you have in your hands. Finally, David Bradford, the production editor, guided me through the author-review process and helped me create a final manuscript that I'm really happy with.

A big thank you also goes to Ed Guy, who wrote the HELLLP! online help tool that's included on the CD. Also thanks to Mike Ward from Microsoft, who helped me during the final stages of the Visual C++ beta. To Bob O'Brian and the rest of the people at Nu-Mega: thanks for writing BoundsChecker, and thanks again for using overnight delivery.

I also could not have written this book without a lot of help at work. My managers, supervisors, and friends provided the support and input I needed while I was writing this book. They have all participated in some way—either by teaching me some part of the development process, by discussing class-library-design issues, or maybe by answering a question about Windows design. In no particular order: Bo Stenlund, Roger Liu, Farnoosh Manouchehri, Cuyler Buckwalter, Peter Claesson, Ayling Hsu, and Joseph Wu— thanks, I couldn't have done it without you.

And the final thanks goes to my wife, René, who not only has a real job as a manager in Marketing but somehow also found time to single-handedly run the household, take care of our daughter, and review my manuscript. We'll go to Banff next year, I promise.

About the Author

Mickey Williams works as a member of the Engineering staff for Ericsson, Incorporated, in Cypress, California. His primary duties currently include developing software for Ericsson's MD110 PBX and other platforms. Mickey has held positions in Marketing, Development, and Support. His interests include intelligent user interfaces, large system development, and class-library design. Mickey received his B.S.C.S. Magna Cum Laude from National University and is a member of the Association for Computing Machinery. He lives in Laguna Hills, California, with his wife René and daughter Alexandria.

Introduction

As you can probably guess by the title, this book is about developing professional Windows applications using Visual C++. The Visual C++ Development System is the most sophisticated environment available for developing applications for Microsoft Windows. The MFC class library and the other development tools provided by Microsoft are a great collection of tools for Windows programming.

However, it takes more than just good tools to develop a professional Windows application. When, like most people, you start learning to program with a new language or develop for a new platform, you probably go through two phases in the learning process:

☐ During the first phase, you are unfamiliar with the language or environment (or both). Most of your time is spent learning about the language syntax, or learning basic information about the environment.

☐ The next phase of the learning process involves applying the knowledge gained in the first learning phase in order to produce a real, working application. This phase may involve learning from other developers, looking at other developers' source code, or learning by experience. This part of the learning process has always taken much longer than the first part.

The Visual C++ compiler and its included tools help make the first step in this process much simpler for today's Windows programmers than it has been in the recent past. It is now possible, using AppWizard, for a beginning Windows programmer to write the skeleton of a Windows program—including toolbars, status bars, help files, and menus—in a few minutes.

The purpose of this book is to help you work through the second part of the learning process, as you become an experienced Windows programmer. This book assumes that you have the basic knowledge of programming under Windows using Visual C++. This book will help you apply your knowledge of Visual C++ and develop a real, fully functional Windows application.

Who Should Read This Book?

This book assumes that you have some knowledge of C++ and Windows programming, and it also assumes that you are familiar with using the compiler and basic tools that are packaged with it. However, developing an application is more than just programming. There's more to producing a robust, well-designed application than knowing the language syntax. Issues such as good architectural design, code reusability, and class-library design are all important parts of real application design.

More important than your level of C++ or Windows knowledge, you should have an interest in learning the process that is used to develop a professional C++ application. This book helps you take an application from the initial idea stage all the way through to its release. If you have an idea that you would like to turn into a real application, this book is for you. But don't worry—if you don't have an application of your own, an example application is provided on the CD-ROM that accompanies this book.

Conventions Used in This Book

The examples used in this book follow the development of a Personal Information Manager called InfoMan. Along the way, steps that might be done differently for other projects are presented also. You can follow along with a project of your own, or develop InfoMan using the examples and documents found on the CD.

The book and its text have been formatted so that it is easy to use and apply the information inside. Most text is formatted exactly as it appears here in this paragraph. Occasionally, a word or phrase may have additional formatting, to give emphasis in the following ways:

- ☐ Code lines, commands, statements, variables, and any text you type or see on the screen appears in a `computer` typeface.

- ☐ Placeholders in syntax descriptions appear in an `italic computer` typeface. Replace the placeholder with the actual filename, parameter, or whatever element it represents.

- ☐ *Italics* highlight technical terms when they first appear in the text and are sometimes used to emphasize important points.

Within each chapter you will encounter several icon boxes, which give additional information or help you pinpoint the current topic's direction:

Note: Here you can find supplementary information that doesn't fit within the structure of the current chapter.

Textbook Tip: Here you can find formal methods and guidance.
For example:

The syntax of the InStr function is

`InStr(start,search_string,find_string)`

 **Developer's Tip:** Here you will find hints, descriptions, and rules of thumb that are gleaned from experience rather than formal learning. For example:

Punching out your customers will have a detrimental effect on your future income.

 **Showstopper:** Look here for warnings and cautions about things to watch out for or avoid. For example:

If you stick the CD-ROM in the floppy disk drive, you will probably break the disk drive.

At the end of each chapter are two special sections. "Modification Notes" describes the differences you would expect to apply to the process if you were modifying an existing application instead of creating one from scratch. "Debugging the Process" describes possible problems to watch out for at this stage of the design and indicates some solutions.

Design and Analysis

Part I requires four days to complete. These four days will discuss how to analyze the requirements and create a detailed design for a Windows application. The topics covered in Part I include the following:

- [ ] Collecting and documenting requirements
- [ ] Test planning
- [ ] Risk analysis
- [ ] Object-oriented design using Booch notation
- [ ] Low-level design of C++ classes

Requirements Analysis

Today, you'll learn how to collect the requirements for a software project. This is where it all starts, and is in many ways the most important part of the entire process.

The first thing you'll learn is the method that you'll use to develop a sample project. Several development methods are introduced today, including the waterfall model, prototyping, and iteration. Prototyping and iteration will be used throughout the book, so you need to pay close attention when they are introduced.

Next, you'll start collecting requirements for the sample project. The process begins when the marketing department sends you some e-mail about a new product.

Later in the day, there's a large section that talks specifically about collecting the requirements for user interfaces. As part of collecting the user-interface requirements, you will create paper mock-ups, or prototypes, of the user interface.

Note: The CD included with this book contains all of the software developed for the project presented in this book, as well as sample documents that you can use along the way to document the different development steps.

The documents are created using Word for Windows. Of course, Word for Windows isn't necessary for Windows development, it's just a very good word processor. Every document also will have a plain-text version with a TXT extension. The versions that are in Word format will have a DOC or DOT file extension.

The Waterfall Model

The traditional phases of software development are analysis, design, coding, integration, testing and debugging, and release. Each of these phases has a well-established place in relation to the other phases, so they are often diagrammed as shown in Figure 1.1. This relationship is referred to as the *waterfall model*.

This development model is in widespread use and has been used to build large software projects for the past few decades. However, projects with the following characteristics will probably have difficulty applying the waterfall model:

- ☐ **Projects where the requirements aren't completely known during analysis.** The waterfall model is best suited to projects where the requirements are completely known. If you have to return to the analysis phase, the model tends to fall apart.

- ☐ **Projects where the requirements might change.** If the user's needs often change during a period shorter than the development cycle, it will be difficult to use the waterfall model.

Figure 1.1.
Relationships between phases in the waterfall model.

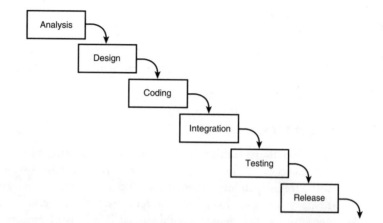

- ☐ **Projects that require a great deal of work during one of the phases.** In a large organization, this bogs the project down in one phase.
- ☐ **Projects that will require new research.** When new research and development is required, often the performance or characteristics of the final product cannot be predicted. This does not follow the structure of the waterfall model, where the performance of the final product is planned during the analysis and design phase.

In order to address these problems, many developers don't strictly adhere to the waterfall model, and instead use some mixture of prototyping and iteration to help develop requirements or test early design options. Other developers don't use the waterfall model at all, and use prototyping and iteration exclusively throughout the entire development process.

Understanding Prototyping

Prototyping is building a model that is a subset of a proposed design. You will want to use prototypes because it is easier to build a quick, semifunctional version of a product than it is to build a full, working product. You can then use the prototype to get feedback about a proposed design. Feedback from the prototype can be used to inexpensively test the suitability of the full design.

Developer's Tip: Always develop a prototype, even if it's on paper. The alternative approach used in the classic waterfall model is to develop a product and unleash it on the world. Unfortunately, it can be very expensive to modify a product after it has been released.

Later today, you'll build paper prototypes of the user interface that you'll use to get feedback from the customer. On Day 6, "Iteration and Prototyping," you will develop a partially working model of part of the user interface. Prototyping can be done at every stage of an application's development. You can prototype to test requirements, designs, and even your application's packaging.

Iteration

Iteration is the repeating of one part, or a series of parts, of the design process. For example, when you collect the requirements from the user, you may have several meetings with them, and after each meeting you may generate a new version of the requirements. You will probably need to refine each new version of the requirements, and each version also is one step closer to the final version. You may have to build several iterations of prototypes when you are developing prototypes. Each new iteration will be closer to the final version that is eventually developed. The build–check–iterate cycle is shown in Figure 1.2.

Figure 1.2.
Iteration has a build–check–iterate cycle.

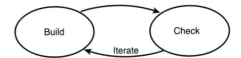

Iteration can be applied to other phases of the development cycle. For example, on Day 6 you'll learn how to use iteration to break up the coding phases into well-defined segments, each of which will become an executable program. Each iteration can be integrated and tested separately from the other parts.

Note: You will use iteration throughout the development of a project and will see how it is used to refine each phase of development.

What are Requirements?

Requirements are the expectations that a customer has about the software you've been asked to develop. The customer in this case is the person who decides that development will start. If you're a consultant, it's usually obvious who your customer is. If you're working for a large company developing shrink-wrapped software, your customer may be the marketing department.

Requirements are the road map that tells you where the customer wants to go with the finished product. There's an old saying, "If you don't know where you're going, all roads take you there."

If you cannot tell from the customer's requirements how the finished product will work, you'll never develop software that meets the requirements.

Requirements Analysis

The process of collecting and assessing requirements for a project is known as Requirements Analysis. This is a very important part of the project development process, but it's often given too little emphasis. If this phase of a project is incomplete or skimmed over, serious problems that may be difficult (or even impossible) to correct can occur later in the project.

For example, an error during the testing phase might let a potential error be released to an end user. Because not all test cases are faulty, the chances that a single mistake during testing could cause a significant failure is relatively small. Hopefully, some of these types of errors are discovered during early field testing. This topic is covered on Day 18, "System-Level and Alpha Testing," and Day 19, "Beta Testing."

An error that occurs during the actual coding phase is likely to cause a fault that is more costly than a testing error. However, this type of fault is easily detected and corrected.

Errors that occur during a design phase are more difficult to detect because test plans will probably be written "as designed." Design errors can be quite expensive because they can lead to large amounts of redesigning, recoding, and retesting.

By far, the worst errors are introduced during the analysis phase. A faulty analysis of the customer's requirements will simply lead to the development of the wrong product. Also, the problem may not be detected until close to the end of the project.

Showstopper: It's not unusual for large projects to be canceled if major faults are found in the requirements analysis late in the development cycle.

Setting Up Requirements

Requirements are the initial step in the software development process. Although it is possible to write simple software programs without taking the time to completely analyze the requirements, larger projects are impossible to complete without a detailed look at the project requirements.

The requirements for a software project will almost always start out as a list of items to be included in the project, something that can best be described as a wish list. The InfoMan sample project covered in this book starts with an electronic message from the marketing department, shown next, asking for an investigation to start on a new project. As is usually the case, there is not enough information in the initial requirements to develop a project.

```
To: M.Williams, Development
From: Anthony M. Peters, Marketing
Hi Guys
For our next product, I'd like us to offer a Personal Information
Manager (PIM), called InfoMan. The product should be ready to
market in 60 days, and have the following features:
    - It should be easy to use.
    - A manager for to-do lists.
    - A Rolodex-style database of names or addresses for contact
      management.
    - A calendar-based appointment manager.
    - It would be nice to be able to print out the database on
      perforated Rolodex label paper, using any MS-Windows
      compatible printer.
    - Several different databases "on-line" at once.
    - On-line help.
    - Also, we've been seeing a lot of those tab-control things
      recently, can you work those in somewhere?
We want to be able to offer the product for $49.95, so don't spend
too much time on it. If you have any questions, call Phil or
myself.
Thanks
Tony
P.S. Please have a project plan and schedule for our next staff
meeting.
```

The initial set of requirements for many projects starts out looking like the preceding electronic message. Tony's message has all the signs of a bad set of requirements: some of the requirements are ambiguous, some are unstated, and some of the information in the electronic message is irrelevant.

Showstopper: Don't fall into the trap of trying to use requirements that are inadequate. It's natural to want to solve a problem, and sometimes there's a tendency, especially at the start of a new project, to just "get started."

If this sounds like you, remember that requirements analysis *is* "getting started." Don't just take off running in a convenient direction. Take a deep breath, sit down, and find out where the customer wants you to go.

1

Ambiguous Requirements

The first problem with the requirements stated in the memo is that they are ambiguous. If you were to attempt to develop a software project based on them, the chances of developing the product that the marketing department has in mind are about zero.

A good way to detect an ambiguous requirement is to ask yourself, "Is this requirement testable?" Table 1.1 lists some of the sample requirements for the project that was started with the previous electronic message. The table also indicates whether or not each requirement is ambiguous.

Table 1.1. Some examples of ambiguous and nonambiguous requirements.

Requirement	Ambiguous?
Include a Calendar Manager	Ambiguous: The functions that make up a Calendar Manager should be spelled out.
The program should be easy to use	Ambiguous: This one will be covered in the section "Using Focus Groups", later today.
The program should manage to-do lists	Ambiguous: The data that make up a to-do list and the functions used to manage the list should be specified.
Include "...those tab-control things"	Ambiguous: More information is needed about exactly how these controls should function.

Obviously, before this project can begin, some work needs to be done on the requirements.

Note: This project will be used throughout the book and is called the InfoMan project.

Unstated Requirement

In virtually every project there are requirements that are initially unstated. As the developer, you are responsible for determining all of the requirements, even if they aren't immediately obvious. In the example project, there are at least two unstated requirements:

☐ **For what platform must the system be developed?**
InfoMan should run on some version of Microsoft Windows.

☐ **What should be printed?**
All of the databases should be printable; printing on Rolodex-style tabs is an extra requirement for the contact manager.

You can read between the lines and assume that the project should target Microsoft Windows, because MS-Windows-compatible printers were specified in one of the requirements. However, the choice of an operating system should not be left up to an assumption made by reading between the lines of an e-mail message.

Textbook Tip: Unstated requirements usually lead to assumptions. Whenever you find yourself making an assumption about anything, document it, and notify anyone affected by your assumption.

For example, the assumption in the example is that the InfoMan project should target Microsoft Windows. This assumption should result in immediate feedback to the person originating the requirements. Furthermore, this sort of information should be part of the written software requirements, which will be covered in the section "Documenting Requirements" later today.

More information about documenting assumptions made during the coding phase is covered on Day 5, "Coding Standards and Work Methods."

Another unstated requirement within the example covers the printing capabilities. One of the three management areas of InfoMan is a contact manager that tracks names and addresses. There is a requirement that the contact manager print out its database in a format that can fit on perforated Rolodex labels, but nothing is mentioned for the other two managers. The assumption here is that probably there are printing requirements for the calendar and to-do list, but that should be verified.

Unstated requirements are to software projects as icebergs were to the *Titanic*. It's not the visible requirements that cause the damage; the headaches come from those that are lurking under the surface.

Collecting Requirements

How can you collect good requirements that are free from all these problems? One way is to use an iterative method to collect requirements. Figure 1.3 shows the typical iterations you can follow when you are collecting requirements for a software project.

Figure 1.3.
The iterations used when
collecting requirements.

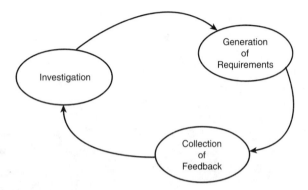

On a large project, there will be a person charged with helping the customer (the Marketing department, in the case of InfoMan) develop a set of specific requirements for the software project. Because InfoMan is a fairly small project, this work would probably be done by one of the development staff. In any case, the work of collecting the requirements is the same.

Using InfoMan as an example, the first step in collecting the requirements is to try to develop them more fully. One way to do this is by using scenarios, discussed next, and by building paper prototypes of your proposed user interface.

Using Scenarios

When you are dealing with a complicated set of requirements, it is sometimes helpful to create a scenario to help the customer or group talk about how a proposed system should work. A *scenario* is a script that can be used to demonstrate the way a person might use the proposed system to carry out a certain task. The process of creating a scenario can help identify unstated requirements and clear up ambiguous requirements.

Discussion about a scenario tends to move very quickly. In fact, the major problem with scenarios is recording all of the information that's generated. There are a few different ways to record a scenario:

☐ Set up a video camera in the corner of the room. This approach has the benefit of not requiring much interaction during the meeting, and it also helps capture visual information from the discussion. Unfortunately, some people may be intimidated by the camera, and it may be a large expense if a video camera isn't available.

☐ Record the meeting on audio tape. This method may be cheaper than the video approach, but some detail is lost because only audio is recorded.

☐ Have someone in the meeting take notes. If you use this method, try to limit the recorder's participation in the meeting. The recorder will be busy enough just taking notes. If the meeting has to slow down so that the recorder can participate and take notes, it won't be as effective.

Figure 1.4 shows a typical room used to develop a scenario. A whiteboard is available for sketching user interface ideas. The video camera is set up in the corner, so that it can record the participants and the whiteboard.

Figure 1.4.

A typical meeting room used to develop scenarios.

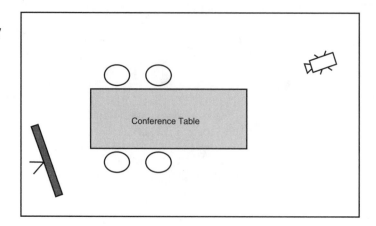

Using InfoMan as an example, one scenario might have the group talk about creating a new to-do list. During the discussion, specific requirements can be identified, and assumptions and unstated requirements brought out into the open. A typical discussion follows:

> **Tony:** So you start up the Task Manager.
>
> **Mickey:** How?
>
> **Tony:** I guess there's a menu, and...
>
> **Phil:** Or a toolbar—can you make one of those dockable toolbars?
>
> **Mickey:** Yep, that comes for free with MFC 3.0.
>
> **Tony:** So the Task Manager comes up.
>
> **Phil:** Does it ask you for the filename or anything?
>
> **Mickey:** No, not yet, it's better if you let the user work with a new to-do list, then save later...
>
> **Phil:** Okay, that's a programming thing. You worry about it.
>
> **Mickey:** So what's in a task? The name, the date...
>
> **Phil:** Well, do we need a name?
>
> **Tony:** Either that or we need to show the whole task somehow.
>
> **Phil:** Can you use a list of tasks?
>
> **Mickey:** If the tasks don't have names, the list can get pretty big.
>
> **Tony**: Maybe we can have task slogans that are displayed instead.

The discussion continues like this until the idea of opening and creating a to-do list has been covered in enough detail. How much is enough? It depends on the project, but nobody should leave the meeting with unanswered questions about any of the scenarios.

Again using the example of InfoMan, the following scenarios might be identified:

- ☐ Printing each document type
- ☐ Starting InfoMan and marking a task in the to-do list as completed
- ☐ Switch between views while using the contact manager
- ☐ With several different files open and minimized, selecting one and working with it

After you've collected all of the scenarios, examine them and look for ambiguous or unstated requirements. If there are some areas that still need to be refined, repeat the process. That's what iteration is all about.

Controlling the Number of Iterations

If this is your first exposure to using iteration during development, you're probably worried about handling the iterations. How do you know how many iterations are needed? When you are iterating, it is dangerous to not stay focused on the goal at the end of the iterations. For today, the goal is to develop a set of requirements for InfoMan. If you allow extra functionality to be defined at every iteration, there is no guarantee that you will ever complete the process.

User-Interface Requirements

The user interface brings up some extra issues. To the end user, the user interface is the system. Communication, whether it's between two people or between a person and a machine, depends on the ability to make a mental "connection." If that connection doesn't happen, the communication will suffer. For this reason, good user-interface design is critical. Fortunately, Visual C++ has some features that can be used to help specify the user interface.

Defining the User Interface

When scenarios are being developed, at least some user-interface ideas will probably be presented. Those ideas can form the starting point for the user interface. The first step in defining your interfaces is to decide the number of interfaces that need to be developed. Remember, this will be an iterative process, so you don't need an accurate number (although it's a good idea to at least be close).

InfoMan has three sets of user interfaces. Each set of interfaces corresponds to the views that are associated with each document type.

Creating Paper Prototypes

Earlier, a prototype was defined as a model with less functionality than the fully functioning product. For a user interface, the ultimate in cheap prototypes is the paper prototype, whether it's a sketch on a piece of paper or a screen shot of the proposed user interface.

A simple way to start modeling a user-interface design is to use a pencil and paper. Afterwards, you can refine your paper prototype by organizing the user interface using the dialog editor included with Visual C++. Figure 1.5 shows the dialog editor being used to create part of the to-do list view.

Figure 1.5.

Using the dialog editor to create a paper prototype.

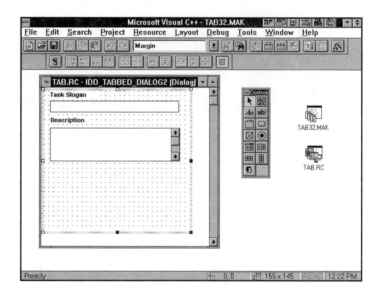

Capture a screen shot of the dialog editor running in test mode. Use Microsoft Paintbrush to help edit the screen shots. If you're planning to use effects or controls that can't be shown using the dialog editor, just edit the screen shot the way you like it. Figure 1.6 shows a reedited version of the to-do list that demonstrates the tab controls.

The paper prototypes for InfoMan are located in the \CHAP1\PROTO\SET1 directory on the accompanying CD. The screen shots are in the PCX PCPaintbrush format.

Using Focus Groups

After all of the screen shots have been edited, they should be evaluated. One way to do that is to use a focus group. Focus groups are made up of users that get together to discuss issues about a product. The focus group may be made up of users of previous products, or they may be potential users of the product that is being developed. It is important that the focus group have an interest in helping you.

Figure 1.6.
*A paper prototype of the
to-do list after editing.*

Using a paper prototype is an ideal way to present a proposed interface to a focus group. You can copy or pass around the screen shots or print them on transparencies and project them. Compare this to trying to get a dozen users to cluster around a computer screen.

Invite comments from the focus group about the proposed interfaces. Show them the screen shots and walk through some of the scenarios that were developed earlier. Comments from actual users like those found in focus groups can be invaluable in finding usability problems early. For example, when the screen shots from InfoMan were shown to some prospective users, one user immediately asked how a to-do item was added or deleted. This is an example of a usability problem that was caught before it caused any problems. Figure 1.7 shows the to-do list with its newly added Add and Delete buttons. The reedited versions of the paper prototypes are in the \CHAP1\PROTO\SET2 directory on the CD.

Figure 1.7.
*The to-do list with added
controls.*

Showstopper: One possible problem with a focus group is that it must be managed. There should be a moderator or facilitator who helps keep the meeting on track. Otherwise, your focus group could easily become side-tracked and focus on other issues.

Documenting Requirements

As the InfoMan project is developed, you'll notice that you create a lot of documentation. Every phase of InfoMan's development has at least one document that is produced. Sometimes (not today), you'll note that some projects can skip a phase, or maybe create an informal document.

You will refer to the system requirements that are written down today throughout the development process. Take the extra time required to document the system requirements well. The following are a few ways to use the system requirements:

- [ ] **It will be used for the high-level and low-level design.** This is probably the most obvious use. This step is covered on Day 2, "System Design," and Day 3, "Test Planning."

- [ ] **The system requirements can be used to start developing test plans.** In fact, some organizations stop right here, developing a functional test plan that will be used to test the final product.

- [ ] **The documents can be used later if the product needs to be modified.** See the "Modification Notes" section at the end of this chapter for more details.

Choosing a Structure for the System Requirements

When you are formatting the system requirements, keep a few basic tips in mind:

- [ ] The document will probably be updated, even during this development cycle.

- [ ] The document may be read by people who are not familiar with all of the technical terms used, so include a glossary.

- [ ] The requirements documents will be used for reference; structure them so that the various parts of the design are easily found.

The format you choose for the requirements document depends on the project. Some projects will have special requirement areas that justify a different format. Whichever format you choose, remember to keep it clear and flexible.

The format chosen for the InfoMan system requirements has the following outline:

- [ ] **Scope.** This section talks about the overall project. It discusses what is included, and also what is not included in the requirements document. Keep this section short. It should only be a document overview.

- [ ] **Project Constraints**. This section should list any special limitations on the overall project. If the project must be completed in a certain time frame or under a certain cost, state it here.

- [ ] **Glossary.** This is an explanation of any technical terms or concepts that are used in the rest of the document.

- [ ] **Functional Requirements.** This section is subdivided into smaller sections that each discuss a single high-level part of the requirements. For InfoMan, the three different management areas each have their own subsection.

- [ ] **Target Platform.** This section focuses on the target environment for your application, if known. If the platform hasn't been decided yet, list the requirements for the platform (if any).

- [ ] **User Interface.** This section describes the user interface. Copies of the paper prototypes should be included in this section.

Reviewing the System Requirements

Studies have shown that critical reviews are a very good way to discover problems during software development. These reviews should be attended by the person developing the requirements, as well as by the customer or someone that represents the customer. The size of the review team depends on the complexity of the project. If you are a single developer and you're dealing with a single customer, the review team has two members. On the other hand, large complex projects should have representatives from all the teams that are involved in the development of the project.

Textbook Tip: Everything that is produced during the development of InfoMan will be reviewed. There are several big advantages to reviewing all of the documents, the code, and test results:

- [ ] The review team is an extra set of eyes that can help catch errors that may otherwise be missed by a single person.

- [ ] Review-team members may be experts in some other part of the development process, and may point out potential problems that would otherwise be overlooked. For example, if your project is developed by a team, include in the requirements review the persons responsible for testing. They can help you find requirements that aren't testable.

> ☐ The review process can be used as an information-sharing tool. If a single person works on the software requirements and decides that the requirements are complete, this means one person in the organization understands the requirements. Because this information must be distributed to other people on the project, why not do it in a way that can help improve the quality of the project?

Modification Notes

Each day will have a "Modification Notes" section like this one, which talks about the issues that are involved with modifying an existing project. If the project is already in use, try to establish a focus group if one doesn't exist already. The focus group can help evaluate prototypes and suggest features for new releases.

If you are modifying an existing project, it's a good practice to follow the documentation style that was used for the existing documents whenever possible. Also, keep in mind that the product's user interface should remain consistent, unless the user interface is changing as part of your modification. The existing product may already have some existing user interface elements that you can capture and edit to create paper prototypes.

Debugging the Process

Each day also has a section like this, which talks about some common problems that pop up.

Spending Too Much Time on Detailed Prototypes

Don't spend too much time developing complicated prototypes during this stage of the project. The purpose of the prototype during the requirements phase is to help illustrate your ideas. Prototypes that grow too complicated early in the process have a tendency to take on lives of their own.

As a rule of thumb, always leave your prototype missing something. If it works perfectly, you are spending too much time on it.

What if the Focus Group Hates Your Prototype?

Congratulations! You've done a great job. You've used a tool and discovered a problem before it escaped into the real world. The first thing to do is always thank the focus group for its feedback. You'll want to use them again for the next design.

What didn't the focus group like? Change it; work with them. One of the advantages to using paper prototypes is that they are fairly easy to modify. Depending on the changes required, you might be able to make changes during a break and re-present the prototype.

2

System Design

Now that you've nailed down the requirements, the system design should be fairly straightforward. Today you investigate the system-level design of InfoMan. The following topics are covered:

- Feasibility studies and risk analysis, using InfoMan as an example
- Booch notation, a method of describing an object-oriented design
- A brief overview of the MFC Document/View architecture, for those of you who might be a little fuzzy on the subject
- How to break the system design of your project down into some candidate classes and try to describe their relationships
- How to take the first cut at a schedule for the rest of the projects development

Textbook Tip: The purpose of system design is to provide a high-level view of the different components that are planned for the system. As part of this process you should produce a list of the larger, "most influential" classes.

Part of considering how your classes will interact with each other is to assign them names and to start identifying interfaces that classes will use for communication. But remember, you're just *thinking* about the classes, not coding them.

Part of the system design also will document the different responsibilities for the identified objects, as well as the planned interactions between them.

The system-design phase is also a good time to start evaluating third-party products that might be available. For example, there are a large number of OLE custom-control vendors offering controls that provide advanced functionality for a relatively small cost.

Performing a Feasibility and Risk Analysis

As soon as the requirements for a project are assembled, two questions are asked by the persons requesting the work:

- Can you develop it?
- When can we have it?

Of these two questions, the most important one is the first. If this question isn't asked, you should ask it yourself. Before you answer, you need to carry out these two steps:

☐ A risk analysis, in which you identify project risks

☐ A feasibility study, in which you put the risks and other factors together so that you can make a decision about continuing with development

Developer's Tip: It's very important that you do a risk analysis at this stage. For many projects, the analysis may be very simple; for others, the analysis may be very in-depth. If you start the schedule before the risk analysis, you are denying yourself a tool that can be used to create a more reliable schedule.

Similarly, the risk analysis can help you identify problems with allocating resources, which includes everything from equipment and developers to raw supplies for packaging. The risk analysis can also help identify any complexities that can impact the system design. Hidden complexity is a real problem for many software projects. Designs that are overly ambitious, have too many dependencies, or rely on un-proven technology are all at risk due to their complexity.

Even if you plan to perform another risk analysis later in the project, do one now; it might save you a lot of time later.

What Is Risk Analysis?

A *risk analysis* looks at all of the visible risks that are associated with a project. Many organizations will run risk analyses several times during a project as it matures. Do a risk analysis for InfoMan now as part of the system-design process to help determine the feasibility of the project. On Day 3, "Test Planning," you will use risk analysis to select test cases.

A risk analysis examines two factors for each possible point of failure in a design:

☐ How likely is this failure?

☐ If it fails, what are the consequences?

For most software projects, the areas of risk fall into three main categories, as shown in Table 2.1.

Table 2.1. Areas of risk in a typical software project.

Risk Area	Examples
Resources	Training issues, quantity of resources, equipment needs
Dependencies	Reliance on outside forces
Complexity	The number of interfaces, changing requirements

Resources

An example of a resource risk is the depth of talent in the programming team. If there are no developers with in-depth experience designing controls, that part of the project is at risk (unless the existing developers are trained, or new developers are hired).

The developer creating the controls for InfoMan has experience with custom controls on similar projects, so the risk for this item is low.

Another example is the number of test or design stations that are available. If you have two PCs and you use one of them for remote debugging while you develop your code, you'll need extra equipment if you plan to have extra help developing your application.

Dependencies

In terms of risk, a dependency occurs when you rely on an event or an input that is outside of your control. External dependencies can occur if you are waiting for a cooperating product to be developed by a supplier.

Nothing in InfoMan depends on outside groups. In the real world, however, these dependencies are everywhere. Some examples of dependencies include the following:

- [ ] The XYZ Widget company has promised to have a Win32 version of their calendar control by next month. However, they've always been late in the past. If you are planning to use their control, then there is a strong risk associated with this dependency.
- [ ] Alex, your control development ace programmer, is currently finishing up another project that's behind schedule already. The other project has a higher priority than yours, and Alex must finish that work before she can start on your project. This is an example of an internal dependency. Even though it is technically within your organization, you may still have very little control over the situation.
- [ ] The company you work for is developing a new "look" to be used on all products for the coming year. The team developing the design style guide isn't finished but hopes to be done next week.

You must calculate the likelihood of any of these potential risks occurring. For example, the fact that the XYZ Widget company has been consistently late in the past indicates that they will probably be late again.

Complexity

The third type of risk is caused by complexity. Complexity in a software project can be caused by changing or unclear requirements or complicated designs.

Consider the project shown in Figure 2.1. Each circle represents a major subsystem that has already been developed. The square box is the proposed project that will control the other subsystems.

Figure 2.1.
A complex project design.

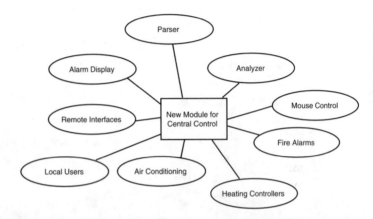

Contrast the design in Figure 2.1 with the project in Figure 2.2. The number of interfaces in the second project are fewer and less complicated. Projects that contain a lot of interface complexity are notorious for hiding problems that become apparent late in the project. You need extra time during the design phase to investigate potential problems in these projects.

Figure 2.2.
A less complex project design.

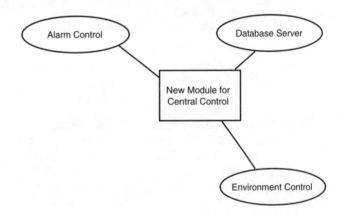

Developer's Tip: In order to identify the risks, it's important to get input from every phase of the project. If the project is developed by a team, get the team together to discuss possible problems or areas that have caused problems previously. One way to have this information handy is to perform a project evaluation at the end of all of your projects. This is covered on Day 21, "Collecting Feedback."

Assigning Weights to Risks

The real benefit from the risk analysis comes after all of the potential problems already described have been identified. Try to find solutions to any risks that have been identified. You should weigh any risks that remain according to the likelihood of the risk being realized. Consider the risk, along with the potential damage that would be caused if the risk does occur. One way to do this without being caught in a numbers game is to place the risks into one of four categories:

- ☐ Risks that are likely to occur and are likely to cause significant problems when they do occur should be assigned the highest weight.

- ☐ Risks that aren't as likely to occur but will have serious consequences when they do occur should receive the next weight.

- ☐ Risks that are more likely to be realized but have lesser consequences are assigned the third category.

- ☐ Risks that are unlikely to materialize and cause small consequences when they do take place are assigned the fourth category.

The relative priority of the second and third categories depends on the project. When you are assigning risk categories, your client may prefer to reduce the total number of risks, and concentrate on bullets one and three from the preceding list. Although this helps concentrate on reducing the total number of risks the project is exposed to, it gives unlikely (but serious) risks a low priority.

Is the Project Feasible?

The next step in the development process is to produce a feasibility report that lists any risks found in either the resource, dependency, or complexity areas, as well as any other risks that have been identified. The feasibility report for InfoMan, found in the \CHAP2\DOCS directory, states that no unsolvable risks were identified.

The purpose of the risk analysis is to bring hidden risks or assumptions out into the open. The most important output from your risk analysis and feasibility report is the identification of these possible risks. Every identified risk should have a solution for avoiding or minimizing that risk. If your risk analysis identifies major risks that cannot be addressed, you should consider stopping the project. Of course, every project is different, and the amount of risk that is acceptable varies from person to person.

Booch Notation

Grady Booch, Chief Scientist for Rational Software, has developed a method for documenting the design of object-oriented programs. Back in the days of punch cards and wire-wrapped core

memory, programmers used flow charts to document how their programs worked. A typical flow chart is shown in Figure 2.3. Flow charts are tedious to create and maintain, and they are a poor way to model an object-oriented design.

Figure 2.3.
A typical flow chart.

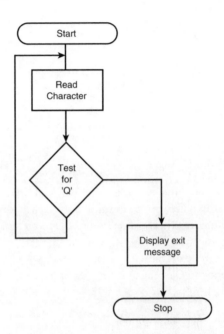

Fortunately, there is a much better way to document your design. Booch notation is well-suited to modeling designs that are meant to be implemented in an object-oriented language, and the resulting documents are easy to both read and maintain. A full discussion of the Booch design methodology is beyond the scope of this book, but you can learn the most common constructions. For the design of most projects, you will use two different types of diagrams: class diagrams and state transition diagrams. Although other diagrams are available in Booch notation, you can express most designs well enough using these two types.

The only problem with Booch notation is that it's very stylized, and it requires either natural artistic ability or a lot of practice. Early versions of Grady Booch's books contained a coupon that entitled you to a plastic Booch notation template to help in your free-hand designs. You also might like to have help drawing some of these figures, so the CD has examples of all of this chapter's design icons in the Microsoft Paintbrush (PCX) format.

Class-Design Templates

The first set of figures used in Booch notation deals with class design. These are the (in)famous "clouds" that you may have seen in other examples, or other books. Without a doubt, these are the hardest of the figures to draw consistently. Somehow, class icons drawn at 3 a.m. never look like the ones drawn first thing in the morning. Figure 2.4 shows all of the class-design icons.

Figure 2.4.

Booch notation class-design icons.

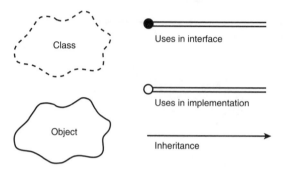

The symbol for a class is a cloud with a dotted edge. When you draw a figure that shows the relationship between a base and derived class, draw an arrow between the two classes, with the arrow pointing in the direction of the base class. In Figure 2.5, the CTask class is derived from CObject.

Figure 2.5.

The CTask class is derived from CObject.

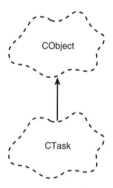

 Note: The Microsoft MFC convention is to use C as the first letter in all of its classes. All of the classes presented as examples in this book also follow this convention.

When you are showing two or more classes that interact with each other in some way, draw a double line between them and label the interaction. In Figure 2.6, the CStudent class "LivesAt" an address, represented by the CAddress class.

Figure 2.6.
The CStudent *class*
"LivesAt" the CAddress
class.

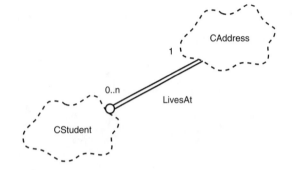

Note that each address may have zero or more students, but each student must have a single address. This is referred to as the cardinality of the relationship. *Cardinality* is defined as the numeric relationship between the classes. If every student has exactly one ID card, and every ID card belongs to one student, they have a 1 to 1 relationship. Likewise, if every student must have an address, and every address must have zero or more students, then there is a 1 to 0..n relationship between the address and student classes. When you see 0..n, it means that any value between 0 and *n* is possible—that is, any nonnegative number. Occasionally, you may see values other than 0 or *n*.

Developer's Tip: Don't waste a lot of time at this stage. Get good candidate classes, review them, and allow yourself to make iterations. The secret to good system design is to allow yourself to make a few iterations. You'll find that Booch diagrams are easily modified and are well-suited to this style of design.

Some operations that can be performed on an object of the CStudent class will need to use CAddress as either an argument or return value. Therefore, the CStudent class uses CAddress in its interface. If CStudent has some classes that are used internally and are not exposed, then CStudent uses those classes in its implementation.

Showstopper: Don't so get wrapped up in drawing the figures that you forget about the design. The purpose of the diagrams is to show the model, not vice versa. If the design starts to follow a diagram, then you'll be left with an artificial design that looks good on paper, but doesn't work in real life.

State Transition Drawings

Identifying the interfaces and classes for your application can sometimes be difficult. Another type of diagram that can be useful as you try to analyze your application is the state transition diagram. All objects have states through which they cycle. By analyzing these states, sometimes you can get a feel for how different classes should interact.

Using InfoMan as an example, some of the states for a task from the to-do lists Task Manager might include the following:

- ☐ New
- ☐ Deleted
- ☐ Unfinished
- ☐ Open
- ☐ Completed

In a state transition diagram, it usually is not possible to reach every state from every other state. For example, a deleted task cannot become new. State transition diagrams aren't unique to Booch notation. Any decent discrete mathematics text should include an in-depth discussion of the subtleties of states and state machines. The icons used to model the states in InfoMan are included on the CD and are shown in Figure 2.7. Note that there are special icons that mark the "start" and "stop" states. Each circle represents a new state. Each line between the states represents an action.

Figure 2.7.
*Icons used for state machines
in Booch notation.*

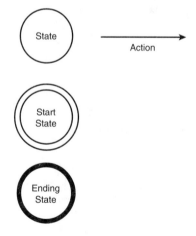

There are just a few simple rules to follow when you are drawing state diagrams. The police aren't going to check up on you or anything; these rules just help you make good models.

- [ ] All diagrams should have starting and ending nodes. The ending node is also known as an *accepting state*.
- [ ] Every action must result in a state.
- [ ] A new state may be equal to the current state.
- [ ] It must always be possible to eventually reach the ending node.

Figure 2.8 is a state diagram showing the different states through which a task can go. Note that some inputs result in a new state that is the same as the current state. The symbol for a state that doesn't change is an arrow that loops back to the state icon, as the Unfinished state does in Figure 2.8.

Figure 2.8.
A state diagram for the task object.

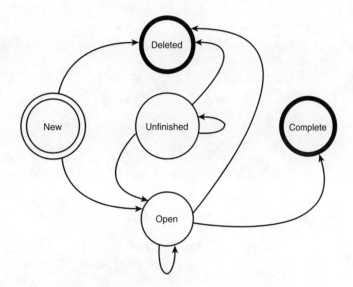

Document/View and MFC Overview

The Microsoft Foundation Classes (MFC) are built around the Document/View architecture. Basically, this is a way to separate a Windows application into four major super objects:

- [ ] The Application object, which controls the application-level interaction with Windows
- [ ] The Frame object, which physically contains the view, menu, toolbar, and other visual elements of the program

☐ The Document object (or objects in an MDI application), representing the data used by the application

☐ The View objects, each of which represents a certain view of a Document object

A Document object doesn't necessarily represent an actual document. It could represent a spreadsheet, a set of motor controls, or the status of a network being monitored by a Windows program.

Using Class Diagrams with Document/View

Figure 2.9 is an early class diagram of the task management portion of InfoMan. The CTaskDoc class represents the document and CTaskView represents the view. Later in the chapter, as you identify the major classes in InfoMan, this figure will be revised.

Figure 2.9.
A class diagram of task management in InfoMan.

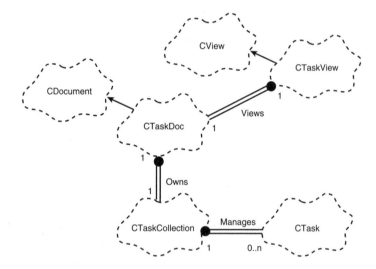

Note that the design covers up to the MFC layer, but no deeper. There isn't much point in documenting the internal relationships of the MFC library, unless it helps to make some part of the architecture clearer.

Identifying Key Classes

The first part of the system design process is to collect a list of possible classes. You may have already started doing this on your own, if you've done much MFC programming.

Classes that Are Required by MFC

The first set of classes that can be identified are the classes that are more or less required by the Document/View architecture. These classes have well-defined interfaces with the framework, so they'll be the easiest classes to start with.

Each document type will require one class, and each view will require a class. You will also need to name the application class. Table 2.2 lists the classes that fall into these categories, using InfoMan as an example. Keep in mind that these are only possible classes at this point. The base class is the MFC class that each of the Document/View classes is derived from.

Table 2.2. Document/View classes used in InfoMan.

Class name	Base class	Description
CInfoManApp	CWinApp	Application class
CTaskDoc	CDocument	Task document
CContactDoc	CDocument	Contact document
CCalendarDoc	CDocument	Calendar document
CTaskView	CFormView	View for CTaskDoc
CContactListView	CScrollView	List view for CContactDoc
CContactCardView	CFormView	Rolodex view for CContactDoc
CContactSplitView	CSplitView	Split view for CContactDoc
CCalendarView	CView	View for CCalendarDoc

Keep in mind that this list is only preliminary; it will change later (I peeked). For example, the CTaskView class will be refined into several smaller classes that provide a tabbed view.

At this point in the design, the idea is just to start identifying the different logical partitions between the classes. There is no need to start drawing formal diagrams, but sketches might help you to see relationships between the classes.

Identifying Other Possible Classes

When identifying possible classes, one good approach to use in your application is to go through the system requirements and underline words that either perform some function or have some function performed on them. Another method is to write out a description of the system and underline all of the nouns.

Like most things in life, identifying classes gets easier with experience. Don't worry about including exactly the "right" classes, just make a list of possible classes. In InfoMan, for example, there are a number of classes in each of the management areas.

Classes Used in Task Management

The task management in InfoMan tracks a task through several different states. The task is created, stored, and (it is hoped) completed. The task might also be deleted, either before or after it is completed.

At this stage of development, you should be concerned only with a high-level system view of the project. You may find it helpful to sketch the relationships between some of the candidate classes on paper, or on a whiteboard. It's also very helpful to interact with other designers and get other opinions on your data model.

Above all, don't be afraid to change the design once you've started diagramming or documenting it. Just as the user-interface specification improved by iteration, the system design can benefit from it as well. As the design is refined and the relationships between different classes become more and more refined, it's normal for some of the candidate classes to be dropped, as well as for some to be added. This doesn't mean that you've done something wrong. Actually, it's a sign that the process is working as intended.

For the task-management part of InfoMan, you can identify two main classes in addition to the one required by MFC. One class will represent the task. This task will be made up of a number of classes that will be determined during the low-level design process. At this point, there's no need to concern yourself with the implementation of individual classes.

The other class will be a collection of task objects. This collection will do most of the work involved in handling individual tasks for the `CTaskDocument` class.

Classes Used in Contact Management

The contact-management part of InfoMan keeps track of a number of contact cards, which you can think of as Rolodex cards. You can remove or add cards from the list, and the entire list can be printed on perforated Rolodex cards.

Contact management contains one basic object, just as in task management: the contact card. Each contact card object will contain a number of other objects that will be handled as part of the low-level design.

There's also a collection class required to handle the individual items stored in the contact document, again just like task management. This collection class will be very similar to the one used for task management.

Classes Used in Calendar Management

The classes used for calendar management are structured a little differently than the classes used for the other two management areas. There's still a single data object, which is called the appointment object. Like the contact-card object and the task object, the appointment object is made up of a number of classes.

The way you store appointments on a calendar is slightly different from the way you store names in a contact list or tasks in a to-do list. Each set of appointments is stored as a collection of appointments for a single day. Each day's appointments are then put into a collection that is controlled by a calendar control.

Classes Used for the Calendar Control

The calendar control is similar to other custom controls used in Windows applications. The calendar control is implemented in the `CCalCtl` class. Of course, there will also be some classes that actually do the work of presenting and selecting the date from the calendar control. These classes are covered on Day 10, "Custom Controls as Reusable Components."

So far you've identified the classes in Table 2.3 for InfoMan. These classes will be your system-level classes, and they will form the top level of the design.

Table 2.3. Top-level classes used in InfoMan.

Class name	Description
`CTaskItem`	An individual task
`CTaskCollection`	A collection of `CTaskItems`
`CContactCard`	An individual contact card
`CContactCollection`	A collection of `CContactCards`
`CAppointment`	An individual appointment
`CDaysAppointments`	One day's set of appointments
`CAppointmentCollection`	A collection of `CDaysAppointments`
`CCalCtl`	The calendar control class

Scheduling the Development Cycle

At the beginning of the day, one of the questions you needed to answer was, "When can we have it?" At this point, you have enough information to provide at least an estimate of the time needed for development. The preliminary schedule that you develop today will be used in the system-design documents and as a starting point for future schedules as the project continues to evolve.

How Much Detail Should be Included in the Schedule?

When you are scheduling the work to be done on any software project, one of the first things you need to determine is how detailed the schedule should be. The schedule should be detailed enough to show an accurate picture of the project's progress. If a schedule is not detailed enough, the project may fall hopelessly behind schedule before a delay is noticed. A detailed schedule will provide a number of checkpoints that allow the project team to have confidence in their ability to meet the planned delivery date.

A plan that is too detailed, however, will bog down the project in a series of minute details that may not be completely necessary. The purpose of the schedule should be to help the project keep on track, not to slow it down.

With these two conflicting goals in mind, the amount of detail in a project schedule will really depend on the project you are developing, and on the team developing it. If you are a single developer working on a three-month project, a large amount of detail is probably not required. If you are in charge of a 25-person team working on medical device software, there is probably one team member that tracks the schedule and resource requirements. That schedule will contain much more detail.

Developer's Tip: Scheduling is one of those tasks that becomes easier with experience. One of the best statistics to keep during the development process is the amount of time that it takes to develop different phases of the project.

If you know from experience that it takes one hour per screen shot to create paper prototypes, then that part of the schedule becomes much easier to create.

On the other hand, sometimes it can be difficult to use that kind of detail for all parts of the project, especially this early in the development cycle. For example, when estimating the time required to develop the classes used in your project, one way to approach it is to categorize the classes as difficult, average, or easy.

Later versions of the schedule will be more specific, but this version will supply a ballpark idea of the amount of time required for development.

The schedule for the InfoMan project needs to cover major deliveries and the development of major system-level classes. An example of a delivery is the handoff that takes place when the project starts functional testing. Because there is still a lot of design left to be done, the schedule will evolve for the next few days.

Using Milestones

For a project of InfoMan's size, a good way to create a schedule is to use milestones. Think of milestones as a point in time when the project has reached a new phase in its development. Table 2.4 shows the highlights for the milestones chosen for InfoMan. The dates that have been chosen are based on preliminary estimates only, and may change over the next few days.

The left column of Table 2.4 refers to the milestone number. Many development organizations use milestone or tollgate numbers during their development process. The method used to divide your project into separate milestones will depend on many factors. Your goal should be to divide your project into a number of smaller subprojects. Plan out the work that needs to be done, including the design, testing, and release of your application, and look for the places where the application makes a transition. For example, when the coding starts, or has been completed, or when the application is sent to beta users.

Table 2.4. Milestones for the InfoMan project.

Milestone	Description	Date
M1	Requirements, design, and prototype all complete	5/05/95
M2	Task Manager complete	5/12/95
M3	Contact Manager complete	5/19/95
M4	Calendar Manager complete; Delivery to functional test	5/23/95
M5	Documentation complete	6/1/95
M6	Online docs complete	6/1/95
M7	Delivery to System/Alpha Test	6/3/95
M8	Delivery to Beta test	6/18/95
M9	InfoMan general release	6/18/95

Even after the schedule has been finalized, it's still subject to change. When unforeseen problems cause dates to slip, you must update the schedule. Day 6, "Iteration and Prototyping," covers

methods you can use to help structure your schedule to minimize the problems caused when one part of the project slips.

The schedule at this point will be very rough. As you gather more information about the details of each class, the testing required, the number of programmers assigned to each task, and so on, the schedule will evolve. At this point, however, you don't know any of those details.

The preliminary InfoMan schedule was written using Word for Windows; it can be found in the \CHAP1\DOCS directory on the CD, as part of the system-design document SYS-DES.DOC. A document template containing all of the styles used for the document is in the same directory, stored as SYS-DES.DOT. An ASCII version of the document is also stored as SYS-DES.TXT.

Design Documents

Take the extra time required to document the system design well, as you did for the requirements on Day 1, "Requirements Analysis." Like the requirements, the system-design document for a software project has many uses:

- ☐ The system design can be used to develop the low-level design.
- ☐ The system design can be used to start developing test plans.
- ☐ The documents can be used later if the product needs to be modified.

The format for the InfoMan system-design document is similar to the system requirements from Day 1. Note that information from the risk analysis is included.

- ☐ **Scope.** This section talks about the overall project. It discusses what is included, and what is not included. Keep this section a short thumbnail.

- ☐ **Glossary.** This is an explanation of any technical terms or concepts that are used in the rest of the document.

- ☐ **Functions.** This section is subdivided into smaller sections that discuss a single high-level part of the design. For InfoMan, the three different management areas have their own subsection. Each subsection includes descriptions of the program operation at a high level.

- ☐ **Target Platform.** The section focuses on the target machine on which InfoMan will be running. Anything required for the software to run is discussed here. Also, any limitations are included in this section.

- ☐ **User Interface.** The user interface is described here. If any modifications had been made to the paper prototypes developed on Day 1, the changes would have been included here.

☐ **Development Period.** This section includes the first cut of the schedule that was developed earlier.

☐ **Risks.** This section includes any issues uncovered during the risk analysis.

Modification Notes

When you are modifying an existing application, the previous system-design documents can be very useful. Hopefully, there are existing documents that describe the existing system design. You can modify existing high-level design documents to show how proposed new classes will fit into the existing architecture.

If the current project doesn't have any documents, you'll need to create some yourself. At a minimum, you should document the modifications to the existing project. If it's possible to create at least an overview of the current project, you will find it useful later in the design process when testing and debugging. Unfortunately, it's a great deal of work to try to re-create complete design documentation for an application that has already been built; because the documentation wasn't used to actually create the application, it's often unreliable. It is often easier to start a new, fully documented project in parallel with the existing one, then throw the undocumented project away.

Debugging the Process

A few problems are likely to come up during system design, especially if any of today's topics are new to you.

Problems Identifying Classes

It takes a few projects to get the hang of class identification. Just remember that the list is always just a list of class candidates. Don't focus on trying to identify every single class; select a few classes and establish their relationship to each other. Remember to keep a high-level view at this stage.

Even though there are clearly more classes to be found for the to-do list, during system design keep your focus on identifying the major classes. This is like going to the circus and looking for the elephants. You'll look for the mice on Day 4, "Low-Level Design."

Problems Drawing Figures

It's not easy to draw some of the figures required by Booch notation. If you have any experience with Paintbrush, use the templates from the CD, and cut and paste the figures into your design.

If you don't have much experience with PC-Paintbrush, take it easy and allow some extra time until you get the hang of it. The advantages of using this notation are worth the learning curve.

Several tools can be used to draw these diagrams for you. If you decide to use one of them, make sure you buy one that allows your initial designs to be easily updated as your application evolves. Some of the more popular tools that support designs using Booch notation are:

- ☐ S-Case, available from Multiquest. At one time, they were sending out free demonstration disks. They can be reached at (708)240-5555, or on CompuServe at 72531,2510.

- ☐ Rational Rose for Windows, available from Rational. This is a more expensive product than S-Case, but it offers more features that are useful for maintaining large software projects. Rational can be reached at (408)496-3600.

Test Planning

Today you will learn about test planning and how the different test phases fit in with the rest of the development process. Two types of tests are planned today:

☐ Functional tests, which test that specific functions are implemented correctly in software

☐ System-level tests, which test the overall performance and stability of the system

Risk analysis is covered again in more detail, and you will use it to help you prioritize different test cases. You will also learn the different ways to decide when to start and when to stop testing, as well as how to create and use the documentation produced during test planning.

Using Structured Testing Techniques

Structured testing is a method for proving that software developed for a project is both correctly implemented and correctly designed. Structured testing is sometimes called *verification and validation*, or just *V and V. Verification* refers to the testing that proves the software is constructed correctly and functions as it is designed. You use validation testing to prove that the system is built as specified. The simpler terms "testing" or just "verification" are sometimes used instead of "structured testing," even though they are not as accurate.

Another term for structured testing is *life-cycle verification*, which means that the application is tested throughout its development. Yet another type of testing is *formal verification*, which relies on formal mathematical proofs to show that a product has been designed and developed correctly. You'll use life-cycle verification to test InfoMan; formal verification techniques are abstract and tend to be not very useful in the real world.

When you do structured testing you test a software system by splitting it into several different phases.

☐ **Module testing.** This phase tests the source code used to implement a source module. This topic is covered in more detail beginning on Day 7, "Basic Class Construction."

☐ **Integration testing.** An integration test verifies that the interfaces between different modules or classes work as implemented and as planned in the design. This phase is sometimes called the design test phase because it tests the design interfaces; it does not test any of the source code. This test phase is covered in more detail beginning on Day 9, "Increasing Reusability with Libraries and Templates."

☐ **Functional testing.** A functional test phase tests part of the system against the system's requirements. You collected and documented the requirements for InfoMan on Day 1, "Requirements Analysis." Developing a functional test plan is covered in more detail later today.

☐ **System testing.** The purpose of a system test is to verify that the entire system functions correctly. Typically, tests in this phase look for performance or feature-interaction problems. Depending on the system, functional and system testing may be combined into a single test phase. You will learn how to develop a system test plan later today.

☐ **Acceptance testing.** This test phase covers alpha and beta testing, where the system is actually put into use. This phase isn't really considered part of structured testing, but is part of the verification process. Beta testing is covered on Day 19, "Beta Testing."

Figure 3.1 shows the different test phases in relation to the rest of the software development process. Note that module testing is closely related to module construction, and the other phases come later. Also, note that some parts of the system might be undergoing functional testing while some parts are still being constructed. This is an advantage of iterative design, which you learned earlier, in Day 1.

Figure 3.1.

Test phases as part of the development cycle.

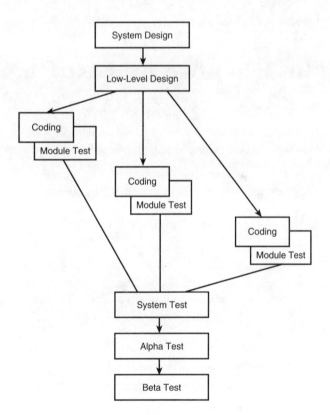

> **Textbook Tip:** One of the important points of structured testing is that it shifts testing emphasis away from the source code and toward the system as a whole. The testing process is split into different phases, each of which tests a different portion of the system. It is not possible to successfully test a system by testing only the source code. For InfoMan, only the module testing phase actually tests the source code, and that phase is actually part of module construction.
>
> Other test phases focus on the system design, how well the different modules work together, satisfaction of the requirements, and system reliability. These important parts of the system tend to be ignored if testing emphasizes only the source code.

The Purpose of Test Planning

Good testing is impossible without a good test plan. In that way it isn't much different from any other part of the development process. Test planning involves determining the tests that should be done, prioritizing them, and estimating the resources required to perform the tests. This information is then used to help refine the overall system project planning.

In order to generate a meaningful schedule, you will need to know how much time you will need for testing. In order to determine this, you must estimate the number of test cases; that's where the test plan comes in. You may use several different test plans in a single project, especially when you use an iterative design. Every test phase should also have a separate set of test plans.

When you do functional testing, it's a good idea to break your tests up into sections. If your requirements are divided into separate sections, divide your test plan into sections as well, with each test plan section corresponding to a section in the requirements specification. The InfoMan project has six main sections in its functional test plan.

- ☐ Serialization
- ☐ Printing
- ☐ Online help
- ☐ To-do list and task management
- ☐ Contact management
- ☐ Calendar management

It is certainly possible to break each of these plans into more detail, or to reduce the number of plans by combining some of them. By separating each of the test plans acording to its area of functionality, it's much easier to modify or reuse the plans if needed.

You should include in the test plan the following items, which will be covered in more detail later:

- ☐ **Test start and stop criteria.** This is a description of the requirements for starting as well as stopping the test phase.

- ☐ **Description of tests to be executed.** The description may or may not actually include detailed instructions for executing each test. You should give each test case a priority; you will learn how to do so later today.

- ☐ **Estimated time required for testing.** This should be broken down by priority. For example, if a test plan used for InfoMan has three different priority levels, the estimate should give the time required to execute tests at each priority level.

- ☐ **Description of the test environment.** You should specify whether you need extra equipment to run a test plan—for example, a second computer or external modems.

Why Plan Now?

It may seem that Day 3 is too early to plan for your functional and system-level tests. Actually, this is the perfect time. On Day 1 you collected the customer's requirements. Day 2, "System Design," covered the high-level design of the system. By creating test plans today, the plans will focus on the requirements and high-level parts of the system. Test plans also can give feedback about the requirements and high-level design.

An important part of the functional test-planning process is to verify each of the customer's requirements. If you discover a requirement that is ambiguous or untestable, it's more easily corrected now than after the coding has been completed. If you delay test planning until after the software is actually implemented, the test planning will take place long after the requirements are discussed. Any problems with the requirements or high-level design discovered during test planning would be discovered after the coding phase.

Setting Up Testing Criteria

An important part of test planning is setting up the entry and exit criteria for a test phase. *Entry criteria* are the conditions that must be met before testing can begin. *Exit criteria* are the conditions that will allow the test phase to end. These criteria may be informal or simple, or they may be very detailed.

Each testing phase may have unique start and stop criteria, which you determine during the test planning phase. This allows everyone involved in the planning process to know which conditions must be met before testing will begin, and which conditions will exist when testing is completed.

The following are the start criteria for all test phases of InfoMan:

☐ The software coding is complete

☐ All previous testing phases have been completed successfully

☐ No more than a specified number of failed test cases exist

☐ All required documentation is available

Determining when to start testing is usually easier than deciding when to stop testing. Because testing is done at the end of the development cycle, there is often a tendency to compress or shorten the amount of time planned for testing. Table 3.1 lists some reasons for ending a test phase.

Table 3.1. Some reasons for ending a test phase.

Bad	Good
Release date moved up	All tests are executed
Out of testing time	Too many faults, go back to previous phase
Time to start beta trial	Fault intensity meets ending criteria

Notice that a good reason for stopping a test phase is poor test results. One of the criteria for stopping a phase should be poor input. Testing alone cannot fix a truly broken system; it can only find the problems. If the number of discovered errors is extremely high, testing should stop, and the product should return to the previous phase.

You should establish two sets of exit criteria. One set outlines reasons for successfully completing the test phase; the other set is a list of conditions that will cause the test phase to fail. The criteria for successfully completing a test phase should include the following:

☐ The minimum number of tests that must be completed

☐ The acceptable error rate

☐ The number of open faults or errors allowed

☐ The maximum number of changes allowed during testing

The minimum number of tests completed may specify a priority level. For InfoMan's functional tests, the minimum test coverage is 100 percent of the priority-one and priority-two test cases, and 50 percent of the priority-three test cases.

The *acceptable-error rate* is the number of test cases that are initially faulty but later corrected. This is an issue because there is a relationship between the number of faults discovered in a system and the number of faults remaining. A larger-than-expected error rate indicates a problem that should be investigated. For InfoMan, the acceptable error rate is five percent of test cases.

Every test phase will probably discover some faults with your application. Sometimes, a complex fault may remain "open," or unsolved for a long period of time. If a test phase was not permitted to end until every single fault was corrected, testing might take far too long. For most projects, a small number of open faults that have low priorities should not hold up the end of the test phase.

You might place a restriction on the maximum number of changes allowed during a test phase, because too many changes indicate an unstable product. With every change you make to a system you risk introducing problems that won't be detected.

Too often, the amount of time spent testing a product is determined by the number of hours available to test it, rather than the amount of testing required to verify that it functions correctly. Later today you will learn a method for balancing the amount of time available based on risk analysis.

Test Documentation

The documentation generated by test planning may vary between projects. Test documentation can consist of the following:

- ☐ A system-level test plan
- ☐ A test plan for each set of tests to be executed
- ☐ A test specification for each test plan
- ☐ A test instruction for each test plan
- ☐ A set of test results for each test plan

If you have a project that is very simple, all of these documents may be combined into a single unified test document. The advantage of using a single document for testing is that all of the information is in a single place. This is great for a single developer working on a project with little likelihood of change.

The advantage of having multiple documents is that all of the information is kept in smaller pieces. This is ideal when you are dealing with large teams or with projects that are expected to change a great deal. Ownership of the documents can be divided easily among several team members, and it's possible to use only the parts of the testing documentation in which you're interested.

Risk Analysis Revisited

On Day 2 you did a quick risk analysis to help plan a preliminary schedule for the InfoMan project. Another use for risk analysis is in test planning. One of the problems a developer has during test planning is distinguishing between test cases that should be executed first and those

that should be given a lower priority. Another problem is identifying areas of the system that should be given a higher priority during test design.

One way to identify which test cases should receive the most attention is to perform a risk analysis. Areas of the system that are most likely to fail, or are most likely to have serious consequences when they fail, are given priority over other parts of the system.

Developer's Tip: An important ingredient in a good risk analysis is your awareness of risks. As a software developer, seek out information that you can use to help determine possible risks. If you have Internet access, read the Usenet newsgroup `comp.risks`, which discusses computer-related incidents.

Technical journals and computer magazines often discuss problems that have occurred in other systems. A very good regular column on computing risks appears in *Software Engineering Notes*, a newsletter published by the Association for Computing Machinery's Software Engineering Special Interest Group.

Relative Risk

The risks identified in risk analysis are relative. The system that you develop may have no areas that are without risk, or your project may be almost entirely low-risk.

Determining High-Risk Test Cases

The actual selection of test cases is covered later in the section, "Functional-Test Planning." For now, assume that you have several test cases and that you want to identify which cases should be tested first. On Day 2 you identified four different risk areas and assigned weights to each of them.

☐ Risks that are likely to occur and are likely to cause significant problems when they do occur should be assigned the highest weight.

☐ Risks that aren't as likely to occur, but will have serious consequences when they do occur, should receive the next weight.

☐ Risks that are more likely to be realized, but have smaller consequences, are assigned the third category.

☐ Risks that are unlikely to materialize and cause small consequences when they do take place are assigned the fourth category.

Each test case should be given a priority that is based on the risk areas just identified. For InfoMan, there will be three testing priorities:

- [ ] **Priority 1.** Test cases that are more likely to be faulty, and will cause significant problems if they are faulty.

- [ ] **Priority 2.** Test cases that are less likely to be faulty, but will cause significant problems if failure occurs. Also, test cases that are more likely to be faulty, but have less severe consequences.

- [ ] **Priority 3.** Test cases that are less likely to fail, and will have less severe consequences if they do.

Showstopper: Remember that all of these priorities are relative and assume that you are developing general-purpose desktop software. Don't let yourself lose sight of the product that you are developing. If your system risks large sums of money, or can cause great inconvenience if it fails, many of your priorities may be high.

Don't get caught in a numbers game. Remember that most of these numbers were made up, and three priorities were assigned here for your convenience. It's very easy to start believing that only three priorities can ever exist, and that is just not the case.

Use informal risk analysis as a useful tool for determining testing order, not as a prediction of the future.

Functional-Test Planning

The purpose of functional testing is to verify that the system meets all of the customer's expectations. Functional testing is only one part of the verification process, which is shown in Figure 3.2. Parts of the development cycle that don't apply to verification are omitted for clarity.

When you perform functional testing with iterative design, some parts of the system may be in the functional test phase whereas other parts are still being coded. Figure 3.3 illustrates this idea.

This "pipelining" of the development process can be very efficient because you can use small teams to do the coding, module test, and functional test phases. This sort of testing is possible with a project like InfoMan, because the system design has identified four main modules.

Figure 3.2.

Verification phases used in InfoMan.

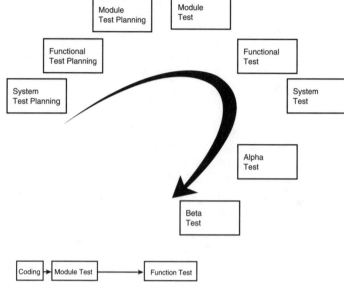

Figure 3.3.

Functional testing of modules that are completed first.

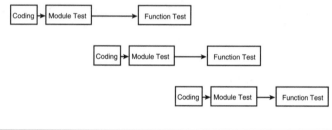

Verifying Requirements

As stated earlier, you should test all of the requirements—all test cases that you develop should be traceable back to the requirements. This means that for every test case, there should be an identifiable customer requirement that justifies the test.

Showstopper: When you are planning the function tests, it's not unusual to discover "obvious" functionality that seems to be missing from the system requirements. Resist the temptation to add functionality only into the test phase. Just because new requirements sound obvious, this is no reason to test for them if they aren't listed in the system requirements. The reason for this is to avoid introducing anonymous requirements during the testing process. If you discover a missing requirement during test planning, the best course of action is to go back and update the requirements.

The low-level design, module construction, and user-documentation phases will all use the requirements as a starting point. If a requirement belongs in the system, go back and add it to the system requirements.

The first step in defining requirements for functional testing is to generate a list of potential test cases. Each test should verify one or more system requirements. Once a function has been tested, it generally doesn't need to be tested again. Figure 3.4 illustrates some functions arranged in a tree hierarchy. Functions in the lower part of the tree depend on functions in the upper part. If each test starts at the top of the tree and ends at the bottom, how many tests are required to completely test all branches?

Figure 3.4.
Functionality graph from a multimedia program.

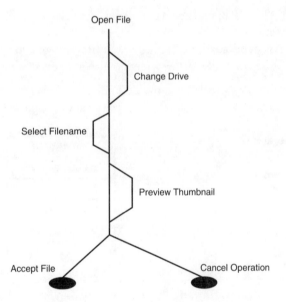

You only need two test cases to get full coverage. It isn't necessary to test several combinations of different paths. For example, a poor selection of test cases might test every permutation of previewing a file, changing the active drive, and either canceling or accepting the selected file.

Developer's Tip: Avoid creating functional test cases that are too complicated. Many developers have a tendency to create as few cases as possible that each test several requirements.

Having less than one test case per requirement is a good goal to strive for, but complicated cases will take longer to set up, longer to execute, and longer to debug if the case fails. A series of simpler test cases often makes better use of your testing resources.

Another problem with complicated test cases is that they are harder to modify and reuse than a series of simple test cases. See the section, "Modification Notes," later today, for a discussion about modifying existing test cases.

Avoiding Over-Testing and Under-Testing

The goal of functional test planning is to create the minimum number of test cases required to test all of the functions specified by the customer. If too many tests are generated, time is wasted on duplicated effort. If too few tests are created, some functions will be left untested. In the worst case, some areas of the system may be over-tested, whereas others are left with poor test coverage.

For your project, you should build a test-coverage matrix to help ensure good test coverage. Figure 3.5 shows a sample matrix used to design some of the function tests for InfoMan.

Figure 3.5.

A test-coverage matrix used for InfoMan.

To-do List Function Tests	1.1	1.2	1.3	1.4	1.5	1.6
1.1.01 Multiple Files Open	X					X
1.1.02 Cascade/Tile	X			X		
1.1.03 Arbitrary Records		X			X	
1.1.04 Prompt for Changes					X	

You can create a test-coverage matrix using pencil and paper, or with a spreadsheet or word processor. The matrix in Figure 3.5 shows the requirements on the left side and test cases along the top. To save space, the requirements have a short slogan, with a number that refers back to the system requirements.

When a prospective test case verifies a requirement, an X is placed at the intersecting box in the matrix. After entering all of the prospective test cases, look for any of the following characteristics in the matrix:

☐ If a row has no check marks, the requirement is untested. A test case should be added for this requirement.

☐ If a row has many check marks, some tests can probably be eliminated.

□ If a column has a large number of check marks, reexamine the test case. It may be too general, or it may be trying to test too many requirements.

Assigning Priorities to Test Cases

Earlier in the section, "Determining High-Risk Test Cases," you learned the concept of prioritizing test cases. Although risk is a major factor when determining the priority of test cases, it's not the only factor. High-risk test cases are usually executed first. However, there are some other criteria that you should consider after the risk analysis.

Test cases that exercise basic functionality should be tested before more complicated cases. In InfoMan, one of the priority one cases tests that a to-do list can be saved. It's a good idea to test cases that verify information can be entered into a to-do list first, because any tests that depend on entered data will definitely fail.

You may also consider setting a goal for the distribution of test priority. Try to assign at least a few cases at every priority level. After all, if every test is priority one, there's not much point in setting any priorities.

Estimating Functional Testing Costs

The amount of time required for testing is a significant part of the budget for building software projects. An accurate estimate during the planning process can help avoid problems late in the project, when pressure sometimes builds to reduce the amount of time spent on the testing phase.

When you are estimating the amount of time required to execute test cases, consider the following:

□ Not every case will be executed on the first attempt; a number of cases will fail and need to be retested. Allow some time for a certain percentage of cases to be retested.

□ Some cases may require set-up time.

□ Allow time for record keeping and other "overhead."

□ Allow time for fault isolation.

After taking all of these items into account, make an honest estimate of the time you will need to execute an average successful test case, and record the results. Then, take that number and at least double it for an unsuccessful test case. If you like, an alternative is to actually walk through a faulty test case.

Of course, the number of test cases that are likely to fail can only be estimated based on your previous experience. If your previous experience says that 10 percent of your cases fail, then use that number. If you are new to Windows programming or are developing a complicated application, you may need to use a higher number. For InfoMan, there are 115 test cases; assume that 10 percent may fail. You can estimate that it takes 15 minutes to execute a successful test case, and 30 minutes to execute an unsuccessful test case. The total estimate for functional test is

```
(115 × .25) + (12 × .50) = 35 hours
```

Developer's Tip: With experience and good record keeping, you can help make all of your estimates more accurate.

An important measurement, or metric, used to measure software development is the amount of time used to execute an average test case. In order to use this metric, you must track the amount of time that is actually spent executing test cases for several similar projects. After several projects, the estimate should become fairly accurate.

As an added bonus, collecting these types of measurements can help you improve your processes by giving you definite targets and goals to reach for.

You will learn metrics in more detail on Day 11, "Error Reporting and Metrics."

System-Test Planning

System testing is an extension of functional testing. Often, the system test and functional test phases are combined into a single test phase.

The tests for InfoMan are separated because they actually are testing two different aspects of the system. The functional tests verify that InfoMan works as specified in the requirements, whereas the system tests verify that InfoMan will work as an entire system.

Separate system-level testing is often used for real-time systems, or systems that must be robust under duress. Reservation systems, telephone networks, and nuclear power plants are some examples of systems that have these testing requirements. These systems require an extra structured test phase that focuses on the entire system before the system moves into alpha or beta testing.

Test cases for the system-level test phase should focus on more that just basic functionality. Tools that add to system load or that simulate system failure are often used during the system test phase. Some areas commonly tested during system testing include the following:

☐ **Performance testing.** These tests verify that under real-world conditions the system can meet performance requirements.

☐ **Feature interaction.** These test cases are used to prove that different functions in the system can work independently of each other without interference.

☐ **System stability.** If the system is expected to survive under stressful conditions, these tests verify that the system degrades gracefully and recovers properly.

Planning Performance Tests

You should plan performance tests with a few targets in mind. These targets, which should come from the system requirements, should be traceable just like the function test cases you learned about earlier.

The goal of performance testing is not to duplicate the performance tests that have been done as part of functional testing. Rather, these tests should focus on performance during real-world conditions. The performance test cases for InfoMan are included in the system test plan in the \CHAP3\DOCS directory. Some test cases used for InfoMan include the following:

☐ Loading and printing a to-do list while STRESS.EXE is running

☐ Opening 10 different to-do lists, calendars, and contact documents

☐ On a machine with the minimum configuration (8MB of RAM, 386-40), starting the application by clicking on a to-do list file with at least 100 entries

Developer's Tip: Try to put the system under real-world conditions as much as possible. That may mean adding to the system load by running other applications or reducing the amount of RAM or disk storage available to the application. Two good tools from the 16-bit SDK are useful for simulating load from other applications: STRESS.EXE and HEAPWALK.EXE. Both of these applications consume system resources and tend to slow down the responsiveness of your application.

Another important thing to remember during the system test is the computer configuration. Try to run the application in a system test with a variety of machines, if they are available. The typical developer's machine is usually more powerful than a typical user's. Try to step into your user's shoes for at least some of the system testing.

Planning for Interaction Testing

Interaction tests target the areas where different functions in the system overlap. Unlike the other system tests, in most cases no special hardware or configuration is needed for interaction testing.

Interaction tests fall into two main areas:

- ☐ Tests that prove that two or more functions that might not be related actually can be used at the same time. An example of this sort of test is printing one file while viewing another in an MDI application.

- ☐ Test cases that simulate user actions that might not normally be expected. An example of this sort of test case is printing a file, then immediately closing it.

Estimating System-Testing Costs

You estimate system-testing costs in much the same way as described earlier for functional testing. However, because system tests are typically more complex, the estimate per test case should be higher.

InfoMan has 14 system-test cases. Because the tests are more complex than the functional tests, the average time per test will be estimated as 30 minutes. Failed cases will be estimated as 45 minutes, resulting in a total estimate of

```
(14 × .5) + (2 × .75) = 8.5 hours
```

Note: As with all of your estimates, you should use values that reflect the amount of time an average test will take for your project. If you don't have any prior experience, work through one of your test cases now using a prototype version or a competing product.

Modification Notes

If you are modifying an existing Visual C++ project, scheduling may be much simpler because you may have information about the amount of time spent executing test cases in previous test phases. If this information isn't available as a formal document, hopefully you have at least some feeling about the amount of time previously spent testing.

If there are test plans available from previous development, try to reuse the existing plans if possible. If the current test plans are usable, it's probably easier to modify them than to create new ones from scratch.

Debugging the Process

One problem that might come up during test planning is the amount of time forecasted for test execution. Sometimes after planning the test cases, more time is needed for testing than was originally budgeted. If this happens to you, you have two choices:

☐ Add more time to the schedule and adjust the budget

☐ Reduce the number of test cases

You really have only one of these two options. Trying to squeeze six weeks of testing into two weeks of schedule won't work.

Showstopper: Skimping on your testing now can result in big problems later. It's much better to put the necessary time and effort into a good test plan now, rather than try to fix the damage caused by a defective product. Many companies have given up their market leadership, or even gone bankrupt, after releasing poorly tested products.

3

Low-Level Design

Today you'll learn about low-level design, sometimes referred to as "detailed design." During the low-level design phase you'll further define the classes used in the project and start making decisions about the classes that are to be coded in the next phases of the project.

Today you'll learn the following:

☐ Details about implementing methods required by the MFC Document/View architecture

☐ Steps you can take to help keep your classes reusable

☐ The documentation generated by low-level design, and how it's used

An Overview of Low-Level Design

Your goal during the low-level design phase is to determine the characteristics of all of the classes involved in the project. This includes all of the interfaces, many of which were identified during system design. It also includes the actions that you should take when you use an interface method.

Ideally, the low-level design phase should result in design documents that could be given to any developer, who could then code the project with no further input. However, if you are not able to produce design documents with that level of detail, you have two options:

☐ Build prototypes to model parts of the application where you lack experience, then use information from the prototype to help your design

☐ Allow flexibility in your design, and be aware that it may change as issues are discovered in areas where the design may be incomplete

When possible, you should try to make the design as complete as possible. If you lack experience in any area of the design, plan for it by giving yourself enough time to either create a prototype or rework the design.

Note: The low-level design of some parts of InfoMan is used today to help illustrate low-level design in an application that uses the MFC class library. There's not enough room to cover the entire design of InfoMan in this chapter, but you can find the low-level design documents on the CD that accompanies this book.

You can find the low-level design for the classes used by InfoMan in the \CHAP6\DOCS directory on the CD. As with the previous documents on the CD, they are included in both Word for Windows and ASCII text formats.

The styles used for the low-level design documents are covered in the section, "Documentation Used in Low-Level Design," later today.

Document Classes

The base MFC document class, `CDocument`, has many member functions and is capable of supporting a wide range of applications. Most `CDocument`-derived classes use these functions to support these key areas:

- ☐ Creating new documents
- ☐ Granting access to data contained in the document
- ☐ Handling serialization of the document to and from the file system

Most `CDocument`-based classes are similar because the primary role of the document class is as an interface for the data used by the application. Think of the document class as an envelope and the data as a letter. The document contains the data model, just like the envelope contains a letter. You can find envelopes that come in all shapes and sizes, but they are still recognizable as envelopes. Classes derived from `CDocument` will also come in all shapes and sizes. The most important property of envelopes and document classes is that they make good containers for their contents.

The document class used for a real-time, stock-trading application may not seem to have much in common with the `CTaskDoc` used by InfoMan, but from the MFC framework's point of view, they both manage data for a Windows application.

4

Separating the Document and View

One of the basic features of the MFC architecture is the Document/View model. The document represents the data object and is implemented in a class derived from `CDocument`. The view is used to display or give access to the document and is derived from `CView`. Although the MFC class libraries offer several types of documents and views for specialized purposes, all documents are used to contain your data and are associated with views that are used to display the document to the user. Figure 4.1 shows the basic idea of this model.

Developer's Tip: This may seem like old news if you've had some experience with Document/View, but there are some subtle issues of which you should be aware. From a design point of view, the view should be truly separate from the document and data model. As a rule of thumb, data and the functions that manipulate the data belong in the document. Visual elements—how the data is presented or manipulated—go in the view.

As the low-level design progresses, look for signs that the view is trying to duplicate the work done by the document or is attempting to store information that is really the responsibility of the document. If the interfaces between the document and the view start increasing, or if you find it necessary to store internal details about the document in the view, that's a good indication that the design is in trouble. For example, although a view class might keep track of the current page number displayed to the user, it should not store low-level details such as the number of bytes contained in a document. If low-level information about the document is required, create an interface for your document class that can be used to fetch it as needed.

Figure 4.1.
The basic MFC Document/
View model.

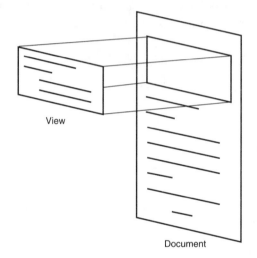

View

Document

Your application's view classes should use the document's interface to collect any information needed and should not depend on the internal construction of the document class. For example, the InfoMan task-management classes that handle the to-do list should not be accessed directly by the CTaskView class. The CTaskView class should not try to store information about the internal status of the data structure used to store the to-do list and should be concerned only with the CTaskDoc interfaces.

Separating the Document and Data Model

The document should be separated from its data model in the same way a document should be separated from its views. The typical saying about class interfaces is that they should be minimal, but complete. This means that there should be a small number of interfaces to a class, but not so few that you have to grant access to internal data members in order to use the class. There also should not be so many interfaces that the class becomes hard to use or maintain.

The goal of reducing the number of interfaces also extends to the number of other classes that each class interacts with. Reducing interfaces almost always reduces complexity, making your design easier to understand and maintain. A class that uses dozens of different classes is harder to use than a class that has contact with only a few other classes.

The conflicting goals of reducing interfaces while providing complete, reusable classes can be a little confusing at first. It can be a bit of a balancing act to satisfy both of these goals, but balancing the desire for added functionality with the need to reduce interfaces will lead to a good, reusable, and maintainable design in the long run.

With this in mind, you should create a minimal interface between the document and the actual data model classes. Provide a well-defined interface between your document class and its data model, and reduce its dependency on the internal details of the data model. Using InfoMan as an example, the `CTaskDoc` class uses well-defined interfaces for access to its data model, just as the `CTaskView` class uses only the interfaces that are presented by `CTaskDoc`.

The primary reason you place data members and functions in the `CDocument` class is to enable the MFC framework to access the to-do list's data model in a standard way. From the other classes, the document will be the interface to the data. Inside the `CDocument` class, however, the document has almost nothing to do with the data; it just delegates methods to the data model's classes.

By restricting the document class to use the interfaces presented by its data model, you must do a small amount of extra work in the design and coding phases. However, the resulting design is more flexible because you can change the implementation of the data model without impacting the document class. Figure 4.2 illustrates the idea of separating the document, view, and data model, using the InfoMan task management classes.

Figure 4.2.
The separation between the document, view, and data model in InfoMan.

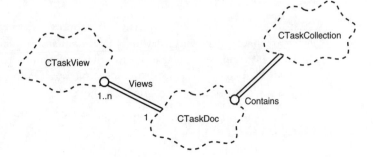

Creating the Document

There are two ways for a user to create an instance of a `CDocument`. To create a new version of a document, the user will generally select File | New from the main menu. In most applications, this creates a new, blank, and untitled document for the user. The second way is for the user to

open an existing document by selecting File | Open from the main menu and selecting the file using the File | Open dialog box.

Most of the work of creating a new document is usually handed off to the data model class (or classes). Most of the low-level design concerned with creating a new document will center around two methods that usually have to be overridden by your document class: `CDocument::DeleteContents` and `CDocument::Serialize`. The MFC *framework*, or classes that support your application, will call `DeleteContents` whenever your document is emptied. The MFC framework will call `Serialize` when an object is stored or loaded from disk.

> **Note:** Today's discussion of the low-level design will use pseudocode and Booch diagrams to discuss any specific parts of the design that need to be shown in detail. The low-level design is never expressed in C or C++. This helps to avoid the tendency to start coding during the low-level design.
>
> If you're not familiar with pseudocode, it's just a method of writing down tasks performed by a function in a structured way. Pseudocode enables you to discuss the work performed by a function using an English-like syntax. Different people will use different "flavors" of pseudocode; the listings here are very Pascal-like. The only firm rule is that the pseudocode must be clear, and not a programming language.
>
> In general, it's a good idea to put most ideas about the implementation out of your head for now. It should be possible to implement your design in languages other than C++; after all, this is the design, not the source code. For that reason, the term *method* is used today to deemphasize the fact that it may be later coded as a C++ function.

When a user opens an existing document, the MFC framework calls the `CDocument::OnOpenDocument` method. The standard implementation calls the methods `DeleteContents` and `Serialize`, and marks the document as "clean," meaning no changes have been made to it since it was loaded. This is the way that most document classes, including InfoMan's, are loaded using the MFC class library.

You will have to provide code to implement the `DeleteContents` and `Serialize` methods for your document class. Listing 4.1 is a pseudocode listing describing these two functions as designed for InfoMan's `CTaskDoc` class.

Listing 4.1. Pseudocode for `CTaskDoc::DeleteContents` and `CTaskDoc::Serialize`.

```
method:CTaskDoc::DeleteContents()
begin
    Call the TaskCollection::RemoveAll() method
```

```
        Call UpdateAllViews() with NULL
    end

    method:CTaskDoc::Serialize( parameter CArchive ar )
    begin
        Call the TaskCollection::Serialize() method with ar
    end
```

When the MFC framework creates a new document (usually because the user has requested it), the MFC framework calls the `CDocument::OnNewDocument` method. Listing 4.2 is a pseudocode example of the typical actions that the InfoMan `CTaskDoc` class should take.

Listing 4.2. Pseudocode for creating a new task document in `CTaskDoc`.

```
    method: CTaskDoc::OnNewDocument()
    begin
        Call CDocument::OnNewDocument()
        if
            the call fails, return false
        else
            Call the TaskCollection::RemoveAll() method
        end if
        return true
    end
```

The pseudocode examples presented here are written using names like `RemoveAll()`, which are similar to the names that will be used when the application is actually coded. Some people prefer to start defining the names for interfaces as soon as possible. When you are working with your low-level design, you may prefer to use descriptive names like "Remove all of the Task Items" for your interfaces, and postpone the final naming decisions until the design is complete. The important thing to remember is to make sure your interfaces are defined before coding begins.

Accessing the Document

When the data model is separated from the document class, many of the interfaces to the document are actually handled by the data model. This helps reduce the amount of work that is required in the document class. For example, Figure 4.3 shows the interfaces that were defined for `CTaskDoc` and `CTaskzCollection` during the system design.

Figure 4.3.

Class diagram showing the interfaces for `CTaskDoc` and `CTaskCollection`.

Note that all of the methods invoked on the CTaskDoc class result in a similar call made to the CTaskCollection class. This enables the document class to delegate to the data model all of the work involved with handling the data model. The document class is free to focus on managing the document, and it does not have to be modified if the structure of the CTaskItem class changes. This follows the design goal of having minimal interfaces between classes.

Two of the methods do need some work to be done by the CTaskDoc class. When a CTaskItem is added to CTaskCollection through the AddTask method, or when an existing CTaskItem is modified by UpdateTask, any views must be updated as well.

Listing 4.3 shows the pseudocode for the GetTask, AddTask, and UpdateTask methods. Note that a pointer to CView is passed as a parameter into the AddTask and UpdateTask methods. This has to do with efficiently updating the views, and you will learn about it later today, in the section titled, "Low-Level Design of View Classes."

Listing 4.3. Pseudocode for the `CTaskDoc::GetTask` and `CTaskDoc::AddTask` methods.

```
method    CTaskDoc::GetTask( parameter WORD taskPosition )
begin
    Call the CTaskCollection GetTask method with taskPosition
    return the result of the call to GetTask
end

method    CTaskDoc::AddTask( parameter pointer to CView
                             parameter pointer to CTaskItem
                             parameter WORD taskPostion )
begin
    Call the CTaskCollection AddTask method with CTaskItem pointer,
                                                taskPosition
    return the result of the call to AddTask
end
```

Low-Level Design of the Data Model

The data models that documents use vary between applications. In fact, they vary to some degree even between the three document types used by InfoMan. The steps that you take to help refine the low-level design, however, are similar for most document types.

The characteristics of the document and view classes are fairly well-defined by the MFC architecture, but the implementation of the data model will vary from document to document. The InfoMan classes are used in this section to show the typical low-level implementation of a data model. There are two aspects to any data model:

☐ The outside appearance of the model, made up of the interfaces that are publicly exposed

☐ The implementation of the data model, consisting of the internal data and methods that are hidden from users of the model

The Visible Parts of the Data Model

When you examine any of the classes at a low level and begin to plan the implementation, the need for additional classes sometimes appears. If you discover the need for a new class, you should add it to the system-design documents, as well as include it in the low-level design.

For example, the InfoMan CTaskItem class has an attribute to hold the priority of the item. During the system design, the priority was defined as a simple attribute, probably defined as an int or WORD, or something similar. Today, during the low-level design, the priority seems to be more complex than it first appeared. It's used to determine the relative priority of different task items in the to-do list, and it's displayed to the user in several different formats. After an object or data item starts to control other objects or have special needs or characteristics, consider creating a class to represent it. It is beginning to look as though it might be better to create a priority class.

How do you know when you should consider changing an attribute into a class? There are several different points, any of which could be a reason to create a new class for the attribute:

☐ The attribute is similar to an existing class used elsewhere, so implementation will be low-cost.

☐ The attribute models a real-world object.

☐ The attribute shows up in many parts of the application and is more complicated than a built-in type (a char or int, for example).

☐ The attribute is difficult to handle if it isn't converted into a class. Doing so will reduce the complexity of the design.

The priority attribute that was a data member for CTaskItem qualifies under all of these categories.

The visible parts of the to-do list data model are represented by the CTaskItem, CTaskCollection, and CPriority classes. The CTaskDoc class deals only with CTaskCollection, because it contains the primary interfaces for the entire data model. Figure 4.4 shows the interfaces exposed by these classes.

Figure 4.4.
The document and data model classes used for task management by InfoMan.

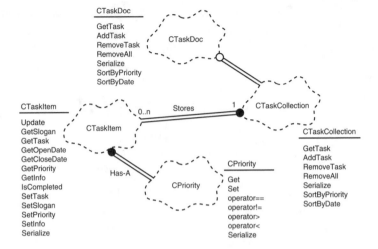

The Hidden Parts of *CTaskCollection*

The primary use of the data model in InfoMan's task management is to collect `CTaskItem` objects held by `CTaskCollection`. The MFC classes offer several different collection classes that can be used as a base class for `CTaskCollection`.

The names used for the `CTaskCollection` interfaces were chosen so that the implementation of the underlying collection could remain flexible. In the future, if you implement the collection as an external map class or as a btree, the interfaces can remain as they are and you will not need to recompile any clients of the class. This is a better approach than creating a collection that is suited to only one type of data structure. As applications get older they always evolve, and keeping the interfaces to your classes generic will help cut down on the number of changes that have to be done when a class is redesigned.

There are several ways to store and retrieve data from an MFC collection. Because the view will store the tasks in the to-do list in a list box, the `CTaskCollection` will store the `CTaskItem` objects as an array. You can coordinate the current status of the array with the list-box control containing the task slogans. This will make selection of the appropriate `CTaskItem` much simpler, because the index of the selected item in the list box control will match the index in the `CTaskCollection`.

There are five main methods for `CTaskCollection`:

- ☐ `Serialize`
- ☐ `AddTask`
- ☐ `GetTask`
- ☐ `RemoveTask`
- ☐ `RemoveAll`

The `CTaskCollection::Serialize` method is forwarded from the `CTaskDoc` class, and is used to store or retrieve the collection to or from an archive. The `AddTask`, `GetTask`, and `RemoveTask` methods are used to manage individual tasks in the collection. Tasks are referred to by their current index, similar to an array. If an item from the collection is removed, all of the indices "above" it are shifted down by one. The `RemoveAll` method removes every task that is contained in the collection.

The Hidden Parts of *CTaskItem*

As discussed on Day 2, "System Design," the `CTaskItem` class is derived from `CObject`, and models a task from the to-do list. Figure 4.5 is a detailed class diagram of `CTaskItem`. It shows the public and private methods, as well as the data used to implement the class.

Figure 4.5.

A detailed class diagram for `CTaskItem`.

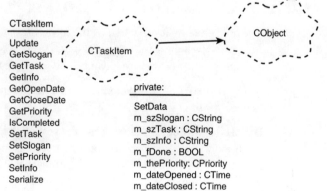

One of the great things about object-oriented design is that you can design and build your classes using other classes as components. You can include an object of any class in your new class just as easily as you would include an `int` or a `char*`. For example, if your class needs to store strings, as `CTaskItem` does, you can use `CString` objects as data members, which greatly simplifies your string handling.

The `CTaskItem` class uses `CString` objects for its members. Methods are provided to fetch or set most of the members, or the data can be set by the constructor. No dynamic allocation is done by the `CTaskItem` class; it's all handled by `CString`, so the construction and destruction steps are very simple.

If the class had used dynamically allocated data, then the constructors and destructors would have been more complicated. On Day 7, "Basic Class Construction," you will implement some classes that need to allocate data dynamically.

Pseudocode for the `CTaskItem::Serialize` method, which is called for each `CTaskItem` in turn by `CTaskCollection::Serialize`, is shown in Listing 4.4.

Listing 4.4. Pseudocode for `CTaskItem::Serialize`.

```
method    CTaskItem::Serialize( parameter CArchive ar)
begin
    If the archive is storing then
        archive the slogan and task description
        archive the open and close dates
        archive the completed flag and notes
    else
        un-archive the slogan and task description
        un-archive the open and close dates
        un-archive the completed flag and notes
    end if
    Call the priority member's Serialize method with ar
end
```

Other Data-Model Issues

You could drop the low-level design of the to-do list data model into almost any application platform. At this level, there isn't any Microsoft Windows-specific code, because you're dealing with a collection of `CTaskItem`s that can be created, updated, managed in a list, or deleted.

Keeping the `CTaskItem` and `CTaskCollection` classes independent from the document and view classes is good for several reasons:

☐ **The classes can be tested without the rest of the application.** During the class-construction phase, the classes must be tested. Because these classes don't have any dependencies on the rest of the application, they can be coded and tested separately from the document and view code. This topic is covered on Day 7.

☐ **The classes are easily reused in other applications.** Looking ahead, if the next product that follows InfoMan uses a to-do list, this class can be reused as is. Even if you don't immediately know of any use for a general-purpose class, it's a good idea to build it so it can be reused because every class is an addition to your toolkit.

☐ **Changes to the application will cause little or no impact to these classes.** As these classes are designed, there is little interaction with the MFC application framework. If you make major changes to the application, there will be very little or no changes to these classes. For example, you could convert the application into an OLE 2.0, mail-enabled application with no change at all to the data-model classes.

☐ **Changes to the class will cause little impact on the application.** If the data model needs to be reimplemented for speed or efficiency, the application will not be affected. On a project where there may be a large number of changes late in the development cycle, this can be a big help.

Low-Level Design of View Classes

As defined by the MFC framework, the two primary jobs for a `CView`-derived class are to accept input from the user and to display information about the document to the user. On Day 2, the `CTaskView` class was described as shown in Figure 4.6. `CTaskView` was derived from `CView`, and it enabled the user to control the `CTaskDoc` document class using tabbed controls.

Figure 4.6.
The original class relation-
ship diagram for `CTaskView`.

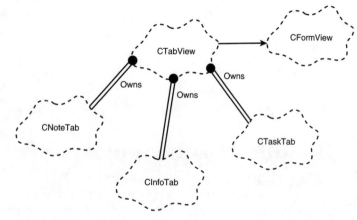

This design would work, but the `CTaskView` class would be very large, very complex, and difficult to maintain. Also, all of the code that maintains the tabs would be part of the `CTaskView` class and would not be easily reusable.

It is usually better to use several small classes as opposed to a few large, complex ones. To refine the original design, separate the functionality of the tabs and subviews into separate classes to help make the design more maintainable. This also creates `CTabView` and `CTab` classes, which can be reused in future designs. Figure 4.7 is a class diagram of the new task-management-view classes used by InfoMan.

The `CTabView` class is derived from the MFC `CFormView` class and is responsible for maintaining the tabs and controls found in the tabbed control area. `CTabView` is responsible for drawing all of the controls and keeping exactly one view visible at any given time.

The `CTab` class is derived from `CWnd` and represents a "page" in the tabbed view. The `CTab` class is responsible for updating the controls contained on each page, as well as for drawing the actual contents of the page. This functionality is similar to the `CPropertyPage` and `CPropertySheet` classes included with MFC, except that these classes will work inside a View class.

Figure 4.7.

Refined class relationship diagram for task management in InfoMan, including the CTabView *and* CTab *classes.*

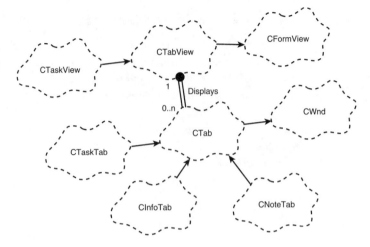

Handling User Input

The *view* handles all of the input that is sent from the user to the document. The low-level design of a view, of course, depends on the type of application, but most views share a few traits in common.

Typically, the view is responsible for mapping the user's actions into calls to the document's methods. For example, with InfoMan's to-do list, if the user presses the Add button, CTaskView should create a new CTaskItem and call CTaskDoc::AddTask. When a CTaskItem is removed, CTaskView determines which of the tasks is highlighted in the list-box control and calls CTaskDoc::RemoveTask.

The CTabView class maintains a list of subviews that represent the contents of each tab. Only one of these views can be visible at any given time. When CTabView receives a message that the left mouse button is down, it performs a "hit test" to determine if the mouse is over a tab. If it is, that tab is made the visible tab, and the contents of its window are displayed. The previous tab's window is hidden.

Handling Updates from the Document

There are two cases in which the document will ask the view to update itself. The framework will call the OnInitialUpdate method to ask the view to prepare itself for a new view, typically when the document is created or initially loaded. The OnUpdate method is called when the document class has called UpdateAllViews.

Developer's Tip: To make your application appear more responsive, you should try to update the view immediately when modifying a document. For example, in InfoMan, if a task is deleted from the to-do list, the view can remove that item from the list box without waiting for the document to request that CTaskView be updated. When this sort of self-updating is possible, it makes the application appear much more responsive.

If a CView pointer is passed to the CDocument::UpdateAllViews method, all views except that CView will be updated. This pointer should be passed to the document whenever a method that will change the view is invoked.

If you want to update all views, including your own, send NULL instead of your own CView pointer. If you do this, be careful not to create an infinite loop. If you update the document during your processing of the update message, you will cause another update message to be sent to your view, causing the document to be updated again, and so on.

In the InfoMan CTaskView, OnInitialUpdate is used to clear all of the private data that is used by the view, and then to retrieve the first CTaskItem from CTaskDoc. OnUpdate uses the hint parameters to determine how to update the view. Listing 4.5 shows the pseudocode for CTaskView::OnUpdate.

Listing 4.5. Pseudocode for CTaskView::OnUpdate.

```
method    CTaskItem::OnUpdate( parameter pointer to CView
                               parameter LPARAM nHint
                               parameter pointer to CObject )
    if pointer to CView == this then
        return
    else if pointer to CObject != NULL then
        cast CObject to CTaskInfo
        insert CTaskInfo into task list at nHint
        Populate controls with CTaskInfo data
    else
        remove entry from task list at nHint
    end if
begin
```

If the pHint parameter is NULL, then the nHint parameter holds the index of the task item to be removed from the to-do list. If the pHint parameter is not NULL, then it points to a new CTaskItem, which should be inserted in the position indicated by nHint.

Showstopper: Views that show true documents in a view—for example, word-processing documents—should not repaint the entire display based on a call to OnUpdate or OnInitialUpdate. Instead, use the hint parameters to identify which part of the view needs to be redrawn, and invalidate only that area of the view. A WM_PAINT message will be generated and sent by Windows at the appropriate time.

Documentation Used for Low-Level Design

The documentation that is produced as part of the low-level design is similar to the documentation that you've created for some of the previous phases of InfoMan. The exact format that is used for the documentation may vary, depending on your needs. At a minimum, the design documentation should have the following attributes:

- ☐ It should be easy to update the design with changes that are required because of new features or enhancements that are made to the design.

- ☐ The design documentation should have a flexible format. It's much easier to reuse a flexible format than to redesign a new document every time you start a new project.

- ☐ It should be easy to look up detailed information about a class or function. The low-level design documentation will be used as a reference, so it should have an index and table of contents.

The low-level design documentation that was created for InfoMan follows the format shown next. Because a project may need to document the low-level design of modules that are not classes, the following document can be used as either a module or class-design document:

Scope. This section talks about the class or module in general terms. It discusses the functionality of the class or module and how it relates to its environment.

Glossary. This is an explanation of any technical terms or concepts that are used in the rest of the document.

Description. A more detailed description of the class or module. This section should be detailed enough to enable a new user of the class to use it successfully. This section should contain figures if needed.

Inheritance. A description of the inheritance tree for the class. You can use Booch class relationship diagrams here. If this design is for a module instead of a class, this section is empty.

Constraints. A list of any problems or special needs of which a user of the class should be aware. For example, if a class cannot be instantiated or if it cannot be created on the stack, you should document it here.

Public methods. A listing and description of the public methods available from the class or module. There should be enough information for each method to enable a user to confidently use the interface without having to read the source code.

Nonpublic methods. This section describes the protected and private interfaces for the class or module.

Data members. A description of the internal data that is used by the class or module.

Usage examples. If the class should be used in a way that isn't immediately obvious, it can be helpful to include some examples of code that uses the class as it was intended.

Modification Notes

When you modify an existing project, the low-level design phase will be much like the design phase for a new project. The only difference is that there are probably a number of classes existing in the project from which the new design can reuse or inherit.

Look for classes that are currently being used that perform similar functions. You may be able to use these classes as is, or inherit from them. It's always a good idea to reuse existing, working code whenever possible.

Debugging the Process

Most problems during the low-level design phase are caused by issues that are discovered when you are trying to implement the classes identified during the system design.

Classes with Interfaces that Seem to Be too Large

A class that is growing too large and complex may actually work better if it's split into two or more classes that are more narrowly defined. Classes that focus on a single task are easier to design and implement, and they are also easier to maintain in the future.

The CTaskView class was a very complex class before it was split into three classes, each of which concentrated on doing a less-complicated job.

Complicated Attributes for Classes

An example of a complicated attribute is the priority member variable that was used by CTaskItem earlier today. As the low-level design progressed, it became easier to think of the priority as a class instead of as a built-in type.

If you find new classes during the low-level design, use them. Don't fight the process just because you hadn't considered that class previously. Just go back to the system-design documents and update them to reflect the new class, then create the low-level design using the new system design.

Construction

Part II is eight days long; during this part of the project, you'll create most of your application's code. This section also discusses coding standards, prototyping, and low-level testing. Some of the topics covered in this part of the book include the following:

- ☐ Instrumenting your code
- ☐ Debugging strategies
- ☐ Creating reusable classes, libraries, and DLLs
- ☐ Error reporting and metrics
- ☐ Integration

Coding Standards
and Work Methods

Today you will look at different ways to help improve the quality of your code by using coding standards and guidelines. Coding standards come in all shapes and sizes, and you will look at two of the most popular ones. You'll also create a coding standard to be used for the InfoMan sample application. Topics along the way include naming conventions, styles for adding comments to your code, and using source-code "boilerplates" to help make it easier to provide standard comments for every source file.

Naming Conventions

A large part of programming deals with names. The names that you pick for variables, functions, and classes will say something about your programming style. It will also have a big impact on the usability of your source code. If you have a naming style that helps others read and understand your source code, the source will be easier to debug and maintain in the future.

If a naming style is inconsistent or makes it difficult to understand a source module, it will, of course, be more difficult to maintain. Also, when you or someone else tries to modify the code in future releases, there is a greater chance for error.

Hungarian Naming

The most common Windows naming convention is Hungarian naming. A Microsoft engineer named Charles Simonyi invented it, and it is used in most of the sample code that comes from Microsoft. Legend has it that it was called Hungarian notation because it was so difficult for a novice to read, but Charles Simonyi is also Hungarian, so who's to say?

The main idea behind Hungarian is that the logical type of a variable is prefixed to the variable name. For example, a variable of type RECT used for a view rectangle is prefixed with the abbreviation rc, creating the name rcView. Table 5.1 lists some sample Hungarian prefixes that will be used in InfoMan.

Table 5.1. Some sample Hungarian prefixes for InfoMan.

Type	Prefix	Example
char[], CString	sz	szAuthor
Pointer to	p	pWnd
RECT, CRect	rc	rcView
SIZE, CSize	s	sTall
POINT, CPoint	pt	ptAnchor
Device Context, CDC	dc	dcStretched
PEN, CPen	pen	penDark
BRUSH, CBrush	br	brGray

The image at the top right shows a "Sams Learning Center" and "SAMS PUBLISHING" logo.

Type	Prefix	Example
WND, CWnd	wnd	wndControl
COLORREF	clr	clrBackground
HANDLE	h	hWndMain
Class name	C	CString
Enumerated type name	E	EColor

Developer's Tip: When using Hungarian naming, it's important to keep your prefixes simple. A general rule of thumb is to use one modifier, like p for pointer, and one data type, like br for a brush, per variable name. For example, the variable

`pbrControl`

is a pointer to a brush used for a control. If you try to encode more than one type and modifier, names become too complicated, like

`phdcrcControl`

which is much less readable than

`pControlHdcRect`

Another problem can occur when you define your own prefixes. Although the prefix s is used for SIZE types and sz is used for strings, there's no conflict because no type starts with z. However, if you defined a z prefix in your project, you may have some readability problems.

A complete listing of the different prefixes is included in the InfoMan coding standard that is developed in the section, "Creating Your Own Coding Standard," and on the CD that accompanies the book. Try to keep the number of different prefixes to a minimum. In particular, don't try to assign a prefix to every single object type. Even a moderately sized MFC project might have hundreds of classes, and the list of prefixes would quickly become unmanageable.

Keep in mind that there are no correct Hungarian prefixes. Even at Microsoft, it's left up to the teams working on a particular project to determine which Hungarian prefixes are used, or even if any are used at all.

Showstopper: Don't fall into the trap of trying to map every single type into a Hungarian prefix. Too many project developers try to find a prefix for every single data type, and that's not what Hungarian notation is for.

> Don't try to map all of the built-in data types based on their actual representa-
> tions (long, WORD, int, etc.). C++ is strongly typed, and the compiler will tell
> you if there's a problem with conversion between types. Also, don't try to map
> the detail of every single class. For example, if your project contains a
> COcxPropPage class, a pointer to that class should not be named poppControl. A
> better name is pOcxPage. It conveys more information and uses the same
> number of characters.

Other Naming Conventions

There are several advantages to using Hungarian with your Visual C++ 2.0 project. It is widely
used in Windows programming, it enables the logical type of a variable to be determined at a
glance, and it fits in with code created by the Visual C++ Wizards, all of which generate
Hungarian.

Of course, some people don't care much for Hungarian because they believe that it makes the
code less readable. When you are writing a paper, for example, you would hardly prefix every
verb with v and every noun with n. Another complaint lodged against Hungarian is that it tends
to place too much emphasis on the actual underlying representation of a variable, rather than
focusing on its use.

Whether or not you should use Hungarian prefixes, and to what degree you should use them,
is a personal decision best left up to the team working on the project. As with many style issues,
it can be counter productive to try to impose a particular style on people.

There are other naming conventions that aren't as well-known as Hungarian naming. Many
programmers with experience in UNIX programming prefer to use a style that's common in that
system, and can be found in many UNIX programming books. A popular UNIX style is used
in the GNU coding standard, discussed later in the section, "Using Existing Coding Standards."
Still others have their own style that has evolved over the years. Listing 5.1 contains two examples
of the same function written with different naming conventions.

**Listing 5.1. Two different versions of a destructor, using different
naming conventions.**

```
//
//Hungarian naming
//
CTabArray::~CTabArray()
{
    // free up tab info
    CObject* pTab;
    int j = GetSize();
```

```
        for(int i = 0; i < j; i++)
        {
            if ((pTab = GetAt(0)) != NULL)
            {
                RemoveAt(0);
                delete pTab;
            }
        }
}
//
//Gnu (UNIX) style
//
tab_arrayT::~tab_arrayT(){
    // free up tab info
    objectT* tab_ptr;
    int j = get_size();
    for(int i = 0; i < j; i++){
        if ((tab_ptr = get_at(0)) != NULL){
            remove_at(0);
            delete tab_ptr;
        }
    }
}
```

Developer's Tip: If you write code that is never seen, used, or maintained by anyone else, then you should use the style that makes you productive. On the other hand, if you work for someone else or if you work on a team, you should consider using a naming convention that makes everyone more productive.

5

Coding Standards

The best way to ensure that all of the code produced for a project is consistent is to implement a coding standard. A good coding standard can improve productivity and quality at the same time, which is something that rarely happens in software development.

Textbook Tip: The choice of which particular coding standard to use is not as important as picking one particular coding style and sticking with it. Everybody needs to use a coding standard, even if you're a single person consulting on your own or just learning to develop C++ projects.

Even if you think you're absolutely sure that you'll never have someone helping you write code, consider the following:

☐ You might grow. Who knows, maybe you'll become successful and have to hire some help. A coding standard you develop now can help cut down on the amount of time it takes for new hires to understand your work model.

☐ On the other hand, you might become unsuccessful (because you are so stubborn about the coding standard and other issues) and have to hire extra help to finish the project. A coding standard would sure come in handy.

☐ More and more customers are becoming interested in their supplier's work methods. Don't be shocked if customers start asking you for a copy of your coding standard and other work methods.

One of the biggest productivity problems on a software project involves the amount of time it takes someone unfamiliar with a block of code to understand it. More than the time spent learning the new code, productivity also suffers when errors are made because a person misunderstood existing code. If you use a consistent coding style, you can reduce these productivity problems.

Speaking of errors, a coding standard can help you eliminate coding errors by providing a kind of pre-review of your code. How many times have you made the error shown in Listing 5.2? What if you were given some code to maintain, and you came across some code constructed as in Listing 5.2? Is the code correct, or is it working accidentally?

Listing 5.2. This code compiles, but is it correct?

```
if( fReturn = FALSE )
{
    throw CExceptInconsistent();
}
```

A coding standard can eliminate these problems by specifying that constants should always be on the left side of conditional expressions, as shown in Listing 5.3. The compiler will catch the error in this case.

Listing 5.3. This error will be caught by the compiler.

```
if( FALSE = fReturn )
{
    throw CExceptAllocationFailure();
}
```

Another approach to preventing this type of error is to not allow assignment inside conditional expressions, such as `if()` or `while()`. That would clearly make the code in Listing 5.2 incorrect according to your coding standard. However, it can still be a source of errors because the compiler will still accept it.

> If you're a member of a development team, a good way to establish a coding standard is to get input from as many members of the team as possible. Remember that the idea is to have a standard that makes everyone productive, and that happens only if everyone on the team can feel efficient when they use the new coding rules.

What's Covered in a Coding Standard?

A coding standard should cover several things. You may find that you are already taking steps in some of these areas.

- ☐ Naming conventions for variables, functions, and modules
- ☐ Language constructions that are recommended against or even forbidden
- ☐ Commenting rules for source modules and functions
- ☐ Code boilerplates (a topic discussed later today in the section, "Using Source-Code Boilerplates"), or blank templates that makes source code look uniform
- ☐ Indentation rules for declarations, functions, and control structures

Using Existing Coding Standards

If you can find an existing coding standard that fits your needs, and everyone on the staff can live with it, great. You'll get the benefit of reusing a proven style, without the expense and hassle of trying to develop one on your own.

A popular coding standard for C++ is available from Ellemtel Telecommunications Laboratories, titled "Programming in C++, Rules and Recommendations," by Mats Henricsson and Eric Nyquist. This coding standard is included on the accompanying CD in straight-text format in the \CHAP5\LMTEL directory. It's also available on the Internet in several locations, including the Ellemtel site by anonymous FTP to `euagate.eua.ericsson.se`.

Ellemtel is partially owned by L.M. Ericsson, a Swedish telecommunications manufacturer with 70,000 employees in over 100 countries. Many of these employees are engineers or scientists developing computer programs. Because the source code that is developed by its employees represents a huge investment, the company has a great deal of interest in protecting it.

The Ellemtel coding style focuses on how maintainable and readable code is, rather than on source-code volume. This makes it ideal for code that must be maintained for a long period of time, like telecommunications software. The rules and recommendations in the Ellemtel coding standard are mainly common-sense issues that have been discovered by trial and error, and by people who have been actively using the language for many years. A good feature is how the standard uses examples to illustrate the rationale behind a rule.

The following is a sample rule from the Ellemtel guide:

☐ Rule 25: A class that uses "new" to allocate instances managed by the class must define a copy constructor.

The guide also provides a source code example for this rule:

```
#include <string.h>

class String
{
    public:
        String( const char* cp = "");    // Constructor
        ~String();                        // Destructor
    private:
        char* sp;
};
// Constructor
String::String(const char* cp) : sp( new char[strlen(cp)] )
{
    strcpy(sp,cp);
}
String::~String()    // Destructor
{
    delete [] sp;
}
// "Dangerous" String class
void
main()
{
    String w1;
    String w2 = w1;
    // WARNING: IN A BITWISE COPY OF w1::sp,
    // THE DESTRUCTOR FOR W1::SP WILL BE CALLED TWICE:
    // FIRST, WHEN w1 IS DESTROYED; AGAIN, WHEN w2 IS DESTROYED.
}
```

One problem with the Ellemtel guide is that it's very platform-independent. There are some rules that are usually handled differently for Windows development, and some issues that don't need to be addressed at all because they simply don't exist. Unfortunately, this means that some Windows or Visual C++ specific issues are not addressed, such as naming conventions for dialog boxes or other resources.

Another popular coding style, used for UNIX, is available from the GNU project for use by persons that contribute to the GNU G++ compiler, a C++ compiler that is in the public domain.

There are also several coding standards that have been published recently. Teams from Taligent, IBM, Microsoft, and others have published books that emphasize coding standards used on their projects.

All of these companies and projects (Ellemtel, GNU, IBM, and Microsoft) have something in common. They have software projects that represent a substantial investment and must be maintained by teams of programmers.

Creating Your Own Coding Standard

If you decide to create your own coding standard, remember to get input from as many people as possible. A good approach is to use an existing coding standard as a base document, if you can find one that fits most of your needs.

As an example, create a coding standard for the InfoMan project. The standard is split into three sections:

- [ ] General structure and naming
- [ ] Visual C++ and MFC issues
- [ ] Class-design issues

You can find the complete style guide on the CD in the \CHAP5\STANDARD directory. Highlights from the rules are listed in the following sections. The coding standard on the CD contains more rules, with explanations and code examples for each of them. Feel free to omit some of these rules in your own coding standard. In fact, feel free to eliminate all of them. Remember, the most important rule is to use a coding standard that makes the team productive, whether you create it or use someone else's.

General Structure and Naming

The rules covered in this section address problems that occur when you are laying out code in the source module, naming identifiers, and tackling other, general code-structure issues.

- [ ] Don't include unnecessary spaces around identifiers and unary operators. Examples of these are the ++, --, ->, . and () operators.
- [ ] Use an "open" bracing style. This leads to code that is more readable and easier to understand than other styles, and may be more compact.
- [ ] Use Hungarian naming for all variable identifiers.
- [ ] Give variables the smallest possible scope, and declare them close to the first time you use them.
- [ ] Use the .h extension for header files. Inside each header file use preprocessor directives to ensure that the file is included only once.

Issues Specific to Visual C++ and MFC:

This section of the coding standard deals with issues that are specific to using the MFC class library and Visual C++. Portability between different Visual C++ platforms is also covered.

☐ Don't assume that the target machine has Intel architecture. The alignment of structures and the size and order of bits may change between different platforms that can be targeted by Visual C++ and MFC.

☐ If code will work properly on only one platform or operating system, you should comment the header file.

☐ When you work with code generated by an automated tool such as the MFC Class Wizard, use the existing naming convention and format instead of editing the generated code.

☐ Don't edit any code reserved for use by a code-generating tool. The message-map entries created by Class Wizard are an example of reserved-code areas.

☐ Don't make assumptions about the order in which messages are received from Windows.

☐ Use the ASSERT and VERIFY macros to test assumptions about pre- and postconditions in functions.

☐ Consider using BoundsChecker or a similar tool to test for memory or resource-usage problems.

☐ Name resources according to the MFC naming convention.

☐ Don't assume any specific screen resolution when you are designing screen elements.

Class-Design Issues

The rules in this section primarily deal with helping you to create robust and reusable classes, instead of pure style issues.

☐ Always define debug and dump functions for classes if memory is allocated with new.

☐ If you don't intend to modify a function argument, declare it as const.

☐ If a function doesn't modify any member variables, declare it as const.

☐ Implement binary operators as friends and unary operators as member functions.

☐ Always define a virtual destructor for base classes. When in doubt, declare the destructor virtual. Listing 5.4 is an example of the problems that can occur with nonvirtual base classes.

Listing 5.4. An example using a base class that has a nonvirtual destructor.

```cpp
class CBadBase
{
public:
    CBadBase();
    ~CBadBase(); // Design error, do not copy this code.
};
class CDerived : public CBadBase
{
    char* pszName;
public:
    CDerived();
    ~CDerived();
};

CDerived::CDerived()
{
    pszName = new char[20];
}
CDerived::~CDerived()
{
    delete [] pszName;
}

int main( int argc, char* argv[] )
{
    // You often need to use a base pointer to access an instance
    // of a class.
    CBadBase* pBase = new CDerived;

    // The next statement DOES NOT call CDerived's destructor,
    // and a memory leak results. If the base class destructor
    // had been declared as : virtual ~CBadBase(), the proper
    // destructor would have been called.
    delete pBase;
}
```

☐ If a class allocates memory with new, always define the default and copy constructors, along with the assignment operator.

☐ Always test for self in the assignment operator. This is a problem because the current contents of the destination are erased during an assignment. If assignment to self were allowed, the original contents would also be destroyed. An example of assignment to self is shown here:

```cpp
CString szName = "Mickey";
szMickey = szMickey;         // Assignment to self
```

Using Source-Code Boilerplates

A *source-code boilerplate* is a template that you follow to make source code more uniform. The advantage to using standard templates is that it makes code maintenance much easier. You should define boilerplates for the comment header at the beginning of source modules. Another boilerplate should be defined for the comments used for function definitions.

The sample boilerplate used for InfoMan source modules is shown in Listing 5.5. Notice that there is an area in which to record changes that have been applied to the source module.

Listing 5.5. The common module boilerplate used in InfoMan.

```
//=================================================================
// Title : SomeModule.cpp
// Author: M. Williams
// Date  : December 16, 1992
// ― ― ― ― ― ― ― ― ― ― ― ― ― ― ― ― ― ― ― ― ―
// Purpose: SomeModule.cpp doesn't exist. The SomeModule header
//          is the common boilerplate for source module comments
//          from Develop Your First Visual C++ Application in 21
//          Days from Sams Publishing.
// ― ― ― ― ― ― ― ― ― ― ― ― ― ― ― ― ― ― ― ― ―
// History: Dec 16, 1992 M.Williams        Created
//
```

The sample boilerplate used for function definitions is shown in Listing 5.6. Try to keep the function boilerplates minimal. It's better to write clearer code than to write large volumes of comments.

Listing 5.6. The common function definition boilerplate used in InfoMan.

```
//=================================================================
// Function : Foo::SomeMemberFunc()
// Author: M. Williams
// Date  : December 16, 1992
// ― ― ― ― ― ― ― ― ― ― ― ― ― ― ― ― ― ― ― ―
// Returns: void
// Parameters: void
// ― ― ― ― ― ― ― ― ― ― ― ― ― ― ― ― ― ― ― ― ―
// Purpose: SomeMemberFunc peforms some sort of action and then
//          returns.
```

Software-Configuration Management

Software-configuration management (SCM) is the process that is used to track changes made to software during its life cycle. It's also used to make sure the different modules that make up the system are stored properly and changes to each module are tracked.

Another feature of SCM is that it tracks executable releases. Every release that is created using SCM is completely reproducible and traceable. This means that if version 1.05 of a particular package works and version 1.06 is known to have a serious error, then there should be no difficulty in creating an executable that is at version 1.05.

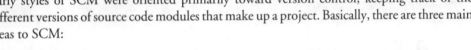

Textbook Tip: If you've ever fixed a bug more than once because a coworker overwrote an updated source file, or if you've ever tried to rebuild a version of a program that used to work but failed because of newly introduced errors, you understand the need for software-configuration management.

SCM can help reduce the rework and lost time caused by these types of problems when you are working in a team environment. If more than one programmer is working with your code over its life cycle, you need to use SCM techniques.

Early styles of SCM were oriented primarily toward version control, keeping track of the different versions of source code modules that make up a project. Basically, there are three main areas to SCM:

- [ ] Identification
- [ ] Control
- [ ] Auditing

Work that is done for the Department of Defense must conform to established SCM procedures that are detailed enough to warrant a book of their own. Without going into that much detail, each of these three areas of SCM are meant to help make a software project more predictable, reliable, and traceable.

SCM Identification

The identification part of SCM is concerned with identifying the parts of the system that should be managed. An easy way to deal with this is to manage everything. For InfoMan, all documents, including requirements, specifications, test plans, test results, and end-user documentation should be managed. This helps during the review process, and it also helps to track changes that are made to the project.

5

SCM Control

Control management is the actual handling of changes that are made to software or documents that are being managed. Among different projects, there will be a wide range in the amount of control that is maintained.

For example, under control management every document is assigned a version number. Current versions of documents should be marked as read-only. Every time the document is updated, the version is incremented. Documents that are written in Word for Windows should include a description of the changes made in hidden text. Tracking changes to documents is covered in more detail on Day 13, "The Design-Documentation Archive."

Source-code modules will also be given a version number and should be kept read-only. Whenever they are updated, the version should be incremented.

When you build executable releases starting on Day 7, "Basic Class Construction," you should document each release by noting which components were used to build the release, including the version numbers.

SCM Auditing

The auditing process refers to creating and reviewing the paper trail that is developed as part of the identification and control processes. For your project, you should document every executable release and list all the components. Every change made to a document or source module causes a new version of that document to be created.

Modification Notes

If you're modifying an existing project, you should try to follow the existing coding rules and work methods whenever possible. Hopefully, the coding standards and work methods used on the project are documented.

If you are trying to introduce the idea of a coding standard for the first time, prepare for some resistance. Programming can be a very personal craft, and people may react to coding standards in a negative way at first. Remember to focus on the benefits of standard styles, and try to minimize unnecessary bureaucracy.

If you are faced with trying to maintain source code that has been previously developed without a standard naming convention, a good approach is to define a naming convention and use it for any new code in the project. Unless the existing source code is completely unreadable, the risks involved with rewriting it aren't worth the benefits.

Debugging the Process

If the current work methods aren't documented, then you've got two choices. Either take the time to document the current work methods if time allows, or follow the established practice for the project as much as possible. Obviously, documenting the existing practice is the preferred method, but that's not always possible.

A common problem that occurs when projects use SCM for the first time is that people will pretend that it doesn't exist. One person changing source code outside of the SCM system can cause serious problems that are very difficult to trace. If you see this happening, make sure that everyone handling managed objects understands the importance of SCM.

5

Iteration and
Prototyping

In previous chapters, you used iteration and prototyping to create the design for your project. You used iteration to help collect the requirements at the start of the project on Day 1, "Requirements Analysis." You also used paper prototypes to help get feedback about the proposed design of the user interface. Today you'll learn about prototyping and iteration in detail. You will use iteration to help divide the construction of your project into easily managed pieces.

Prototyping comes in all forms. The paper prototype from Day 1 was one of the simplest prototypes you'll use in a Microsoft Windows project. Later today you'll actually build a partially functioning prototype using Visual C++ and the MFC classes.

Improving Your Development Process Using Iteration and Prototyping

Prototyping and iteration are two methods that you can use to reduce the amount of time spent developing your application. One of the things both methods have in common is that they emphasize concentrating on smaller parts of your application, rather than attacking the entire project at once.

Understanding Prototyping

A prototype can take many forms; a common way to use prototyping is to develop a user-interface model with limited functionality. This way, you can test its usability before the actual system is built, while there's still time to easily modify the design. You did this on Day 1 when you built paper prototypes that could be used to show InfoMan's user-interface design.

Prototypes are not unique to software design; the aerospace industry often uses prototypes. Before a complex project like the space shuttle actually completed a real mission, a full-size prototype was used to evaluate the flight performance of the shuttle's design.

The space shuttle project is an example of a prototype that tested a large number of the project components. For most people, this prototype seemed to be completely functional. However, most prototypes aren't as complete and test only a limited subset of the planned project.

Developer's Tip: The following are important rules to keep in mind when you are developing a prototype:

- ☐ Keep the prototype focused. Don't let it become a full working model.
- ☐ Keep the prototype low-cost. The prototype is a tool, not a finished product.

☐ Decide how feedback from the prototype will be used *before* it is developed. The feedback from the prototype may indicate that a design decision or assumption won't work. If so, reanalyze the assumptions rather than ignore the feedback.

Visual C++ is well-suited for prototype development. By using the integrated resource editor and ClassWizard, along with the MFC class library, you can keep the cost of the prototype low, and the prototype can be easily changed to react to user feedback. Later today you will build the prototype for the user interface for the Task Manager so that you can gather some early feedback regarding the design.

Understanding Iteration

On Day 1 you used an iterative technique to help you zero in on the project's final software requirements. Even after you started the low-level design, you updated the system design on Day 4, "Low-Level Design." This is what iteration is all about; you divide parts of the project, or even parts of a development phase, into smaller pieces that are attacked one at a time. This may mean that you take three or four iterations to develop a system design or low-level design. Iteration can also be used to divide the actual construction phases into a series of executable releases that each contain a little more functionality.

Each construction iteration becomes a working executable product, and each included software module is completely functional. Some modules may be incomplete. However, in an ideal iterative process you include each module once into the project, and you do not recode it unless you discover faults. In the real world, however, some modules will be needed before they are completely ready. You will sometimes need to use stub modules with limited functionality, which are replaced during development. A *stub* is a small piece of code that is a temporary placeholder for a function to be coded later.

The advantage of iterative development is that each of the design-code-test cycles is shorter than if the entire project was developed using the waterfall model, which was discussed on Day 1. You can act on the feedback from early phases during the development of later phases, you can add new requirements more easily with iterative design, and each of the phases is much shorter and simpler than when the waterfall model is used.

The C++ language is well-suited for iterative development. By using the data hiding and abstraction properties of C++, you can design and construct well-defined modules without interacting with other modules.

You will use an iterative cycle for the construction phases of the InfoMan project. Iterative development cycles are often drawn in a spiral pattern to emphasize the phases through which the project cycles.

If the InfoMan project cycle was drawn as the waterfall was drawn, it would look like Figure 6.1. After the analysis and design phases are developed, the project is developed in three iterations. The scheduling details are covered later today.

Figure 6.1.
The development cycle used for InfoMan.

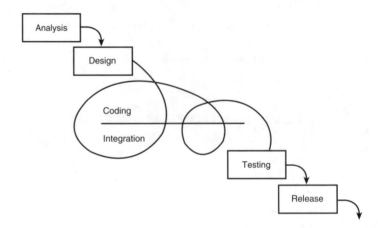

The number of iterations you use depends on the type of project you are developing. For your project, there may be some obvious candidates for iteration. If there aren't, try to divide the project along the following lines:

- Look for separate, functional areas. For example, the three different types of documents used by InfoMan make natural dividing lines for the planned iterations. Because the documents have no dependency on one another, it's easy to split them up into different iterations.

- Another way to plan iterations is to look for functional layers. For example, if the project has several interrelated functions that can't be separated, try to plan a development cycle that provides limited features to the entire project in limited steps.

- If there still aren't a set of clear iterations, consider using simulations or stubs to help create different development phases. If the project has a strong dependency on outside development, you can build a simulator to help reduce that dependency during development. As the project matures, you can enhance the simulator to provide more functionality. These enhancements can be the starting point to help you plan your iterations.

If you follow these steps and still have trouble planning the construction iterations, you have two options:

☐ Reconsider the design, and look for ways to make it more iteration-friendly

☐ Look for another way to construct the project

Using iteration is not the only way to building software. If your project doesn't fit into the model, don't force yourself to use it. If your project really needs the waterfall model for some reason, use it.

Candidates for Prototyping

Several parts of your project may be candidates for modeling with prototypes. If the database design is unusual or needs to meet some specific performance targets, a prototype could help demonstrate the performance of the proposed design. If the help system is complex, or if the menu structure is unusual in some way, those parts of your system can be modeled and tested with users to evaluate that part of the design.

As discussed on Day 1, prototyping is often used to develop early working models of a user interface. In some systems, 100 percent of a proposed user interface might be developed as a prototype and tested in a usability lab, or shown to a focus group as a way to do early testing of a design.

For InfoMan, a good candidate for prototyping is the user interface for the Task Manager. Because it has only one view, it's the easiest of the three managers to model.

The purpose of the prototype will be to test the usability of the multiple tab and list-box interface. Because the tabs that are being used are slightly different from the typical MFC Property Pages used for a "tabbed" look, the prototype will display a dialog box similar to the proposed Task Manager view, and each prototype user will be given a script of actions to be applied to the prototype. By judging user reactions to the tasks they are given, you can address any rough spots in the user-interface design now, before the code has been written.

Designing the Prototype

The prototype for the Task Manger user interface is built around a dialog box and a standard MFC skeleton application. There are three main classes in the prototype, which makes it similar to the design of the Task Manager that you created on Day 2, "System Design," and on Day 4. A Booch diagram showing the relationships between these classes is shown in Figure 6.2.

Figure 6.2.
The major Task Manager prototype classes.

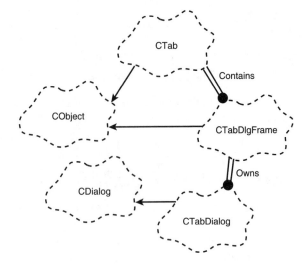

The CTabDialog class is derived from CDialog and is the main interface for users of the tabbed dialog box. The CTabDialog object contains any controls inside the dialog box that are not in the tabbed area. Messages to and from these controls are handled by CTabDialog. It is also responsible for forwarding messages to the CTabDlgFrame member that it contains. The CTabDialog class doesn't have any logic for drawing the tabs or selecting any tabs to be active.

The CTabDlgFrame class contains the actual tabs and draws the tabs on the face of the dialog box. When the CTabDialog needs to know anything about the state of the tabs, it queries the CTabDlgFrame object.

Each CTab object represents an individual tab included in the dialog box. Each CTab object contains a pointer to the CDialog object that is displayed inside the dialog box when its tab is active.

Implementing the Prototype

For InfoMan, the first user-interface prototypes were the paper prototypes built during Day 1. Today, you will build the prototype around an MFC dialog box that has some of the same features as the project's to-do list. The prototype Visual C++ project can be found on the CD in the \CHAP6\PROTO directory. Because of the size of the project, only highlights from the source code are presented today.

The actual steps that you take to build the prototype depend on the project you are developing. However, the main goal when you are developing an early prototype should be to keep the cost low. Whenever possible, use the MFC classes or reuse classes from other projects. Try to keep new development work to an absolute minimum.

Showstopper: The most important thing to keep in mind when you are planning a prototype is to have a focus point. A prototype that starts as a side project to demonstrate the project can easily consume too many resources if you don't limit its functionality. Remember to keep the prototype low-cost.

One way to keep a prototype low-cost is to narrowly define the scope of the prototype. This means to define exactly what the prototype should demonstrate, as well as what will not be included in the prototype.

The purpose of the InfoMan prototype is to demonstrate what the three-dimensional tabs will look like, and show how the different tab views can be switched by using the controls. What is specifically excluded is the capability to add or delete any tasks from the to-do list.

By limiting the amount of work that is used to create the prototype, you can focus on one or two main areas of the project. The main work on the to-do list can be done later, but the focus of the prototype is on the tab controls.

Creating Three-Dimensional Tabs

Figure 6.3 shows an expanded, three-dimensional view of part of the Task Manager prototype. The lowest level of the figure shows the controls and other items that belong to the dialog box. The middle level contains the parts of the dialog box that are controlled by the `CTabDlgFrame` object. The top layer is the currently active tab, which positions its `CDialog` object inside the border provided by the frame.

Figure 6.3.
A three-dimensional view
of the prototype.

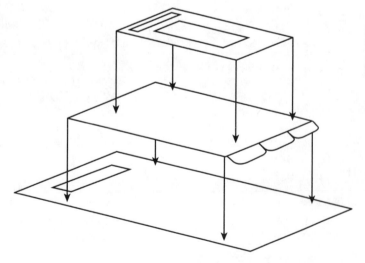

The three-dimensional tabs that are used by both the prototype and the final InfoMan program aren't really controls in the conventional sense. They are actually just areas on the face of the dialog box that are hit-tested whenever a `WM_LBUTTONDOWN` message is received.

When a `WM_LBUTTONDOWN` message is received by the dialog box, indicating that the left mouse button is down, the message is always forwarded to the `CTabDlgFrame` object, which tests the mouse position to see if it's within the boundaries of one of the tabs. If it is, that tab is made active by `CTabDlgFrame`, which tells the `CTab` object to show the subdialog window inside that tab, causing the switching effect.

The `CTabDlgFrame` object has two main functions: tracking the active tab and drawing the three-dimensional tabs. Keeping track of the active tab is simple and takes only one member variable that is used as an index by one of the MFC collection classes that stores the `CTab` objects.

A good way to learn about drawing your own three-dimensional objects is to use the ZOOMIN.EXE utility included in the SDK. Most 3-D objects in Windows are drawn so that the light source appears to be above the upper-left corner of the screen. Figure 6.4 shows a close-up view using ZOOMIN of an upper-left corner from the prototype, and Figure 6.5 uses ZOOMIN to examine a lower-right corner from the prototype.

Each of the edges actually consists of several lines, and each individual line is drawn with a different color. Edges along the left and top side of 3-D surfaces are drawn lighter than the bottom and right edges. This gives the surface a raised look. Each of the tabs along the bottom of the prototype dialog box are drawn using this method along the bottom edge of the area controlled by the `CTabDlgFrame` object.

Note: A great deal of source code will be used to create the InfoMan project. All of the source code is provided on the CD. When a class or section of this code is general enough to be useful for most projects, or if it illustrates a point, it will be included as a source-code listing in the book.

For example, a lot of code in the prototype handles the drawing of the 3-D effect for the tab surfaces. If you're interested, the complete source code can be found in TAB3DFRM.CPP in the \CHAP6\PROTO directory.

Figure 6.4.
Using ZOOMIN to examine 3-D shading on the upper-left corner of the prototype.

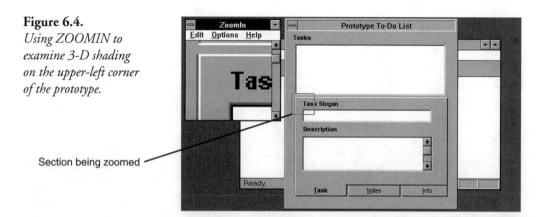

Figure 6.5.
Using ZOOMIN to examine 3-D shading on the lower-right corner of the prototype.

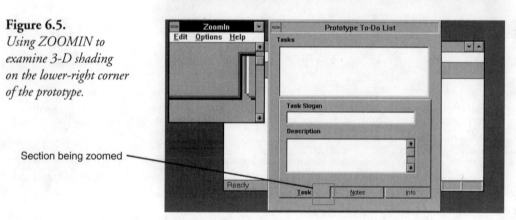

Candidates for Iteration

As discussed earlier in the section, "Understanding Iteration," you should look for either functional areas or functional "layers" when planning your iterations. A good candidate for iteration is a well-defined portion of your application that can be developed separately from the rest of the application without a lot of rework. A good example of functional layers are printing and help functions. Although these functions may be located in several places in your code, the function they perform can be added in a single step without disturbing much of the other code in the application.

You will construct the InfoMan project using an iterative cycle. You defined several main parts of InfoMan on Days 2 and 4.

☐ Basic skeleton

☐ Task Manager

☐ Contact Manager

☐ Calendar control

☐ Calendar Manager

☐ Help system

You can see the relationship between these elements in Figure 6.6. Most of the major identified parts of InfoMan have little interaction with each other.

Figure 6.6.

The relationship between the various InfoMan modules.

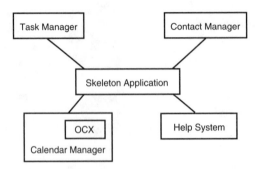

The basic skeleton consists of the toolbars, icons, and basic program structure that are primarily built with the help of AppWizard.

The Task Manager consists of a single view that tracks a list of tasks to be performed. It contains a tabbed view and an owner-drawn list box. Because it has only a single main view, the only complicated parts of the Task Manager are the tabbed subviews.

The Contact Manager has three views: one view showing a list of contacts, one view showing a single contact at a time, and a split view showing both. Because of the multiple views, the Contact Manager is a bit more complicated than the Task Manager.

The calendar control enables a user to select a date with a control that can be used in any view or dialog box. The currently selected date is displayed on the control, and the user can also use the control to select a different date.

The Calendar Manager is probably the simplest of the three manager views, except for the calendar control that it contains. It has only a single view, and its primary function is to be a user (or consumer) of the calendar control.

The help system consists primarily of the help source that will be compiled into a help file.

Planning the Iterations

When you are planning the iterations, it's important to keep in mind any dependencies that exist between different modules or subsystems. For example, the Calendar Manager should be coded at the same time as the calendar control, because the Manager has a strong dependency on it.

Developer's Tip: As you complete each iteration, the modules that are added to the project should be as complete as possible. Whenever you change a design or modify a source module, there is a good chance that you will introduce an error. By planning the iterations so that complete modules are added, modules already included in the project can avoid unnecessary changes.

You will create the basic skeleton with the help of the Visual C++ development environment. By using AppWizard, building the basic skeleton consists mainly of filling in the blanks and responding to questions posed by the Wizard. The only real work done for this iteration is to create an icon for InfoMan. After you create the basic skeleton, it will serve as a base for the rest of the iterations.

The Task Manager is the first "real" iteration for the project. For this phase, you will implement the first user interface and databases. You create the Task Manager first because it is one of the simplest modules. It has a single view, and the user interface has already been tested with the prototype.

The Contact Manager shares some characteristics with the Task Manager but is slightly more complicated because it has three views. One of the three views needs a Rolodex-type card to be displayed, which will require some advanced GDI work.

When the Contact Manager is added to the project, some source modules from the Task Manager will be changed so that template-based versions of some classes will be shared with the Contact Manager. Recoding an already integrated module goes against one of the design goals, but there are good reasons for doing so:

- [ ] The change is very straightforward and doesn't affect other modules, or affects them in only a minor way.
- [ ] The change will result in more general use for some common source modules.

After you integrate the Contact Manager and convert the Task Manager so that is uses the template version of some classes, both of those modules are considered complete. You will not recode them unless you discover faults during testing.

The Calendar is the most complicated of the three views, primarily because of the calendar control that is developed. Some of the code used in the previous iterations, such as the owner-drawn list-box code, is reused for the calendar view, so most of the new code developed for this iteration is limited to the calendar control.

After you add the three managers to the project, the last major iteration will add the help system to the project. This iteration adds very little code, and primarily it will consist of developing the help topics and compiling the help text into a help file.

Project Scheduling

The schedule that has been developed for your project will continue to evolve throughout the entire development cycle. Today, after planning the major iterations, you can adjust the schedule as needed. When you update the schedule, it's usually a good idea to create a new schedule instead of just distributing the changes.

So far, none of the InfoMan schedule has slipped. However, it is fairly common for the schedule to have a lot of adjustments at this stage as you discover classes or find new dependencies.

At this point in the development cycle, the schedule is probably being distributed to a number of people in the organization. The actual distribution list will depend on the organization, but it will definitely include groups outside the development organization, such as the Marketing or Sales departments.

Refining Milestones

At this stage of your project, you should take another look at your schedule and adjust your milestones and dates if needed. The schedule for InfoMan is shown in Table 6.1.

Table 6.1. Milestones for the InfoMan project.

Milestone	Date	Description
M1	5/05/95	Requirements, design, and prototype all complete
M2	5/12/95	Task Manager complete
M3	5/19/95	Contact Manager complete
M4	5/23/95	Calendar Manager complete, delivery to functional test
M5	6/1/95	Documentation complete
M6	6/3/95	Online docs complete

Milestone	Date	Description
M7	6/4/95	Delivery to System/Alpha test
M8	6/18/95	Delivery to Beta test
M9	7/1/95	InfoMan general release

Depending on the amount of complexity in your project, you might want to add some documentation to your schedule that specifies the tasks that must be carried out to meet each milestone. For example, for the M2 milestone the following items must be completed:

- ☐ Skeleton project
- ☐ CTab class
- ☐ CTabView class
- ☐ CTaskView class
- ☐ CTaskTab class
- ☐ CNotesTab class
- ☐ CInfoTab class
- ☐ CTaskCollection class
- ☐ CTaskItem class
- ☐ CTaskDoc class

These classes were all defined on Day 4. As the project and the schedule evolve, you may want to consider the amount of detail that is included in the schedule. One approach is to cut down on the amount of rework needed for the schedule by listing only the high-level items on the schedule, and refining it during a later phase when the project has been well-defined.

You might go into more detail for a more complex project by listing beginning and ending dates, details about class testing and documentation time, the number of programmers assigned to each task, and so on. Because InfoMan is a relatively simple project, that much detail isn't needed. If you choose to include that level of detail in your schedule, make sure that you have the resources to maintain the information; otherwise, you'll only be adding overhead to the project.

Developer's Tip: If you include information about start and stop times, documentation, and testing, you can use that extra information to help plan future projects. By tracking the resources used for this project, you can estimate future projects more easily.

The InfoMan schedule was written using Word for Windows and can be found in the \CHAP2\DOCS directory on the CD (as part of the system design) in file SYS-DES.DOC. A document template containing all of the styles used for the document is in the same directory, stored as SYS-DES.DOT. A plain-text version is also stored as SYS-DES.TXT.

Modification Notes

When you are modifying an existing project, there are several topics covered today that you might do differently.

Modification Prototypes

Prototypes are just as useful when you are modifying existing projects as when you are developing new ones. Prototypes of proposed changes often can take advantage of classes or other code that is already being used in the project.

If the project is already a Visual C++ project, it is much easier to demonstrate proposed changes by coding the prototype using Visual C++ and integrating it with the existing source code. This sort of tight integration isn't possible when you use other tools for prototyping. If the project is under software-configuration management, the best approach is to copy the existing current source modules and start a new source system for the prototype.

If for some reason you must use the existing source modules and update them with the prototype source code, make sure to clearly mark each changed block of source code for conditional compilation. The source code in Listing 6.1 shows a segment of prototype source code with conditional compilation marks used so that the prototype can be "backed out" if needed.

Listing 6.1. Using conditional compilation to isolate prototype code.

```
    GetSearchKey( pKey );
#ifdef PROTO_3D_INCLUDE
    // New code for 3D prototype. We need to get
    // the border color for the tabs.
    COLORREF clrBorder;
    GetBorderColor( clrBorder );
#endif //PROTO_3D_INCLUDE
```

Iterating Modification Changes

When you are determining which modifications should be done together and which changes should be done first, you should follow the same guidelines used for new projects:

☐ Keep iterations as small as possible.

☐ Keep iterations complete.

☐ Don't rework iterations that have been integrated.

Modification Scheduling

If the project that is to be modified had a project schedule that was used during its development, it may be easier to plan the proposed changes. If the old schedule is available, examining it might help you judge a realistic schedule. Also, if the previous schedule didn't have the proper level of detail, the modification schedule can either include or exclude some detail.

The modification schedule should include enough information so that anyone using it does not need to refer back to the original schedule. This may mean creating a new schedule and highlighting changes, or it may be enough to have just a list of schedule changes.

Debugging the Process

There are two main problems that can present themselves when you work with prototypes. Either the prototype can be a problem to develop properly, or it might work too well.

Prototypes that Don't Work

What if the prototype just doesn't work very well? This can happen if the prototype starts out as a quick project that is too ambitious. Because one of the guiding principles behind a prototype is to keep it low-cost, a developer may tend to just start hacking at the prototype. If you find yourself in this situation, take another look at the prototype. What can you do to narrow the focus of the prototype? Are there any third-party tools or libraries that you can use to reduce the size of the project?

Another option is to simply cut the functionality out of the prototype. For example, in the Task Manager prototype, no attempt was made to create an owner-drawn list box containing the icons and tasks. It would have increased the complexity of the prototype and not really helped in the evaluation of the tab controls.

Prototypes that Work too Well

Sometimes, after you demonstrate a prototype to a prospective user, things will go so well that you get a response like, "That's perfect; don't spend any more time on it." This sort of problem is most likely to occur if too much functionality was included in the prototype, or if the user is not extremely sophisticated about software development. It's important to stress that the prototype is just a tool, and not a finished product.

Problems Planning Iterations

If you have problems identifying iterations that can be used for your project, take another look at your design. If the design has a large number of dependencies that make it difficult to isolate individual classes or parts of the application for iteration, consider reworking your design. Designs with many cross-dependencies are difficult to construct and maintain. A good design will usually have components that can be built in several steps.

Basic Class
Construction

Today you'll learn the basics of how to create reusable classes. The discussion is divided into four main parts:

- ☐ Reusable classes: what they are and how to construct them
- ☐ Getting feedback from other programmers and having design reviews to help increase class reuse
- ☐ An introduction to programming by contract, a class-design method that helps make classes more robust
- ☐ Class documenting and commenting conventions

As always, the day ends with the "Modification Notes" and "Debugging the Process" sections.

Reusable Classes

During the InfoMan design process covered on Day 2, "System Design," and Day 4, "Low-Level Design," you broke the InfoMan project down into the classes that you will use to create the project. As part of the design process, it's a good idea to look for common traits that are shared by more than one object type. For example, all of the owner-drawn list boxes used by InfoMan work in similar ways. You can place the functionality that is common to all of the list boxes into a single base class called COwnerDrawListBox.

COwnerDrawListBox is an example of a class that is used several times in one project. Reusing classes within a project in this way is one type of reuse, and it helps improve the entire development cycle in two ways:

- ☐ After you develop the class, very little work needs to be done to use it, compared to the time spent to develop it. When you code classes so that they can be used in other parts of the project, the classes will be immediately available when you need them, reducing the development time required for later phases of the project.
- ☐ After the code for the class has been tested, it becomes "trusted." This code doesn't require testing at a low level again, which reduces the amount of time you need for the verification phase.

Reusing classes within a project is important, but you can also reuse classes in more than one project. The benefits of designing and building classes so that they can be used by future projects is much more rewarding than simply rebuilding the same classes over and over again for each project.

Creating Reusable Classes

Reusable classes don't just happen; you need to work on them, at least for the first project in which you use them. The benefits of reuse pay off only for projects that can reuse classes developed during earlier development cycles.

In order to create classes that can be used in the future, you need to focus on more than just the current application. When you are working on a problem, you might have a tendency to tailor classes to fit the current project. As a result, you create specialized tools that need to be slightly modified every time you use them. This wastes resources and makes you do unnecessary testing and debugging. Try to focus instead on building components that can be used in future projects.

One analogy often used for software components is the integrated circuit. Hardware designers have a seemingly endless supply of integrated circuits that they can mix and match to create devices. They rarely need to design their own custom circuits unless they have special requirements that can't be met with off-the-shelf components. In contrast, most software designers must build their own components that make up their programs. Fortunately, you're using C++ and MFC, which make the job easier. By coding your classes so that they can be reused as components later, you can cut down on your development costs and increase your quality at the same time.

Textbook Tip: In literature, a character that is capable of change is called *round*, and characters that are one-dimensional and unlikely to change are called *flat*.

A flat class can't be used outside of its current application. It may depend too much on other parts of the project, or it may not have general and complete interfaces that could be used by future applications.

Try to make your classes *round*—that is, design them with the capability to be used in more than one context. It's helpful to try to think of at least one other use for a class during the low-level design and coding phases. A round class that's added to your library will be much more useful than a flat one.

One tool that can help you create reusable components is other programmers. By discussing proposed designs or classes with other programmers, you can get input that can help you create classes that can be used in more than one context.

Don't Code Yourself into a Corner

After creating system-level and low-level designs at the beginning of a project, many programmers may feel the itch to start some "real work," and begin coding soon after the project starts. Avoid the temptation to start coding right away. It's much better to examine your low-level design and look for ways to make your classes more general and reusable. The time you spend now will pay off in the long run.

Figure 7.1 shows a class diagram of the CTaskListBox class, along with the methods that are supported by it. The original low-level design as discussed on Day 4 had a DrawItem method that was invoked whenever you needed to draw an instance of CTaskItem.

Figure 7.1.

Class diagram for
CTaskListBox.

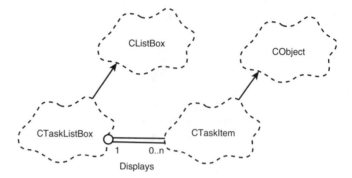

A possible implementation for CTaskListBox::DrawItem is shown in Listing 7.1. The WM_DRAWITEM message is sent from Windows to tell the control to repaint itself. The MFC framework maps this message to a CListBox::DrawItem function call. The CTaskListBox::DrawItem member function is used to draw a CTaskItem directly.

Listing 7.1. A first cut at drawing a list-box item.

```
void CTaskListBox::DrawItem(LPDRAWITEMSTRUCT lpdis)
{
    // Get the rectangle for the item, and calculate the rectangle
    // for the focus rectangle. Also, create a temporary CDC object
    // from the one passed in to us.
    CRect rc = &lpdis->rcItem;
    CRect rcFocus = rc;
    rcFocus.left += m_nHeight;
    CDC *pdcTmp = CDC::FromHandle( lpdis->hDC );
    //
    // If the item ID is LB_ERR, we are getting this DrawItem
    // call to set the focus for the entire list box. We do
    // not want to dereference itemData, since it is invalid.
    //
    if( LB_ERR ==lpdis->itemID )
    {
        CWnd *pWndList = GetDlgItem( lpdis->itemID );
        if( pWndList )
        {
            pWndList->GetWindowRect( rc );
            pdcTmp->DrawFocusRect( rc );
        }
    }
    else
    {
        COLORREF      clrBkgrnd, clrTxt;
        CTaskItem *pTask = (CTaskItem*)lpdis->itemData;
```

```
if( lpdis->itemAction & (ODA_DRAWENTIRE | ODA_SELECT) )
{
    // If we are gaining or losing the selection status,
    // choose the proper color for the background. Since
    // we have a bitmap, we are going to have to paint
    // under it.
    if( lpdis->itemState & ODS_SELECTED )
    {
        clrBkgrnd = GetSysColor(COLOR_HIGHLIGHT );
        clrTxt = GetSysColor(COLOR_HIGHLIGHTTEXT );
    }
    else
    {
        clrBkgrnd = GetSysColor( COLOR_WINDOW);
        clrTxt = GetSysColor( COLOR_WINDOWTEXT);
    }
    //
    // Now that the color has been selected:
    //    - Fill the item's rectangle with the selected
    //      color.
    //    - BitBlt the bitmap onto the colored rectangle.
    //    - Draw the text on top of the rectangle.
    DrawCheckBox( rc,
                  pdcTmp, pTask->IsCompleted(),
                  GetSysColor( COLOR_WINDOWTEXT) );
    ColorRect( rcFocus, pdcTmp, clrBkgrnd );
    CString szTaskItemText = pTask->GetPriority() + "\t" +
                             pTask->GetSlogan();
    DrawItemText( rcFocus,
                  pdcTmp,
                  szTaskItemText,
                  clrBkgrnd,
                  clrTxt );
}
else
{
    //
    // We are doing something other than drawing the
    // whole rectangle, and we aren't doing anything
    // with the selection status, so just set the colors
    // to the normal background colors.
    clrBkgrnd = GetSysColor( COLOR_WINDOW );
    clrTxt = GetSysColor( COLOR_WINDOWTEXT );
}
//
// Draw the focus rectangle around the item. This works
// just like an XOR, so we don't have to keep track of
// the focus state, since drawing the rectangle again
// will make it disappear.
if( lpdis->itemAction & ODA_FOCUS )
{
    pdcTmp->DrawFocusRect( rcFocus );
}
    }
}
```

7

Although Listing 7.1 shows a perfectly valid way for the task list box to draw itself, it is actually a rather poor implementation. The reason goes beyond the actual coding, which works well enough. What if the next project that you implement also uses an owner-drawn list box? The CTaskListBox and CTaskItem classes are very tightly coupled, so one cannot be reused without the other.

The solution is to create objects that manage their own behavior. By moving the logic for drawing a list-box item out of the list box and into the item that is contained in the list box, the code can be more easily reused. Figure 7.2 is a class diagram of the new list-box classes used for task management.

Figure 7.2.

An improved version of CTaskListBox *and* CTaskItem.

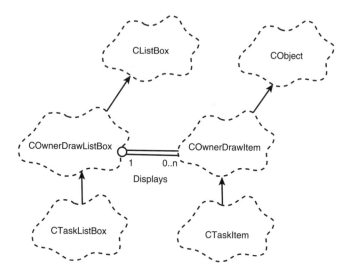

The code in CTaskItem::Draw is the same code that was previously in the CTaskListBox::DrawItem method presented in Listing 7.1. However, now it is located in the class that defines how the item should be drawn. The CTaskListBox class does not implement a DrawItem method, because the one provided by the COwnerDrawListBox class is all that's needed in most cases. COwnerDrawListBox::DrawItem is shown in Listing 7.2.

Listing 7.2. The DrawItem method from the COwnerDrawListBox class.

```
void COwnerDrawListBox::DrawItem(LPDRAWITEMSTRUCT lpdis)
{
    // Get the rectangle for the item, and calculate the rectangle
    // for the focus rectangle. Also, create a temporary CDC object
    // from the one passed in to us.
    CRect rc = &lpdis->rcItem;
    //
    // If the item ID is LB_ERR, we are getting this DrawItem
    // call to set the focus for the entire list box. We do
```

```
    // not want to dereference itemData, since it is invalid.
    //
    if( lpdis->itemID == LB_ERR )
    {
        CWnd *pWndList = GetDlgItem( lpdis->itemID );
        if( pWndList )
        {
            pWndList->GetWindowRect( rc );
            pdcTmp->DrawFocusRect( rc );
        }
    }
    else
    {
        COLORREF        clrBkgrnd, clrTxt;
        COwnerDrawItem* pOwnerDrawItem;

        pOwnerDrawItem = (COwnerDrawItem*)lpdis->itemData;
        if( pOwnerDrawItem )
        {
            pOwnerDrawItem->Draw( lpdis );
        }
    }
}
```

The Draw method is declared as a pure virtual function in COwnerDrawItem. This means that no instances of COwnerDrawItem can be instantiated, because the Draw method doesn't exist in COwnerDrawItem. By declaring Draw to be a virtual function, the correct version of Draw will be invoked at runtime. By declaring Draw as a pure virtual function, a class derived from COwnerDrawItem must implement this method.

Testing Class Reusability Through Reviews

One way to tell if the classes that you've designed and constructed are reusable is to get input from other programmers who are potential users of your classes. At the lowest levels of class design and construction, reviews can work wonders in improving reuse, both within and outside a project. Not all of the following benefits of code reviews are obvious:

☐ Design reviews can help educate junior members of a team by introducing them to coding techniques used by more senior programmers.

☐ Reviews can help spread the word about classes that are available for reuse. This is more beneficial in larger design efforts, or in situations where several projects are developed at the same time.

☐ Of course, reviews can help discover faults in the design or coding phases. This is probably the most obvious benefit, but it's not necessarily the most valuable.

7

If you're working alone, you can simulate a review by consciously "wearing different hats." Make a point to schedule a self-review, and look at each class in terms of its reusability. The following are some important things to look for in a review:

- ☐ **Completeness of the documentation.** Approach the documentation as a potential user of the class. Is the documentation complete enough to enable a person to use the class without examining the source code?

- ☐ **Clarity of the interfaces.** A class user that is familiar with the objects modeled by the class should be able to immediately identify all of its interfaces. If you need to explain object names, the class is not as usable.

- ☐ **Interface completeness.** Consider another application that might reuse this class. Are the interfaces complete enough to support reuse, or will the class have to be salvaged and rewritten to be reused?

- ☐ **Interface complexity.** Are the interfaces easy to understand? Does the class truly help simplify the problem being solved or does it get in the way?

- ☐ **Attention to coding guidelines.** Does the construction follow the standards that have been established for the project?

Minimal Versus Complete Classes

Classes should be minimal, but complete. These two conflicting goals create a kind of healthy tension when it comes to class design. A properly constructed minimal class will have a small number of well-defined interfaces. The class itself should model one well-defined type of object or behavior.

The advantage of having a minimal class is that it's much easier to maintain a class with a few, well-defined interfaces than a class that has a large number of interfaces. It's also much easier for a potential user of the class to understand how it can be used.

Listing 7.3 is a minimal version of a birthdate class and is a good example of a class that's built with a particular use in mind. There is only one type of constructor, no conversion operators, and a bare minimum of Get and Set methods.

Listing 7.3. An example of a minimal class.

```
class CBirthdate : public CObject // A minimal class
{
    public:
        CBirthdate();
        ~CBirthdate();

        Set( const CString& szName, const CString& szDate );
        CString& GetName() const;
        CString& GetDate() const;
```

```
private:
    CString m_szName;
    CString m_szDate;
};
```

The CBirthdate class probably works great in the application for which it was originally used, but the lack of member functions may be a problem if this class is ever needed in the future. The following are some additions to this class that might make it more usable:

☐ A constructor that enables the class to be fully constructed in one step instead of two

☐ A method that enables the name to be changed

These additions don't come for free, however. Let's say that you have a code review with some fellow programmers, and during the review you're asked by a potential user of your class to make some additions to the CBirthdate class. Afterward, you decide to make your CBirthdate class the model of reusability. The new improved CBirthdate class shown in Listing 7.4 will have something for everyone.

Listing 7.4. The new and improved CBirthdate class.

```
class CBirthdate : public CObject // An overweight class
{
    public:
        CBirthdate();
        CBirthdate( const CString& szName, const CString& szDate );
        ~CBirthdate();

        Set( const CString& szName, const CString& szDate );
        Set( const CString& szName, const CTime& theTime );
        void SetName( const CString& szName );
        void SetDate( const CString& szDate );
        void SetDate( const CTime& theTime );
        CString& GetName() const;
        CString& GetDate() const;

        operator CString() const;
        operator LPCTSTR() const;
        int operator <( CBirthdate& rhs ) const;
        int operator >( CBirthdate& rhs ) const;
        int operator==( CBirthdate& rhs ) const;
        int operator!=( CBirthdate& rhs ) const;
    private:
        void SetBuffer();
        CString m_szName;
        CString m_szDate;
        CString m_szFormattedBuffer;
};
```

7

CBirthdate is now a classic example of a maintenance nightmare. There are many more interfaces to test, document, and debug, so every one of them will be a possible problem in the future if the class is ever reused. Testing classes at the module level is covered on Day 8, "Instrumenting Code and Debugging," where you'll see that every line of code that is added increases the testing load.

The improved CBirthdate also has every possible interface, but has become much more complicated to use. The class originally had only a handful of interfaces; it now has so many that it's impossible to remember them all. Classes like CBirthdate, which are difficult to reuse, rarely get a second glance when class reuse is optional.

Listing 7.5 is a CBirthdate class that is a little bit more reasonable. It strikes a good balance between the first two attempts, and is complete enough to make reuse attractive without becoming a burden to maintain later.

Listing 7.5. A minimal and complete version of CBirthdate.

```
class CBirthdate : public CObject // A minimal and complete class
{
    public:
        CBirthdate();
        CBirthdate( const CString& szName, const CString& szDate );
        ~CBirthdate();

        Set( const CString& szName, const CString& szDate );
        void SetName( const CString& szName );
        void SetDate( const CString& szDate );
        CString& GetName() const;
        CString& GetDate() const;

    private:
        CString m_szName;
        CString m_szDate;
};
```

This version of CBirthdate represents a compromise between the first two versions. There are, of course, other ways to represent a birthdate class. Some might have more or less functionality than the class presented in Listing 7.5.

Designing Classes by Contract

Bertrand Meyer, designer of the Eiffel programming language, is a strong advocate of programming by contract. Although C++ doesn't have direct support of this method built in to the language definition, you can still use the basic ideas by following a few guidelines in your class construction.

Basically, *programming by contract* means that the interface definition is the contract between the user and implementor of the class. Every characteristic of the class that will impact the user should be documented in the class header.

As a key part of this method, the class designer must define preconditions that should exist before a class method is called, and postconditions that will be true after the method returns. The user of a class is expected to adhere to the preconditions, while the class itself will guarantee that the postconditions are true.

> **Note:** Today, the term *user* refers to another programmer using the class, not the user of the final application. It might help if you think of the next programmer to use your classes as similar to an application user. Ease of use is just as important when programming as it is when you are using a spreadsheet or word processor.
>
> A major focus during Part II of this book, "Construction," deals with making the classes that are developed easy to use, and easy to reuse in the future.

The following C++ language features will play an important part in your implementation of programming by contract:

- ☐ **Constant class methods.** Declaring class methods as const is a good example of establishing a contract between the class designer and user. This declaration is a promise that the method will not change the state of an instance.

- ☐ **Constant formal parameters.** In a similar fashion, a const declaration assures a user that a parameter will not be changed during a function call.

- ☐ **Macros used to test program consistency.** The ASSERT, VERIFY, and TRACE macros provided by MFC will be used to verify pre- and postconditions. This topic is covered on Day 8. For now, just be aware that these macros will be used to help enforce the class contract.

- ☐ **Exception handling.** This is a relatively new way to handle errors that occur during program execution. Exception handling is also covered on Day 8.

You probably have been exposed to most of these techniques. What may be new to you, however, is using them together in a way that makes your code more reliable and easier to reuse.

7

Using the Header To Document the Class

When using programming by contract, the header for a class is used not only to hold declarations for the compiler, it is also a document that defines the user's interface for the class. Listing 7.6 is the header for the CPriority class from InfoMan.

Listing 7.6. The header for the `CPriority` class.

```
/////////////////////////////////////////////////////////////
// CPriority                   version PA1 14 November, 1994
/////////////////////////////////////////////////////////////
// Copyright 1994, by Mickey Williams for SAMS publishing
//
// The CPriority class is used to represent the priority of
// another object. Typically, the CPriority class will be used
// by another class so that the class can have its priority
// set and/or tested.
//
// The priority is made up of two components:
//    - the 'major' part is a character.
//    - the 'minor' part is an integer.
// Some examples of priorities are A1, A2, B3, Z9.
//
// Various operators are overloaded that allow two CPriority
// instances to compare their priority.
// -------------------------------------------------------------
// History       04 November, 1994 Started.
//               11 November, 1994 Module Test completed.
//               14 November, 1994 Released to archive.
/////////////////////////////////////////////////////////////
class CPriority : public CObject
{
//Constructors
    public:
        // Basic constructors. Nothing special, except that if the
        // default ctor is used, the priority will be set to 'Z0'.
        CPriority();
        CPriority( const CPriority& otherPriority );
        CPriority( const TCHAR chMajor, const int nMinor = 0 );
        virtual ~CPriority();

//Attributes
    public:
        // The only preconditions for the attribute methods are
        // the priority values are not allowed to be negative.
        // It is allowed to change the priority at any time. None
        // of these methods are thread-safe.
        void Set( const TCHAR chMajor );
        void Set( const int nMinor );
        void Set( const TCHAR chMajor, const int nMinor );
        CString Get() const;

//Operations
    public:
        // Only Boolean operators are provided for CPriority. The
        // == and != operators compare both the major and minor
        // parts of the priority if needed.
        BOOL operator==( CPriority& rhsPriority ) const;
        BOOL operator!=( CPriority& rhsPriority ) const;
        // The < and > operators do not attempt to collate based on
        // the current language. They only perform a numerical test
        // on the major and minor components.
```

```
        BOOL operator<( CPriority& rhsPriority ) const;
        BOOL operator>( CPriority& rhsPriority ) const;
        // The standard MFC serialization support.
        virtual void Serialize( CArchive& ar );
#ifdef _DEBUG
        void Dump( CDumpContext &dc ) const;
#endif

//Implementation
    // Everything below this line is subject to radical change in
    // the future.
    private:
        void Initialize( TCHAR chMajor = 0, int nMinor = 0 );
        int m_chMajor;
        int m_nMinor;
};
```

You can use the CPriority header to answer most questions that might come up when the class is used. An important aspect of the header is the way that guarantees are made about the condition of the object before and after functions are called.

For example, if the Get member function is called, as in Listing 7.7, the compiler can ensure that the internal state of the objects isn't changed, because Get was declared as a const member function.

 Textbook Tip: Be careful to make your comments readable and to form complete sentences. Remember, even though you know what you mean, the person reading the comments may not.

Listing 7.7. A code fragment using Get with CPriority.

```
CPriority    pPriority = pHeap->GetHighestPriority();
CString      szPriority = pPriority->Get();
AfxMessageBox( szPriority );
```

It's important to document the class header well. Remember, reuse isn't going to be as cost-effective as possible if everyone must read through all of the source. Unfortunately, when looking for examples of good commenting style, it can be difficult to find good examples. The best way to determine if your comments are easily understood is to have them reviewed by another programmer.

Using Comments to Document the CPP File

The coding style you use when you program by contract also extends to the class-implementation files. Just like contracts in real life, programming contracts need to be verified and enforced. One of the major differences between coding for a single project and coding a reusable class library is that you can't always make assumptions about how the class is used when you are creating a reusable class library.

For example, the CPriority documentation and header state that the components that make up the priority value cannot be negative. So what happens if someone can't follow directions, and tries to give an instance of CPriority a value of "A-1"? By documenting the classes well and using the programming-by-contract techniques, you can make your code more robust and try to catch problems like this before they happen.

On Day 8 you'll see how to use exceptions and MFC macros to handle these situations. Using an exception to notify a calling function that something has gone wrong is called *throwing an exception*. Because you can't always throw an exception, one simple way to handle cases like this is shown in Listing 7.8.

Listing 7.8. Testing for invalid parameters.

```
//
// Initialize
// Called by different constructor when the instance needs
// to be initialized.
void CPriority::Initialize( TCHAR chMajor, int nMinor )
{
    // Actual parameter values must be non-negative.
    if( chMajor >= 0 && nMinor >= 0 )
    {
        m_chMajor = chMajor;
        m_nMinor = nMinor;
    }
    else
    {
        // Set members to default values in case of error.
        m_chMajor = 0;
        m_nMinor = 0;
    }
}
```

If you were writing a class for a single application and you knew (or thought you knew) how CPriority objects were used, you might be tempted to skip the parameter testing. After all, it would reduce the line count by about half and reduce the amount of testing required. Do yourself a favor, and always verify that parameters are within the required ranges.

Note: Premature optimization is the root of all evil. Studies have shown that programmers often spend a lot of time optimizing code that rarely gets executed.

After the project has been integrated, you can profile it and determine which functions can benefit from optimization. Running function-timing tests using the Profiler is covered on Day 12, "Module Testing and Integration." For now, concentrate on writing code that is clear and easily understood.

You might be tempted to put error messages or dialog boxes directly into the class source code. It might seem like a good idea, but introducing specific error-handling methods inside a class will cause problems for you later. The next time you use a class—CPriority, for example—it may be a console application. Even worse, CPriority might be used in a situation where it's clearly not appropriate for a low-level class to handle any errors.

On Day 8 you'll learn some techniques that will make it easier for your classes to tell the user that an operation has failed.

Listing 7.8 also demonstrates different ways to use comments inside classes. In the class header, comments were meant to be used primarily by users of the class, while in the class's implementation, the comments are used by the source-code maintainer.

The comments at the beginning of the function are sometimes called *strategic comments*, because they address important aspects of the function as a whole. Comments that are located in the body of the function are called *tactical comments*. They are used to address a much smaller part of the source code, typically one or two lines.

Note: When you are writing comments for source files, resist the temptation to write a comment for every single line. The purpose of comments is to add some value to the source code, not provide a running narrative. An overabundance of comments won't make unreadable source code easier to manage.

By using meaningful names for variables and functions, and by avoiding overly clever code, your source can be made more reader-friendly, and you can reduce the need for line-by-line comments.

As a good rule of thumb, try to rely more on strategic, rather than tactical, comments. Too often, tactical comments are only used to restate the obvious.

7

Modification Notes

If the project already has a number of well-documented classes that are available, you should try to use them in your new construction. If the classes are not well-documented, try to improve or create the documentation, if possible. The fact that they are being reused at least once makes them good candidates to be reused in the future.

Debugging the Process

The biggest problem that you are likely to face today is organizing the code reviews. Code reviews are a great help, whether they are formal or informal. They can help you find any trouble that might be lurking in your design, and can be a great source of new ideas when you are trying to solve problems. The problem with code reviews is that they don't offer an immediate payback. You aren't actually writing any code, so it may look like you're not productive.

In fact, the amount of time spent reviewing your code is easily paid back the first time that an error is discovered before the code is released. Or the first time that someone attending your review has to take responsibility for the code in the future.

If you're working alone, the best approach is to sit down, forget everything that you know about the code, and review it with a critical eye. There are going to be several times during the project when you have to "change hats" like this if you're working alone. It may not be easy, but it's important.

Instrumenting Code and Debugging

Today you'll learn how to use the tools provided by the Visual C++ development environment and MFC that can help make your life easier. By taking some simple steps now, while you are building your classes, your code will be much easier to test and debug later in the verification phases.

You first learn about assumption testing. All code has some built-in assumptions. By documenting and testing them, you can avoid those "whoops" feelings at the end of a project. Low-level, or "white-box," testing techniques are covered at the end of this section. *White-box* testing is performed with in-depth knowledge about how the code works (in contrast to black-box testing, where the implementation of a function or class is not important).

You will complete the code for the first part of InfoMan by the end of today; this marks the completion of M2, a major milestone.

Documenting and Testing Assumptions

All source code will have some built-in assumptions about how it is used, or what sort of parameters are passed to it. An example of an assumption is a function that takes a pointer to a CRect as a parameter, and assumes that the rectangle is valid. On Day 7, "Basic Class Construction," the CPriority class made some assumptions about the values used for the priorities; specifically, only nonzero values could be used.

It is perfectly OK to make assumptions about the way a class will be used, as long as the assumptions are reasonable and are well-documented. If assumptions aren't documented, users of your code may be forced to track down hard-to-find bugs that are created when the user does not understand the restrictions placed on the class.

For example, Listing 8.1 shows the CPriority class being used with invalid values. In the version of CPriority presented on Day 7, default values are substituted when negative values are detected. If the user decides that the negative values should be allowed, they might create bugs that are very hard to track down.

Listing 8.1. Using CPriority incorrectly might introduce hard-to-find errors.

```
// Using CPriority with bad ctor arguments, don't do this !
CPriority    thePriority( 'A', -5 );
CPriority    otherPriority( 'A', -8 );

// The test always fails, since negative values aren't allowed
// as part of the priority.
if( thePriority != otherPriority )
{
    AfxMessageBox( "Test Worked" );
}
```

```
else
{
    AfxMessageBox( "Test Failed" );
}
```

An assumption that is present in much of the MFC library is that many operations can be performed only on window-based objects after the window has been created. For example, you can't use `CListBox::SetFont` until the list box has actually been created because of the way the MFC `CListbox` class is implemented. Although this is a perfectly reasonable restriction, it is not documented anywhere, and most people don't know how the `CListBox` class is implemented unless they read the source code. This could cause a problem with programmers who use `SetFont` before the list box was actually created.

What the MFC libraries do, however, is turn the assumptions into requirements by causing assertion failures whenever assumptions are violated in debug builds. Although this lets you, as a programmer, know that something is wrong with your code, you're forced to search through the MFC source code and discover the reason for the assertion failure yourself. A better approach to preventing programming errors is to both document and generate assertion failures. Guaranteeing proper program execution by using the `ASSERT` and `VERIFY` macros is covered in the next section.

Turning Assumptions into Requirements

Programmers are only human, so a large number of them may not read your carefully written documentation filled with details about preconditions, postconditions, and other assumptions. Face it, there are a lot of people who won't even read the header file unless you force them to.

On Day 7 you used defensive coding to prevent faulty parameters from being passed into `CPriority`. This helped prevent faulty data from being used by an instance of `CPriority`. However, it didn't do much to help the person sending you the faulty data, because you just ignored it. The sender of the information received no indication that an invalid parameter was being used. If the information contained in `CPriority` was checked by the caller, he or she would discover that the information stored was inaccurate. However, detecting errors this way is neither reasonable nor efficient. Clearly, you need to have a better way to catch the faulty use of your classes.

A good way to enforce proper use of classes and to detect runtime errors is by treating the assumptions like requirements to turn them into errors. This is another part of the programming-by-contract technique that was presented on Day 7. The MFC classes let you use three different macros when you are running debug versions of your program:

1. The `ASSERT` macro can be used to test an assumption that should be true. You can easily test pre- and postconditions by using the `ASSERT` macro.

2. The VERIFY macro is used to test a line of code that needs to be executed in both the release and debug versions of your program.

3. The TRACE macro is used to send messages to a debug terminal. This is called *instrumentation*, or *instrumenting your code*. If you're not familiar with this topic, don't worry—you'll learn about it later in the section, "Using the TRACE Macro."

Using the *ASSERT* and *VERIFY* Macros

One of the key points in programming by contract introduced on Day 7 was the idea of preconditions and postconditions. This idea isn't new—it has been around since structured programming was introduced in the 1970s. What is relatively new, however, is using programming constructs to help enforce preconditions and postconditions.

There are two different macros you can use with the MFC library to test for conditions that you place on program execution. As discussed earlier, you can use the ASSERT and VERIFY macros to test whether or not a statement is true. Figure 8.1 shows the dialog box that is displayed when an ASSERT macro fails.

Figure 8.1.
A failed assertion brings up a dialog box that is difficult to ignore.

Use the ASSERT macro whenever a statement is a precondition that will be tested only in debug builds. An example of a statement used only in debug builds is shown in Listing 8.2. The ASSERT macro is used to test the preconditions required for CPriority::Initialize. This code will create an assertion failure if negative priority values are used. However, these checks are removed when a non-debug version of your application is built.

Listing 8.2. A new version of CPriority::Initialize that uses the ASSERT macro.

```
// Initialize
// Called by different constructor when the instance needs
// to be initialized.
void CPriority::Initialize( TCHAR chMajor, int nMinor )
{
    // Actual parameter values must be non-negative.
    ASSERT( chMajor >= 0 && nMinor >= 0 );
    if( chMajor >= 0 && nMinor >= 0 )
    {
        m_chMajor = chMajor;
        m_nMinor = nMinor;
    }
```

```
    else
    {
        // Set members to default values in case of error.
        m_chMajor = 0;
        m_nMinor = 0;
    }
}
```

Any statements that are included inside an ASSERT macro are removed unless the source module is compiled with the debug options enabled. This means that you can be very liberal with your ASSERT statements, and still have a slimmed-down executable as your final release. Listing 8.3 shows an example of multiple ASSERT statements used inside the CTaskItem::Draw function.

Listing 8.3. The `CTaskItem::Draw` function implemented using ASSERT and VERIFY.

```
void CTaskItem::Draw( LPDRAWITEMSTRUCT lpdis )
{
    // Test that the pointer is valid
    ASSERT( lpdis );
    CRect rc = &lpdis->rcItem;
    // Make sure we have a valid rect.
    ASSERT( rc.Height() > 0 );
    CRect rcFocus = rc;
    rcFocus.left += rc.Height();
    CDC *pdcTmp;
    // Test to make sure that we get a CDC*
    VERIFY( pdcTmp = CDC::FromHandle( lpdis->hDC ) );
    //
    // If the item ID is LB_ERR, we are getting this DrawItem
    // call to set the focus for the entire list box. We do
    // not want to dereference itemData, since it is invalid.
    // The listbox class should trap this case for us, and
    // we shouldn't see it.
    ASSERT( lpdis->itemID != LB_ERR );
    if( lpdis->itemID != LB_ERR )
    {
        COLORREF        clrBkgrnd;
        COLORREF        clrTxt;

        if( lpdis->itemAction & (ODA_DRAWENTIRE ¦ ODA_SELECT) )
        {
            // If we are gaining or losing the selection status,
            // choose the proper color for the background. Since
            // we have a bitmap, we are going to have to paint
            // under it.
            if( lpdis->itemState & ODS_SELECTED )
            {
                clrBkgrnd = GetSysColor(COLOR_HIGHLIGHT );
                clrTxt = GetSysColor(COLOR_HIGHLIGHTTEXT );
            }
            else
```

continues

131

Listing 8.3. continued

```
                        {
                            clrBkgrnd = GetSysColor( COLOR_WINDOW);
                            clrTxt = GetSysColor( COLOR_WINDOWTEXT);
                        }
                        //
                        // Now that the color has been selected:
                        //    - Draw the checkbox for the item.
                        //    - Fill the item's rectangle with the selected
                        //      color.
                        //    - Draw the text on top of the rectangle.
                        CString szTaskItemText;
                        DrawCheckBox( rc,
                                      pdcTmp,
                                      IsCompleted(),
                                      GetSysColor( COLOR_WINDOWTEXT) );
                        ColorRect( rcFocus, pdcTmp, clrBkgrnd );
                        szTaskItemText = GetPriority() + "\t" + GetSlogan();
                        DrawItemText( rcFocus,
                                      pdcTmp,
                                      szTaskItemText,
                                      clrBkgrnd,
                                      clrTxt );
                    }
                    else
                    {
                        //
                        // We are doing something other than drawing the
                        // whole rectangle, and we aren't doing anything
                        // with the selection status, so just set the colors
                        // to the normal background colors.
                        clrBkgrnd = GetSysColor( COLOR_WINDOW );
                        clrTxt = GetSysColor( COLOR_WINDOWTEXT );
                    }
                    //
                    // Draw the focus rectangle around the item.This works
                    // just like an XOR, so we don't have to keep track of
                    // the focus state, since drawing the rectangle again
                    // will make it disappear.
                    if( lpdis->itemAction & ODA_FOCUS )
                    {
                        pdcTmp->DrawFocusRect( rcFocus );
                    }
                }
            }
```

Notice the use of VERIFY statements around the call to CDC::FromHandle. You can use the VERIFY macro to test a statement that is present in both the release and debug builds for a module. There are two ways to test a return value from a function call like CDC::FromHandle. You can either test the return value in a separate statement using the ASSERT macro, or you can place the entire function call inside a VERIFY macro.

Note: If you are building a non-debug version of your application, ASSERT statements are removed by the preprocessor when your source code is compiled. In non-debug builds, VERIFY statements are left untouched, although the statement is not tested as it is in debug builds.

Be sure you understand the difference between the ASSERT and VERIFY macros. The following line of code will be removed in non-debug compilations, leading to disaster if the pdc variable is used later:

```
ASSERT( pdc = CDC::FromHandle( lpdis->hDC ); );
```

You have two options if you want to perform an assertion test on the variable pdc. One way is to test the value of pdc in a separate line using the ASSERT macro.

```
pdc = CDC::FromHandle( lpdis->hDC );
ASSERT( pdc );
```

The other method is to use the VERIFY macro.

```
VERIFY( pdc = CDC::FromHandle( lpdis->hDC ); );
```

Both methods cost the same in terms of program execution. The method that's right for you depends on your preferred coding style. Remember, when you use the ASSERT macro to test a function return value, the actual ASSERT statement must not include the function call unless you want that function call to be removed for release-mode builds.

Using *ASSERT* and *VERIFY* When Debugging

When you're debugging or running low-level tests, you can start the Visual C++ Integrated Debugger from the dialog box that's displayed when the assertion fails. Just press the Retry button and the debugger will start up and put you right at the offending line. You can use this feature to examine the Call Stack or Watch windows and determine the cause of the failure. Figure 8.2 shows the dialog box that is used to indicate a failed assertion. Figure 8.3 shows the debugger running after Retry has been selected.

Figure 8.2.

A failed assertion in the CPriority *class.*

Figure 8.3.

The Visual C++ Integrated Debugger running after the assertion failure.

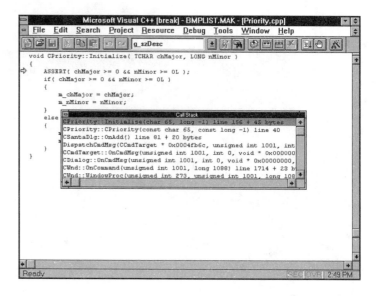

Note that you can use the Call Stack window to trace backward to see which functions were involved in generating the assertion failure. The actual parameters that were passed in at the function entry are also displayed. If you double-click a line in the window, the cursor is taken to the point in the code referenced in the Call Stack window.

Textbook Tip: All of the windows that are available during debugging have extra functionality that might not seem obvious at first glance. The Watch, Call Stack, and Locals windows are all fully editable, and you can cut and paste or drag and drop just as if they were text-editing windows.

For example, if you're having problems with a particular assertion failure, it's easy to copy the information from the Call Stack window into a trouble or fault report for later use. Just launch the debugger from the assertion failure dialog box, open the Call Stack window, and copy the contents to the Clipboard.

Another trick you can use in the Call Stack window is to set a breakpoint inside the window. This enables you to easily return to a point listed inside the Call Stack window, just by pressing the debug icon on the toolbar. This is useful if you don't want to return to a previous location in the Call Stack by single-stepping the debugger.

Using the *TRACE* Macro

You can use the TRACE macro to send output to a debugger to trace program execution. This macro is helpful when you are testing and debugging code that does a lot of work while "hidden" from the user. Just like the ASSERT and VERIFY macros, TRACE macros are active only in debug builds of your application. The format for the TRACE macro is exactly the same as for printf from the C runtime library. Listing 8.4 shows an example of how to use the TRACE macro.

Listing 8.4. Using `TRACE` to send information to a debugger.

```
void DisplayTask( CTestSetBag& theTests, int nIndex )
{
    TRACE( "Test index=%d\n", nIndex );

    CTaskItem*  pTask;
    pTask = theTests[nIndex];
    pTaskWnd->SetWindowText( pTask->GetLabel() );
}
```

Exception Handling

A new addition to the C++ language is exception handling. Exceptions are used to notify a caller that an error condition has occurred in a function. When the error condition is detected, the code that detects the error condition "throws" an exception to the calling function. The calling function will usually "catch" the exception, and handle the error as necessary. There are also a number of special cases that are examined in this section. The phrase "throw" is used to represent passing an exception back to the calling function, and "catch" is used when the calling function receives the exception.

Exceptions make your code much easier to read, maintain, and use, and they also make it possible to allow constructors to fail gracefully and reliably. Listing 8.5 shows a version of the CTaskListBox constructor that does not use exception handling. Note that it does use the ASSERT and VERIFY macros to help catch errors that might pop up in debug builds.

Listing 8.5. A constructor without exceptions.

```
CTaskListBox::CTaskListBox()
{
    // Get a temporary DC that will be deleted by framework later.
    CDC *pdcTemp;
    VERIFY( pdcTemp = AfxGetMainWnd()->GetDC() );
    int cyPixelsPerInch = pdcTemp->GetDeviceCaps( LOGPIXELSY );
    int cxFont = -::MulDiv(8, cyPixelsPerInch, 72);
```

continues

Listing 8.5. continued

```
        // create font to be used for the item text
        BOOL fCreate = m_fontItem.CreateFont( cxFont,
                                              0,
                                              0,
                                              0,
                                              FW_NORMAL,
                                              FALSE,
                                              FALSE,
                                              FALSE,
                                              DEFAULT_CHARSET,
                                              OUT_DEFAULT_PRECIS,
                                              CLIP_DEFAULT_PRECIS,
                                              DEFAULT_QUALITY,
                                              VARIABLE_PITCH | FF_SWISS,
                                              "MS Sans Serif" );

        // if we can't create the font we want, try to create a system
        // font.
        if( fCreate )
        {
            BOOL f;
            VERIFY( f = m_fontItem.CreateStockObject(SYSTEM_FONT) );
        }
        // Get the character size info.
        TEXTMETRIC tm;
        VERIFY( pdcTemp->GetTextMetrics(&tm) );

        // Now calculate the character size used for the item text.
        CFont *pFontOld = pdcTemp->SelectObject( &m_fontItem );
        m_sText = pdcTemp->GetTextExtent("M", 1);
        pdcTemp->SelectObject( pFontOld );
}
```

This class will work fine when it is compiled with the debug flags enabled. What about when it's released into the real world? This version without exception handling can easily result in a partially constructed object. If the call to AfxGetMainWnd()->GetDC fails, the results of the following function calls will be unreliable, resulting in an object that is partially constructed. And there's not much you can do about it; it's fairly awkward to pass failure information back from a constructor, because constructors are not allowed to have a return value.

When you do not use exceptions, the safest approach to constructing your objects is to use a two-step construction process. First, create the object, using only operations that cannot fail; then, use a second function to actually perform any complicated construction. Listing 8.6 has the same functionality as the original constructor, but it is split into two functions. Whenever a CTaskListBox is constructed, the user has to use the CTaskListBox::Init function to construct the object.

Listing 8.6. Two-step construction without exceptions.

```
CTaskListBox::CTaskListBox()
{
    //Perform any initializations that can't fail.
}

BOOL CTaskListBox::Init()
{
    BOOL fReturn = FALSE;
    // Get a temporary DC that will be deleted by framework later.
    CDC *pdcTemp;
    VERIFY( pdcTemp = AfxGetMainWnd()->GetDC() );
    if( pdcTemp )
    {
        int cyPixelsPerInch = pdcTemp->GetDeviceCaps( LOGPIXELSY );
        int cxFont = ::MulDiv(8, cyPixelsPerInch, 72);

        // create font to be used for the item text
        BOOL fCreate;
        fCreate = m_fontItem.CreateFont( cxFont,
                                         0,
                                         0,
                                         0,
                                         FW_NORMAL,
                                         FALSE,
                                         FALSE,
                                         FALSE,
                                         DEFAULT_CHARSET,
                                         OUT_DEFAULT_PRECIS,
                                         CLIP_DEFAULT_PRECIS,
                                         DEFAULT_QUALITY,
                                         VARIABLE_PITCH | FF_SWISS,
                                         "MS Sans Serif" );

        // if we can't create the font we want, try to create a system
        // font.
        if( fCreate )
        {
            fReturn = m_fontItem.CreateStockObject(SYSTEM_FONT);
            ASSERT( fReturn );
        }
        // Get the character size info.
        TEXTMETRIC tm;
        VERIFY( pdcTemp->GetTextMetrics(&tm) );

        // Now calculate the character size used for the item text.
        CFont *pFontOld = pdcTemp->SelectObject( &m_fontItem );
        m_sText = pdcTemp->GetTextExtent("M", 1);
        pdcTemp->SelectObject( pFontOld );
    }
    return fReturn;
}
```

Much of the MFC library was written before exception handling was added to Visual C++. That's why most of the MFC classes use the two-step construction approach. For instance, CFont, CDialog, and all of the GDI objects are created in two steps.

You do not gain a lot of obvious benefits by throwing exceptions. You still have to test for an error condition, then take appropriate action. However, because you can now pass failure information back to the user of the class, it's possible to use single-step construction. Listing 8.7 is a version of CTaskListBox that uses exception handling.

Listing 8.7. Single-step construction with exceptions.

```
CTaskListBox::CTaskListBox()
{
    // Get a temporary DC that will be deleted by framework later.
    // If the DC isn't allocated, throw an exception.
    CDC *pdcTemp;
    VERIFY( pdcTemp = AfxGetMainWnd()->GetDC() );
    if( pdcTemp == FALSE )
        throw CCtorException( "Couldn't get a device context" );

    int cyPixelsPerInch = pdcTemp->GetDeviceCaps( LOGPIXELSY );
    int cxFont = -::MulDiv(8, cyPixelsPerInch, 72);

    // create font to be used for the item text
    BOOL fCreate = m_fontItem.CreateFont( cxFont,
                                          0,
                                          0,
                                          0,
                                          FW_NORMAL,
                                          FALSE,
                                          FALSE,
                                          FALSE,
                                          DEFAULT_CHARSET,
                                          OUT_DEFAULT_PRECIS,
                                          CLIP_DEFAULT_PRECIS,
                                          DEFAULT_QUALITY,
                                          VARIABLE_PITCH | FF_SWISS,
                                          "MS Sans Serif" );

    // if we can't create the font we want, try to create a system
    // font. If that doesn't work, throw a CtorException.
    if( fCreate )
    {
        BOOL f;
        VERIFY( f = m_fontItem.CreateStockObject(SYSTEM_FONT) );
        if( f == FALSE )
            throw CCtorException( "Can't Create Font" );
    }
    // Get the character size info.
    TEXTMETRIC tm;
    VERIFY( pdcTemp->GetTextMetrics(&tm) );
```

```
    // Now calculate the character size used for the item text.
    CFont *pFontOld = pdcTemp->SelectObject( &m_fontItem );
    m_sText = pdcTemp->GetTextExtent("M", 1);
    pdcTemp->SelectObject( pFontOld );

    m_fItemsDrawn = FALSE;
}
```

The CCtorException class is shown in Listing 8.8. A CCtorException will be thrown by any class in InfoMan that fails when it is constructed. This helps simplify the catching of exceptions when several could be thrown back to a single point, such as when dialog boxes or form views are constructed. It's possible to add failure information using a CString parameter when throwing the exception, or, as always, you can derive your own class from CCtorException.

Listing 8.8. The `CCtorException` class, thrown when constructors fail in InfoMan.

```
class CCtorException : public CException
{
    //Constructors
    public:
        //Two constructors are provided. One allows an
        //exception reason to be stated, the other doesn't.
        CCtorException();
        CCtorException( const CString& szReason );
    //Attributes
    public:
        //GetReason allows the exception reason to be fetched.
        CString GetReason() const;
    private:
        CString m_szReason;
};

//Constructors
CCtorException::CCtorException()
{
    m_szReason = "";
}

CCtorException::CCtorException( const CString& szReason )
{
    m_szReason = szReason;
}

CString CCtorException::GetReason() const
{
    return m_szReason;
}
```

You will see the big advantage with exception handling when you use classes that throw exceptions. All of your code that is used for normal, nonfault cases can be placed in a try block.

All of your fault-handling code can be located in one part of your function, in catch blocks. It's much easier for a user to read and write code that handles error cases properly when exceptions are used. Listing 8.9 shows how CInfoApp::OnFileNew uses try and catch blocks to handle error cases.

Listing 8.9. Error handling in `CInfoApp::OnFileNew`.

```
void CInfoApp::OnFileNew()
{
    // Create a new form for the InfoMan application. If
    // a CCtorException is thrown, display the cause. Otherwise
    // just tell the user that there was an error.
    try
    {
        CWinApp::OnFileNew();
    }
    catch( CCtorException e )
    {
        CString szCause = "Couldn't create form " + e.GetReason();
        AfxMessageBox( szCause, MB_OK | MB_ICONSTOP );
    }
    catch( CMemoryException )
    {
        CString szCause = "Couldn't create form. Out of memory";
        AfxMessageBox( szCause, MB_OK | MB_ICONSTOP );
    }
    catch( CException )
    {
        AfxMessageBox("Couldn't create form", MB_OK | MB_ICONSTOP );
        // Re-throw exception, since we don't know what it is.
        throw;
    }
}
```

The code in Listing 8.9 is typical of exception-handling cases. The function is split into two parts: the top half handles the "normal" case and takes care of the real work for the function, whereas the bottom half handles any exceptions that might be thrown. An important point here is that the exceptions will be caught, no matter what throws them. There is no apparent connection between calling CWinApp::OnFileNew and catching a CCtorException a few lines later. Any exception that is thrown and not handled during the execution of OnFileNew will be caught by the exception handlers in OnFileNew. Figure 8.4 shows how exceptions are thrown and handled in CInfoApp::OnFileNew.

Note: Exception handling is meant to be used in the case of errors. Don't get in the habit of using exceptions to handle ordinary conditions. Improper use of exceptions will lead to code that is hard to maintain and less robust than code that doesn't use exceptions.

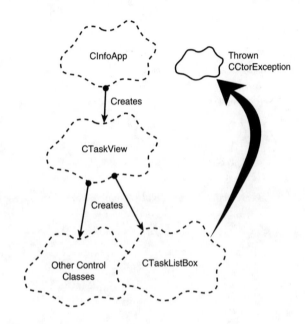

Save exceptions for cases that are truly difficult to handle without them, such as construction failure, range errors, or out-of-memory conditions.

Figure 8.4.

Exception handling in
`CWinApp::OnFileNew.`

Defining Exceptions

The simplest form of exceptions are character strings. Listing 8.10 shows a string being used to carry exception information between two functions.

Listing 8.10. Throwing a char string as an exception.

```
void GetLabelMetrics( TEXTMETRIC& tm )
{
    CDC *pdcTemp = AfxGetMainWnd()->GetDC();
    if( !pdcTemp )
        throw "GetDC Failed";
    pdcTemp->GetTextMetrics(&tm);
}

Test::Test()
{
    try
    {
        TEXTMETRIC tm;
        GetLabelMetrics( tm );
    }
```

continues 141

Listing 8.10. continued

```
catch( const char* pszMsg )
{
    AfxMessageBox( psgMsg );
}
```

In most cases, throwing a simple string doesn't provide enough information to the calling function. If a user wanted to take recovery measures based on the type of exception thrown, the user would have to compare the string to different error messages in order to determine the type of exception. For example, with CInfoApp::OnFileNew, the exceptions are divided into three categories:

☐ **Constructor failures.** If a CCtorException is caught, OnFileNew knows that something went wrong with the construction of one part of a document or view. In this case, a dialog box is displayed with information about the failure.

☐ **Memory exhaustion.** If CMemoryException is caught, you tell the user that you've run out of memory. You don't rethrow the exception. If you do, the program will be terminated by a call to unexpected.

☐ **Other exceptions.** If any other type of exception is caught, you catch it, pop up a dialog box so that the user has at least a small clue where the error came from, and rethrow the exception. The application may terminate because of an unhandled exception. You may not want to rethrow in your applications, depending on your personal preference. Alternatively, you can set up a new handler for unexpected by using set_unexpected.

Because the three kinds of exceptions listed here are different classes, it is easy to separate and handle them appropriately. If the classes that make up InfoMan just threw char strings, exception handling would be much more difficult.

Note: Don't start adding exceptions without some thorough planning. When you are defining your exception classes, it's a good idea to keep a good formal list of them. Know what each of them represents, what throws them, and what the exception hierarchy is. If you want to make good use of exceptions, it's important for everyone to be on the same wavelength.

For example, if you (or another team member) decide to use CNoSpaceException when your widget is out of space, and someone else uses CExceptionNoRoom for their widgets, your classes aren't going to be very easy to use.

Because exceptions can be objects, it makes sense to arrange them in a hierarchy just like other classes. An object that is thrown can be caught if the catch statement specifies either the same class or a base class for the thrown object. Figure 8.5 is an exception-class hierarchy for collection access exceptions.

Figure 8.5.

A hierarchy of exceptions used for collections.

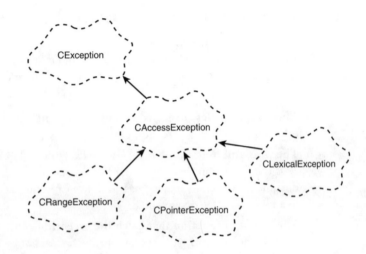

You can use the CAccessException class to catch any access exception, because all other access exceptions are derived from it. You can use the CRangeException, CPointerException, and CLexicalException classes whenever you know the type of access. Listing 8.11 shows the typical way a class library's user can use this exception class.

Listing 8.11. Using a collection that throws exceptions.

```
void DisplayTask( CTestSetBag& theTests, int nIndex )
{
    try
    {
        CTaskItem*  pTask;
        pTask = theTests[nIndex];
        pTaskWnd->SetWindowText( pTask->GetLabel() );
    }
    catch( CAccessException );
    {
        AfxMessageBox( "Display Task - Internal Access Error" );
    }
}
```

An advantage of hierarchy-based exception handling is that the user doesn't necessarily need to know what the exact exception is. This makes it possible to define new types of exceptions without changing the client code. For example, if CTestSetBag is implemented as an array, the

CRangeException might be thrown. If CTestSetBag is later reimplemented as a hash table, a CHashErrorException might be added to the CAccessException hierarchy. If CHashErrorException is derived from CAccessException, you would not need to edit any code that uses CTestSetBag.

Documenting Exception Handling

The classes that are thrown as exceptions typically don't have a lot of functionality. Generally, they just save information when they're thrown, and that information is retrieved if and when they are caught. Documentation is still very important. There are three places where you should document exceptions:

- ☐ **The exception class itself.** You should document the exception class just like any other class, including preconditions and postconditions.
- ☐ **The class and function that throw the exception.** The set of exceptions thrown by a class is information that is essential to any user of that class. You don't need to document exceptions that are passed only within the class, but all exceptions thrown to a user should be documented.
- ☐ **The class and function that catch the exception.** This is primarily a maintenance issue. By documenting the exceptions that are caught by a class, you make it easier to update that class if something about the exception hierarchy changes.

Profiling and Low-Level Testing

As part of the class-construction process, you should test the code at a low level. All source code should be tested at the implementation, or source code level. Sometimes this sort of testing is called *white-box* testing (in contrast to black-box testing, where the implementation of a function or class is not important).

For every class written for InfoMan, a test driver was written that tests every interface and every function. This is the minimum amount of testing that's acceptable for low-level testing. There's nothing quite as embarrassing as releasing source code that has obvious bugs in it into a library.

For low-level testing, you should run your tests so that as much code as possible is actually exercised. Some organizations involved in mission-critical work actually require 100 percent code coverage during low-level testing. The required code coverage for InfoMan will be somewhat lower. Because a lot of code in Windows programs just tests for error cases, it can be very difficult and costly to test every single line of code. The required code coverage for InfoMan will be 75 percent during low-level testing.

Writing a Test Driver

A *test driver* in its simplest form is a function that exercises every interface in a tested class. Depending on the code coverage percentage required, you may need to simulate error cases as well as normal operation. When you are writing a test driver, you should focus on testing the code. Later in the project, the focus will be on testing the integration of different classes or testing the application's functionality. Low-level testing is the only test phase where the code is all that matters.

In order to cut down on the amount of test-driver code required, it's a good idea to use an existing application to test any Windows-specific classes. If you don't have the source code to any applications lying around to hack up, create a skeleton application using AppWizard. Just run AppWizard, answer a few questions, and a few minutes later you've got an application that you can use as a base for test drivers.

Listing 8.12 is part of a test driver that can be used to test the CPriority class. Figure 8.6 shows the About coverage box displaying the results.

Note: The test program used for this example can be found in the \CHAP8\COVERAGE directory.

Listing 8.12. A test driver that displays its results in the About coverage box.

```
void CAboutDlg::OnTest()
{
    BOOL fResult = FALSE;
    // Get a pointer to the result window.
    CWnd* pWndResult = GetDlgItem( IDC_RESULT);
    // Test default ctor and two of the SetPriority overloads.
    CPriority   aPriority;
    aPriority.Set( 'A' );
    aPriority.Set( 27L );
    // Test the full-load ctor, the copy ctor, and the remaining
// SetPriority method. The test objects will be set in order,
    // with thePriority and aPriority being 'nearly' equal. This
    // will give us a chance to exercise the operators completely.
    CPriority   *pPriority = new CPriority( 'C', 10 );
    CPriority   thePriority = CPriority( *pPriority );
    thePriority.Set( 'A', 26 )
    pPriority->Set( 'B', 10 );
    // Serialization and Dump tests. The file "Test.txt"
    // should be checked manually.
    char* szFile = "Test.txt";
    CFile file;
```

continues

Listing 8.12. continued

```
    fResult = file.Open(szFile, CFile::modeCreate¦CFile::modeWrite);
    if( fResult )
    {
        CDumpContext dc( &file );
        thePriority.Dump( dc );
        dc.Flush();
        file.Close();
    }
     // Remaining code tests serialization and operators.
}
```

Figure 8.6.

The results from the
CPriority test driver.

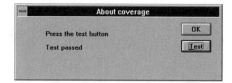

Collecting Code-Coverage Information

As part of the testing process, you should collect code-coverage statistics. *Code coverage* is the amount of code that has been executed during a test period. This is an important measurement, because it tells you how much of your code has been executed. If you pass a series of tests but execute only 25 percent of your code, 75 percent of your code has never been tested. Code coverage is expressed as a percentage of your total amount of code. To calculate it, take the number of lines executed and divide that number by the number of source lines in the module.

Textbook Tip: As with test drivers, it's a good idea to test only a single module at a time. In fact, a good practice is to run your module with its test driver until all tests pass, then start running coverage tests using the test driver. There's not much point in running a coverage test on a module that's not completely debugged.

Depending on the amount of code coverage you're aiming for, you may want to edit the test driver to create extra test cases. The test driver for CPriority originally didn't have any cases where priority "A26" was compared to "A27." By using code-coverage tools it became obvious that there was a hole in the module tests.

Before starting a code-coverage test, you must relink the project with profiling enabled. Enabling profiling disables incremental linking, so you don't want to leave this flag set longer than

absolutely necessary. You can enable profiling by opening the Project Settings dialog box on the Linking property page.

To start a code-coverage test, select Profile from the Tools menu. The Profile dialog box enables you to choose several different tests, including Function Timing and Function Coverage tests. Using the Profiler for Function Timing tests is covered on Day 12, "Module Testing and Integration."

Select the Line Coverage radio button and add a command argument in the Advanced Settings edit control. The command to start a line-coverage test on the `priority.cpp` module is

```
/EXECALL /INC PRIORITY.CPP(0-0)
```

To start a test on a module other than `priority.cpp`, substitute that name in place of `priority.cpp` in the preceding code. The Profile dialog box is shown in Figure 8.7.

Figure 8.7.
The Profile dialog box with code-coverage options selected.

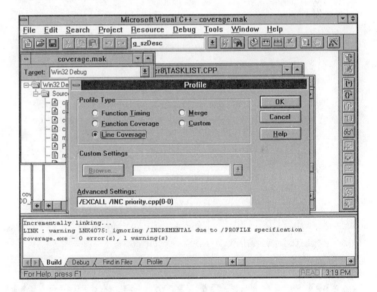

Click OK to start the profiling session. Run whatever tests you've planned to exercise the module, then quit the application. The profiler will display the results for you in the output window. Listing 8.13 is part of the profiler output from the `CPriority` test.

Listing 8.13. A fragment of the Line-Coverage test output from the profiler.

```
prep /nologo /lv /EXECALL /INC priority.cpp(0-0) C:\chapt8\coverage
profile /nologo /nc C:\chapt8\coverage
prep /nologo /m C:\chapt8\coverage
```

continues

Listing 8.13. continued

```
plist /nologo C:\chapt8\coverage
Profile: Line coverage, sorted by line
Date:    Tue Dec 27 18:51:11 1994


Program Statistics
------------------
    Command line at 1994 Dec 27 18:50: C:\chapt8\coverage
    Total lines: 81
    Line coverage: 91.4%

Module Statistics for coverage.exe
----------------------------------
    Lines in module: 81
    Module line coverage: 91.4%


163:          void CPriority::Initialize(TCHAR chMajor, LONG nMinor)
164:    *     {
165:    *         ASSERT( chMajor >= 0 && nMinor >= 0L );
166:    *         if( chMajor >= 0 && nMinor >= 0L )
167:              {
168:    *             m_chMajor = chMajor;
169:    *             m_nMinor = nMinor;
170:              }
171:    *         else
172:              {
173:    .             m_chMajor = 0;
174:    .             m_nMinor = 0L;
175:              }
176:    *     }
```

This particular test achieved 91 percent code coverage. Because of some idiosyncrasies with the way that the profiler calculates the coverage, it's almost impossible to get 100 percent coverage reported, even if every line is executed.

You've Reached a Milestone!

Congratulations! After you've completed the low-level testing and code coverage for your classes, you've reached M2, the first milestone that becomes executable code. After you compile all of your classes for the first time, that executable becomes the M2 release and can be tested at a higher level. Day 12 covers the steps that are required to actually integrate different iterations into a "Golden" release.

Note: Beware when distributing this release because it probably has a fairly large number of bugs in it. The project used to make the M2 release can be found in the \CHAP8\INFO directory on the CD-ROM.

Modification Notes

Most of the techniques used for new projects can be extended to cases where you're modifying some existing code. There are two places, however, that need special attention when you are modifying an existing project.

Coverage on Existing Modules

It can be very difficult to get acceptable code-coverage results when you're modifying an existing module. If you're lucky, an old test driver used for the original module might be available for use. If it is, use it and immediately buy a Lotto ticket, you're HOT.

If there isn't an existing module test driver, you'll have to build one yourself. Unfortunately, this can be quite a job. One option is to run several tests using the existing program structure to exercise the code. By examining the results, you can try to create cases that increase your coverage percentage.

Using Exceptions in Modified Code

It's almost always a bad idea to start using exceptions in an existing project. If you really need to add exceptions, the best thing to do is analyze which exceptions you need. Then design an entire hierarchy of exceptions and rewrite your existing error-handling code to use them.

Debugging the Process

What could possibly go wrong on a day titled "Instrumenting Code and Debugging"? One common problem that can pop up is deciding on a code-coverage target.

Deciding on a Coverage Metric

At first, everyone wants to shoot for 100-percent code coverage during low-level testing. In fact, any number close to 80 percent is a very good number to achieve. The reason that 80 percent

coverage is difficult to achieve is that a large percentage of the code in any program is used to handle cases that almost never happen. It's often much more efficient to "test by examination" parts of the code that are difficult to execute.

Of course, you should consider using risk analysis to decide on a code-coverage target. If you're building airplanes or medical devices, you should probably take the extra steps needed to test every line of code.

Increasing
Reusability with
Libraries and
Templates

Today you will continue building your application, and you will look into more ways to improve your ability to reuse classes. Static libraries, templates, and file-version marking are the primary topics you will learn in this section.

Static libraries are a convenient way to create building blocks for your projects. You'll learn how to create, document, and use static libraries.

One of the new features added to Visual C++ is support for templates. You'll learn how to create and use templates, as well as learn some advanced uses of the built-in templates from the MFC library.

You are using an iterative development cycle to create your project, so today you will develop and release the code for the InfoMan project for its next iteration. At the end of the day you will add a version of InfoMan with contact management to the existing project and release it. The contact-management classes include support for a split view, variable-tab list boxes, and multiple views for a single document. The classes are all on the CD-ROM, and you can reuse them in your own project.

Note: As with the earlier chapters, you will use the InfoMan project as a workbench to try out the topics you learn. The source code for the InfoMan project, as well as the code for more general examples, is included on the CD-ROM that accompanies the book.

Static Libraries

On Day 7, "Basic Class Construction," you concentrated on creating classes that were general enough to enable the source code for the class to be reused. When classes are reused as is or as base classes, they are often reused in their source code form; you can then compile and link them into a project.

If you can design, build, test, and debug a stable set of classes to the point that you can trust them, there is another way to package the classes that improves their reusability. Hardware designers use integrated circuits, or ICs, to assemble large designs in reusable packages. By taking the code from the trusted classes and compiling it into a library, the code really does become a "software IC," and it can be used just like a component.

Using a library helps project development in several ways:

☐ **The code is hidden.** You only provide the interface; the actual implementation code is hidden from the class user.

☐ **The number of modules in a project can be reduced.** Because several classes can be grouped into a library, compilation time is reduced.

☐ **Responsibility for a library can be given to a person or team outside of the main project flow.** The library or set of libraries can be maintained as a separate shared component by several projects.

Types of Libraries

Libraries for Windows come in two basic styles: Dynamic Link Libraries (DLLs) and static libraries. The difference between the two types is illustrated in Figure 9.1.

Figure 9.1.
Dynamic Link Libraries versus static libraries.

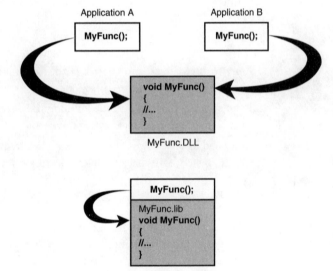

DLLs are often used when functions are needed by multiple applications on a single machine. They are mapped into the calling program's process space and "linked" at runtime. A good example of a DLL that you may be familiar with if you have used Visual C++ is MFC30.DLL, which is used by most programs built using MFC 3.0. Most of the core MFC code is located in MFC30.DLL; because it is a shared DLL, several different applications can use the DLL at the same time. This reduces the time required to load your application, as well as its size. DLLs are covered in more detail on Day 10, "Custom Controls as Reusable Components."

Static libraries are used when the functions can't be dynamically linked. For example, classes or functions that use CTime can't be placed in a DLL. Some parts of the C runtime library can't be used in a DLL.

Another reason to use a static library is cost. If a set of functions is small, it may not be worth the trouble to create a DLL for it. A static library is very easy to create and use, and the behavior of the final program remains the same.

153

The only difference you'll experience when moving some of your project out into a static library is that your compilation times will be reduced. That's the kind of side effect that you can probably live with.

Identifying Library Contents

Now that you're ready to put all of your code into libraries, let's cover some ways to determine library packages. There are a few steps that you can take that will help you define the contents of library modules.

Obviously, not everything in a project is suitable for inclusion in a library. Basically, you're looking for groups of stable functions and classes that are reusable without modification. These groups of functions can then be placed into libraries.

Showstopper: Don't put evolving code into a library. The code that's distributed in a library should be trusted, or at least trustable.

If you start out a project by recompiling the libraries or having multiple versions of libraries released at the same time, you're in for serious headaches.

It's a good idea to release libraries much less frequently than the main executable. If you can't do that, consider releasing the code in source form until it's stable.

Using InfoMan as an example, the exception classes are a set of classes that address a single function; namely, exception handling. Because the exception classes are so naturally grouped, they make excellent candidates for an exception library.

In your projects, look for similar groupings. Look for groups of classes that do the following:

- ☐ Share similar functions
- ☐ Are known to be stable, or are relatively stable
- ☐ Are good candidates for reuse without modification

The exception classes in InfoMan are made up (so far) by five classes. Creating an exception-class library will help the exception classes to be reused in future projects because it reduces the amount of work needed to include them in a project. A Booch diagram of the `infox` exception library is shown in Figure 9.2. The exception library used in your project is probably similar.

Figure 9.2.
A class diagram for the exception library used in InfoMan.

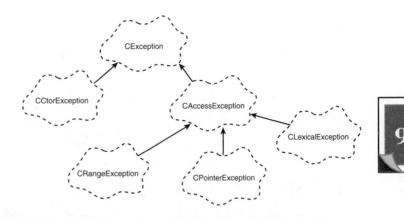

Creating a Static Library

A static library is created in much the same way as any other project. From the New Project dialog box, choose Static Library as the Project Type. Figure 9.3 shows the new project dialog with `infox` as the new project name.

Figure 9.3.
Starting a new project to build a static library.

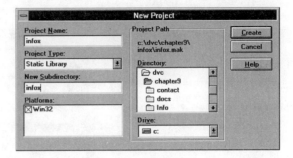

There's no AppWizard to help you add any fancy options or bells and whistles because, quite frankly, there are none to add. After completing the dialog box, a directory and makefile will be created for you, and that's all you need.

The next step is to copy the files that are needed into the project directory. Add the files to the project, just as you would for any other user-supplied files for a Windows project.

Compile the project, just as you would compile a normal Windows project. The resulting lib file will be generated in the `WinDebug` subdirectory.

> **Developer's Tip:** It's a good idea to create a single header file for each of your static libraries. If you're combining several classes together into a static library, like you did for infox, it's likely that there are several headers, one for each class. Combining these headers will make life easier for the users of your library, and easier for you to maintain. This is another reason to build libraries from stable classes.

Using Static Libraries

To replace the source files in your Windows project with a static library, follow these easy steps:

☐ Open your project that targets Windows.

☐ Remove any source files from the project that were used to build the static library. They don't need to be compiled again if they're in the library.

☐ Copy the static library into your project directory.

☐ Include the static library as a file to be linked into the executable. You can do this by opening the Project/Settings dialog box, and selecting the Link tab. Figure 9.4 shows the infox.lib added to the InfoMan project as a static library.

☐ Compile your Windows executable.

Figure 9.4.

Adding a static library to the InfoMan project.

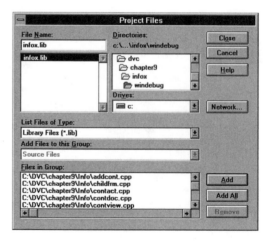

Using the infox.lib static library in new projects is even easier. Add the library just as you would add an extra source file to the project tree. Any source files that use the exceptions defined in infox.lib must include the infox.h header file.

Libraries that you create for your project also can be reused for future projects. That's why it's important to build libraries where possible, using completely generic classes and functions. Including project-specific functions or classes into a library will limit the library's reusability later.

Documentation Required for Static Libraries

The documentation required for a static library is similar to the documentation required for the classes that make up the library. In fact, most of the library documentation will just refer to the class documentation for details about the individual classes or functions.

A good approach is to leave the class documentation mainly as is, note that the class is part of a static library, and refer the user to the library documentation for high-level information. The static-library documentation can refer users back to the class documents for details about the individual classes. This helps reduce the amount of work you must do when you are updating your documents.

Compared to the documentation that you've created for other parts of the project, the requirements for the library are much smaller. The documentation for the static library should conform to the following minimum format guidelines:

Scope. This section talks about the library in general terms. It discusses the library functionality and how it relates to its environment, in a brief high-level summary.

Glossary. This is an explanation of any technical terms or concepts that are used in the rest of the document.

References. This section should contain the names of documents used by classes and other functions included in the library.

Description. Provide a more detailed description of the library here. This section should be detailed enough to help a new user of the library, but it should not replace the documentation for the individual classes.

Constraints. An optional section here provides a list of any problems or special needs that a user of the library should be aware of. For example, if the library has to be explicitly initialized, it should be noted here.

Usage Examples. Include some examples of code that use the library. For example, the `infox` documentation includes some code examples that use exceptions supported by the `infox` library.

Templates

Support for templates, which is new in Visual C++, provides a new way for you to write code that is more robust and easy to maintain. Code that is written using templates tends to be general-purpose by its nature, and is very reuse-friendly.

When you are using templates you can increase robustness by eliminating a large number of casts. In large systems, casts are usually the root of all evil, or at least a good portion of it. For example, if you use a nontemplate MFC container, you will have a great deal of code that looks like the example in Listing 9.1. This code is not type-safe, and it is an excellent place to introduce an error that is difficult to trace. Later, you'll see an example of a type-safe collection using the MFC collection templates.

You can think of type safety as a guarantee by the compiler that objects passed as parameters and results really are what you expect them to be. For example, if you have a function that returns a CRect pointer declared as

```
CRect* GetNextPointer();
```

the compiler will complain if you try to assign the return value to a CWnd pointer like this:

```
CWnd* pWnd = GetNextPointer();  // Error, can't convert
```

The practice of casting is not type-safe. In fact, the following code will not be caught as an error by the compiler because an explicit cast is used:

```
CWnd* pWnd = (CWnd*)GetNextPointer();  // Ooops
```

One common place where casts are often used is in collections. Using template-based collection classes helps to eliminate casts, and it enables the compiler to check for type safety during compilation. Later, in the section, "Using MFC Templates," you'll learn how to use the template-based MFC collections.

Listing 9.1. Using casts with nontemplate-based collection classes.

```
void CParentList::AddChild( CObject *pObj )
{
    // make the new child last
    CChildObj* pChild = (CChildObj*)pObj;
    pChild->SetLastChild( TRUE );
    m_pos = GetTailPosition();
    // make the current last child not last
    if( m_pos != NULL )
```

```
    {
        CChildObj* pLast = (CChildObj*)GetTail();
        pLast->SetLastChild( FALSE );
    }
    AddTail( pChild );
}
```

Whenever possible, you should use the template-based collection classes provided in the MFC library. You should also try to generalize your classes and global functions into templates whenever you can.

Using MFC Templates

There are three classes at the root of the MFC template-based collection hierarchy: CMap, CArray, and CList. Each of these classes has a different use and each of them is completely type-safe. All three of these collection classes are used in similar ways; for now, look at the CArray class, using some code from InfoMan as an example.

The CArray class is used to implement a dynamic array of any type. You can create a CArray of ints, CObjects, CWnds, or anything else that needs to be stored as an array. InfoMan uses CArrays in the CHeader class to store the tab positions and labels used in the contact list view.

When you declare an instance of CArray, you provide two type arguments: the first argument specifies the storage type; the second argument is the parameter type used to pass values to and from the array. Table 9.1 contains some examples of different CArray arguments.

Table 9.1. Examples of arguments used to create instances of CArray.

Declaration	Contains	Arguments
CArray<int,const int&>	int	Reference to const int
CArray<CString*,CString*>	CString*	Reference to CString
CArray<CRect, CRect&>	CRect	Reference to CRect

Listing 9.2 contains some code fragments from InfoMan that show how a CArray can be declared and used. As you can see, much less code is needed to use template-based collections compared to the nontemplate versions. The other MFC template collection classes, CList and CMap, are used in a similar way.

Listing 9.2. Using the `CArray` collection class in InfoMan.

```
// From the contdoc.h source file
CArray<CContactItem*, CContactItem*> m_setOfContacts;

//
// From the contdoc.cpp source file
void CContactDoc::UpdateContact( CContactItem* pItem,
                                 CView*        pView,
                                 int           nIndex )
{
    TRACE( "Updating item in document\n" );
    ASSERT( nIndex < m_setOfContacts.GetSize() );
    if( nIndex < m_setOfContacts.GetSize() )
    {
        CContactItem* pOldItem = m_setOfContacts[nIndex];
        m_setOfContacts[nIndex] = pItem;
        delete pOldItem;
    }
     else
    {
        throw CRangeError( "GetContact - Out Of Range" );
    }
}
```

In the preceding code fragment, you can see that the `CContactDoc` class uses an instance of `CArray<CContactItem*, CContactItem*>` to store the contact items contained in the document. After the template is declared, it is just as easy to use as an array of a built-in type.

Helper Functions

When you use `CArray`, `CList`, or `CMap`, you may need to implement one or more of the MFC collection helper classes. The *helper classes* are used by the template-based MFC collections to create, destroy, or serialize members of the collection.

The most common helper function to be implemented is `SerializeElements`. If you store pointers to objects in a `CArray`, `CList`, or `CMap`, you must implement this function if the collection is serialized. Otherwise, the collection will write the values of the pointers to the stream when it is serialized to the stream, and will attempt to read those pointers when serialized from the stream. The default behavior is known as *bitwise reading and writing*. The individual data elements are serialized exactly as they are stored in the collection. Our function will override this behavior and serialize the objects that are pointed to, not the pointers themselves.

The collection class will call the `SerializeElements` function with a signature based on the elements that are stored in the collection. If `CRect`s are stored in the collection, a `CRect*` will be passed to `SerializeElements`. In the case of `CContactDoc`, pointers to `CContactItem` are stored in the `CArray`, so the address of a pointer to `CContactItem` is provided to `SerializeElements`. Listing 9.3 is the version of `SerializeElements` used for `CArray<CContactItem*, CContactItem*>`.

Listing 9.3. The `SerializeElements` function used by `CArray<CContactItem*, CContactItem*>`.

```
void AFXAPI SerializeElements( CArchive&       ar,
                               CContactItem**  pItem,
                               int             nCount )
{
    for( int i = 0; i < nCount; i++, pItem++ )
    {
        if( ar.IsStoring() )
        {
            TRACE("CContactSet-Storing %d elements\n",
                nCount);
            (*pItem)->Serialize(ar);
        }
        else
        {
            //Create a new element and store the pointer in
            //the collection.
            TRACE("CContactSet-Loading %d elements\n",
                nCount);
            CContactItem* pNewItem = new CContactItem;
            pNewItem->Serialize(ar);
            *pItem = pNewItem;
        }
    }
}
```

There are a total of six helper functions for the MFC collection classes, all of which are implemented as global (nonclass member) functions. You will probably not have to provide new versions for all of them in your application. In InfoMan, the convention for helper functions is to implement them in the CPP file for the class that uses the collection.

Creating Your Own Class Templates

When you implement a class as a template, your first step should be to create a nontemplate version, if you haven't done so already. Because of the syntax used by templates and the difficulty involved in debugging them, it's much easier to get a nontemplate version working first, and then convert it.

A *CStack* Class Template, Created While You Wait

An example of a simple template-based class is a stack template. Even though a stack is a very simple data structure, review the steps of creating a simple nontemplate version first. A stack is a "last-in, first-out" data structure. A good way to visualize a stack is to think of a stack of plates in a cafeteria. If a plate is placed on the top of the stack, that plate will be the first plate removed.

The first version of the stack class is shown in Listing 9.4. The `CStackInt` class is fully functional, but it can store only integers. If you want to store a `double`, a `CString`, or any other type, you'll have to recode the class completely.

161

Listing 9.4. `CStackInt`, a stack class for integers.

```
class CStackInt
{
    //Constructor
    public:
        CStackInt();
        virtual ~CStackInt();
    private:
        // Copies not allowed.
        CStackInt( const CStackInt& ){};
    //Operations
    public:
        BOOL    IsEmpty() const;
        int     Pop();
        void    Push( const int& item );
    //Implementation
    private:
        int*    m_p;
        int     m_nStored;
        int     m_nDepth;
        enum    { GROW_BY = 5 };
};
//Constructors
CStackInt::CStackInt()
{
    m_p = 0;
    m_nStored = 0;
    m_nDepth  = 0;
}
CStackInt::~CStackInt()
{
    delete [] m_p;
}
// Operations
BOOL CStackInt::IsEmpty() const
{
    return m_nStored == 0;
}
void CStackInt::Push( const int& item )
{
    if( m_nStored == m_nDepth )
    {
        int* p = new int[m_nDepth + GROW_BY];
        for( int i=0; i < m_nDepth; i++ )
        {
            p[i] = m_p[i];
        }
        m_nDepth += GROW_BY;
        delete [] m_p;
        m_p = p;
    }
    m_p[m_nStored] = item;
    m_nStored++;
}
int CStackInt::Pop()
```

```
{
    ASSERT( m_nStored );
    m_nStored--;
    return m_p[m_nStored];
}

int main( int argc, char* argv[] )
{
    CStackInt theStack;

    int i = 0;
    while( i < 5 )
        theStack.Push( i++ );

    while( theStack.IsEmpty() == FALSE )
        cout << theStack.Pop() << endl;

    return 1;
}
```

After you're confident that the CStackInt class works as expected, it's easy to convert it or any other class into a template version. First, change the class declaration to refer to a generic class, class T, instead of int. Listing 9.5 shows the new class declaration for CStack.

Listing 9.5. The declaration of the CStack template.

```
template <class T> class CStack
{
    //Constructor
    public:
        CStack();
        virtual ~CStack();
    private:
        // Copies not allowed.
        CStack<T>( const CStack& T){};
    //Operations
    public:
        BOOL    IsEmpty() const;
        T       Pop();
        void    Push( const T& item );
    //Implementation
    private:
        T*      m_p;
        int     m_nStored;
        int     m_nDepth;
        enum    { GROW_BY = 5 };
};
```

The next step is to change all of the member functions so that their definitions indicate that they are members of a template class. Most of the changes are just cutting and pasting to add the template information for each function and changing all of the int parameters to type T. Listing 9.6 shows the definition of the CStack member functions.

Listing 9.6. Member functions from the `CStack` class.

```cpp
//Constructors
template <class T>
CStack<T>::CStack()
{
    m_p = 0;
    m_nStored = 0;
    m_nDepth  = 0;
}
template <class T>
CStack<T>::~CStack()
{
    delete [] m_p;
}
// Operations
template <class T>
BOOL CStack<T>::IsEmpty() const
{
    return m_nStored == 0;
}
template <class T>
void CStack<T>::Push( const T& item )
{
    if( m_nStored == m_nDepth )
    {
        T* p = new T[m_nDepth + GROW_BY];
        for( int i=0; i < m_nDepth; i++ )
        {
            p[i] = m_p[i];
        }
        m_nDepth += GROW_BY;
        delete [] m_p;
        m_p = p;
    }
    m_p[m_nStored] = item;
    m_nStored++;
}
template <class T>
int CStack<T>::Pop()
{
    ASSERT( m_nStored );

    m_nStored--;
    return m_p[m_nStored];
}
int main( int argc, char* argv[] )
{
    int i = 0;
    CStack<int> theStack;

    while( i < 5 )
        theStack.Push( i++ );

    while( theStack.IsEmpty() == FALSE )
        cout << theStack.Pop() << endl;

    return 1;
}
```

A *COwnerDrawListBox* Class Template

The owner-drawn, list-box example that was created on Day 7 can easily be converted to a template class. This template version can be used for the contact management part of InfoMan and will not need list-box items to be derived from COwnerDrawItem.

The CTaskListBox::DrawItem method assumed that each list-box item was derived from COwnerDrawItem, and made a cast to COwnerDrawItem* whenever an item needed to be drawn or measured. The code for CTaskListBox::DrawItem was shown on Day 7 in Listing 7.2.

The template version of COwnerDrawListBox uses the template parameter to determine the type of items stored in the list box. This not only simplifies the code, it reduces the chances for errors due to faulty casting, and makes the class more flexible. The listing for COwnerDrawListBox<T>::DrawItem is provided in Listing 9.7.

Listing 9.7. COwnerDrawListBox<T>::DrawItem relies on a template parameter to determine the type of items stored in the list box.

```
template<class T>
void COwnerDrawListBox<T>::DrawItem(LPDRAWITEMSTRUCT lpdis)
{
    // Get the rectangle for the item, and calculate the rectangle
    // for the focus rectangle. Also, create a temporary CDC object
    // from the one passed in to us.
    CRect rc = &lpdis->rcItem;
    //
    // If the item ID is LB_ERR, we are getting this DrawItem
    // call to set the focus for the entire list box. We do
    // not want to dereference itemData, since it is invalid.
    //
    if( lpdis->itemID == LB_ERR )
    {
        CWnd *pWndList = GetDlgItem( lpdis->itemID );
        if( pWndList )
        {
            pWndList->GetWindowRect( rc );
            ::DrawFocusRect( lpdis->hDC, &lpdis->rcItem );
        }
    }
    else
    {
        T*              pOwnerDrawItem;

        pOwnerDrawItem = (T*)lpdis->itemData;
        if( pOwnerDrawItem )
        {
            pOwnerDrawItem->Draw( lpdis );
        }
    }
}
```

Any class can be used as a template parameter for an instance of COwnerDrawListBox, as long as the class supports the Draw and Size functions. If you attempt to use the COwnerDrawListBox template with a class that doesn't support Draw and Size, a compilation error will result.

Note: The complete version of the COwnerDrawListBox template class can be found in the \CHAP9\INFO directory. It's not shown completely here because of the size of the listing.

Creating Your Own Function Templates

Function templates are used whenever a function can be generalized over more than one class. Think of a function template as a general-purpose kitchen blender. A good kitchen blender can chop ice, carrots, bananas, and almost anything else. The results after using the blender depend on what was placed into it, but it will always be a blended version of the original.

An Example of a Function Template

The textbook example of function templates are type-safe versions of the min and max macros. Examples of min and max are available in the Visual C++ online help. A more complex (and reusable) use of function templates is to provide general-purpose sorting functions. Listing 9.8 is an example of a bubble-sort algorithm implemented as a template function.

Listing 9.8. A bubble-sort function implemented as a function template.

```
// Simple textbook bubble sort. Slow, but stable, and easy to
// explain. Works for any CArray<T,const T&>.
template< class T > void BubbleSort( CArray<T, const T&>* pArray )
{
    ASSERT( pArray );
    int cArray = pArray->GetSize();

    for( int nHead = 0; nHead < cArray; nHead++ )
    {
        for( int nTail = cArray - 1; nHead < nTail; nTail-- )
        {
            if( pArray->GetAt( nTail ) < pArray->GetAt( nTail-1 ) )
            {
                // The tail is never allowed to reach zero.
                ASSERT( nTail > 0 );
                // The tail is never allowed to dangle past the
                // end of the array.
                ASSERT( nTail < cArray );
```

```
            // Swap nTail and nTail-1...
            T t = pArray->GetAt( nTail );
            pArray->SetAt( nTail, pArray->GetAt( nTail - 1 ) );
            pArray->SetAt( nTail - 1, t );
          }
        }
      }
    }
```

9

The BubbleSort template function will take a pointer to any CArray<T,const T&> and sort it in ascending order. Listing 9.9 is an example of using BubbleSort to sort an array of ints and display the result to the console.

Listing 9.9. Using the **BubbleSort** function template to sort an array of ints.

```
    CArray< int, const int& > rgInt;
    rgInt.SetAtGrow( 0, 18 );
    rgInt.SetAtGrow( 1, 7 );
    rgInt.SetAtGrow( 2, 4 );
    rgInt.SetAtGrow( 3, 8 );
    rgInt.SetAtGrow( 4, 12 );

    BubbleSort( &rgInt );
    for( int i = 0; i < rgInt.GetSize(); i++ )
    {
        cout << rgInt[i] << endl;
    }
```

Note: The complete source code for this template example can be found on the CD in the \CHAP9\TEMPL directory. Due to the size of the source, it's not completely included in the text. If templates are a new topic for you, a good exercise would be to compile the example and play around with it, changing the declarations and base classes.

Using BubbleSort as an example, you can create other general-purpose sorting templates for CArray. By identifying areas of your design that can reuse function templates like BubbleSort, you can help improve your project's quality at a very low cost.

Remember: *typedef* Is Your Friend

Just when you got the hang of pointers to functions, along come template declarations. Although template declarations are very similar to other class declarations in C++, the individual

declarations tend to be longer, and therefore more complicated. If you're having trouble separating the different parts of a template declaration, don't worry, you're not alone, and there is a way to make your life easy again. Listing 9.10 is an example of some template declarations.

Listing 9.10. Some examples of complicated template declarations.

```
class CFoo
{
    // Declarations here
};

// Class CMyArray - A class that has the initial size of the array
// as a template argument.
template <class T, int cSize> class CMyArray : public CArray< T, T&>
{
    // Declarations here
};
// Constructor for class CMyArray
template <class T, int cSize> CMyArray<T, cSize>::CMyArray()
{
    SetSize( cSize );
}

//Declaring an instance of CMyArray< CFoo, 5 >
CMyArray< CFoo, 5 > rgFoo;

// A function declaration that returns a pointer to an instance of
// CMyArray< CFoo, 5>
CMyArray< CFoo, 5 >* GetArray();

// A function declaration that takes CMyArray<Foo, 5> as a parameter
void PrintArray( CMyArray< CFoo, 5 >& rg );
```

An easy way to simplify a template declaration is to use typedef to create a new type. By creating new type names when you use templates, you can reduce the amount of baggage that gets in the way of your declaration. Listing 9.11 is similar to Listing 9.10, but the definitions are easier to read because a typedef is used for CMyArray< CFoo, 5 >.

Listing 9.11. Using typedef to simplify template declarations.

```
// Class CMyArray - A class that has the initial size of the array
// as a template argument.
template <class T, int cSize> class CMyArray : public CArray< T, T&>
{
    // Declarations here
};
// Constructor for class CMyArray
template <class T, int cSize> CMyArray<T, cSize>::CMyArray()
{
    SetSize( cSize );
}
```

```
typedef CMyArray< CFoo, 5 > CFooArray;

//Declaring an instance of CMyArray<Foo, 5>
CFooArray rgFoo;

// A function declaration that returns a pointer to an instance of
// CMyArray<Foo, 5>
CFooArray* GetArray()

// A function declaration that takes CMyArray<Foo, 5> as a parameter
void PrintArray( CFooArray& rg )
```

As an example, the CContactView and CHeader classes in InfoMan use CArray<int,int> and CArray<int,int>* to track the column size used in the list-box control. Using typedef, the new type names become CTabArray and CTabArray* and are much easier to read, especially when they are passed as parameters.

Version and Release Marking

Today marks the second executable release of InfoMan. If you're following along with your own project, you've probably reached your second release. With more releases coming, it's important to be able to tell them apart. Because some releases may appear very similar to each other, you should start using the Version and File Installation APIs if you're not doing so already. You can add version information to any Win32 executable, DLL, or font file.

You can use the file-version information to help determine which files should be replaced during an installation. This information will be very useful when you start your testing, but for now you'll also use it to identify versions during the construction phase.

Adding version information is easy, and it takes only a few minutes. To take advantage of the File Installation APIs, you must define a version-string resource. Just create a new resource and select Version as the resource type. Fill in the information for each of the string resources. Figure 9.5 shows a version resource being edited.

Figure 9.5.
Editing a version resource.

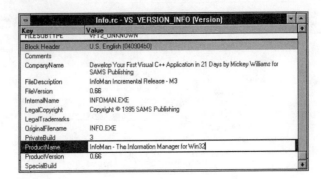

That's all you have to do to mark your file with a version number. You can use the File Manager to see the file version and to view the File Properties dialog box. An example of that dialog box for InfoMan is shown in Figure 9.6.

Figure 9.6.

Version information for INFOMAN.EXE displayed by the File Manager.

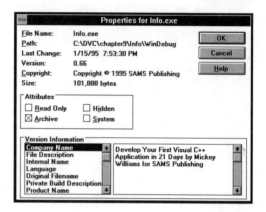

If you want to display the file-version information yourself like InfoMan does in Figure 9.7, things get a little more complicated. In fact, it's so complicated you'll provide a CVersionInfo class to do the work for you. The CVersionInfo class can be found on the disk, in the \CHAP9\INFO directory.

Figure 9.7.

The About InfoMan dialog box, with version information included.

The interface for the CVersionInfo class is given in Listing 9.12. When an instance of CVersionInfo is created, it collects version information regarding the file of which it is a part. This class is easily reusable in your application.

Listing 9.12. The interface for the CVersionInfo class.

```
class CVersionInfo : public CObject
{
    //Constructors
    public:
        CVersionInfo();
        ~CVersionInfo();
        CVersionInfo( const CVersionInfo& );
    //Operations
    public:
        CString GetVersion() const;
        CString GetCopyright() const;
```

```
        CString GetCompanyName() const;
        CString GetDesc() const;
        CString GetInternalName() const;
        CString GetOriginalName() const;
        CString GetProductName() const;
    //Attributes
    private:
        const static CString m_szID;
        LPVOID   pvVersion;
}
```

9

Congratulations! Your project has completed another milestone. The InfoMan project is now at its third major milestone, M3. InfoMan can now store contacts with the new contact-management classes added today, as well as track tasks with the task-management classes that were finalized on Day 7. Figure 9.8 shows the dialog box used to add a contact, with one of the contact views in the background.

Figure 9.8.
The Contact Management view from InfoMan.

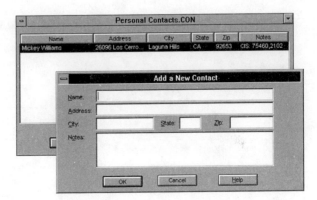

Your project is probably far enough along that you can start distributing a few copies to friends and getting some feedback about its user interface and operation. Remember, the code hasn't been thoroughly tested, so don't let too many copies out just yet.

Modification Notes

If you're modifying an existing project, there are a large number of candidates that could be made into templates or static libraries. Look for low-level, common functions that could be made into libraries. If your modification adds functionality that's similar to some existing part of the project, look for parts of the code that can use templates. Because Visual C++ has only recently supported templates, there may be many specialized sort routines that can be converted.

Above all, make an effort to version mark all of your EXEs and DLLs. It's the only way to create reliable installation routines, and you can use this information yourself during the verification process, later.

Debugging the Process

If you have problems creating template classes, make sure that you've created a nontemplate version first. After you get the nongeneric class working, you can go on to the template version. However, it's not unusual to find an error in a base class when you convert it into a template. If this happens to you, it will probably happen when you try to create an instance using the template. For example, the CStack template might not work if you tried to use it with CStrings like this:

```
CStack< CString > m_stackOfStrings;
```

The best approach to this problem is to convert the template into a nontemplate version, using CString in place of the template argument. This will result in a CStackString class, much like the CStackInt class that the CStack template was based on. By working backward, it's often possible to find those hard-to-track errors in the template.

Custom Controls
as Reusable
Components

One way to leverage your Windows code is to reuse classes from one project in others. This is the type of reuse that you learned about in earlier parts of this book. Today, you'll investigate a slightly different type of reuse, where the reuse occurs at a higher level. This reuse centers around building your controls as reusable components.

You'll take the tabbed list box from InfoMan that you created on Day 9, "Increasing Reusability with Libraries and Templates," and create several different types of reusable controls based on it. There are also several sample programs provided on the CD to help with today's discussion.

The Advantages of Using Controls as Components

In previous chapters you learned the benefits of reusing your source code. On Day 9 you learned the advantages of creating classes that were general and reusable. In these discussions, the unit of reuse was the C++ class. When you are developing Windows applications, it can be helpful to design your classes so that the unit of reuse is larger than the individual class.

Today, you'll learn how to reuse your code at a higher level. By investing a small amount of extra work when you create specialized controls for your applications, you can easily reuse those controls in later projects.

Textbook Tip: The use of components is one of the favorite topics of discussion in software engineering. Studies have shown that a large amount of work on software projects consists of "ordinary" work.

An example of this is *repetitive coding,* or work that is copied from previous projects with little modification. Moving to component-based design and using automated design tools are two ways to help reduce the amount of time spent on repetitive, low-level coding.

An Overview of Controls in Windows

User-friendly controls are the mark of a well-designed Windows application. Choosing the right control for each task is an important part of the overall design of your Windows application. Most of the time, the standard Windows controls will provide enough functionality for your application.

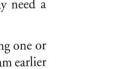

However, sometimes your user interface may need more functionality than the standard controls offer. You might need a control that provides different feedback to the user, or that has slightly different functionality than the standard control. At other times, you may need a completely new type of control for some specialized purpose in your application.

One straightforward way to deal with specialized controls is to implement them using one or more MFC-based classes. This is the approach taken for the InfoMan example program earlier in this book. Although this method enables the building blocks for each control to be reused, it forces you to deal with the implementation of the control at a rather low level.

Reusing Controls

Reuse can occur at several different levels. At its lowest level, you can cut and paste code from an existing project into a new one. Although, strictly speaking, this is code reuse, it's not very efficient and is prone to errors. Anyone who uses the raw source code in this way must understand how each line of code works in detail. Additionally, the code must be completely retested every time it is used. This should be called text reuse, not code reuse.

On Day 9, you learned the process of creating classes that were general enough to be used in future projects. This takes more time and effort, because the class must be designed in an open way and tested in more general conditions than if it were built for a specific, narrow purpose. However, building classes that can be trusted to work without modification in the future is an effort that is usually worthwhile. If you reuse a class in another project right away, the time spent making the class more reusable is quickly recovered.

You can apply the same approach to controls that are developed for your applications. By spending a small amount of extra time when the control is initially developed, it can be easily reused in future projects. This is useful, because a large part of the coding effort in many Windows applications is devoted to the user interface.

When you program in Visual C++ using controls in Windows, you have several options:

- ☐ Using a standard control
- ☐ Using an owner-drawn control
- ☐ Subclassing an existing control class
- ☐ Creating an aggregate control
- ☐ Building a custom-control DLL
- ☐ Building an OLE custom control (OCX)

Each of these options is well-suited to creating specialized controls in Windows. For complex controls, each of these options offers a different degree of reusability. As shown in Figure 10.1, you can achieve the most reuse by building custom controls. These controls can be used in Visual C++, as well as in other Windows C++ environments. OLE custom controls also can be used in Microsoft Access and Visual Basic version 4.0 and above.

Figure 10.1.
Different types of advanced controls offer different degrees of reusability.

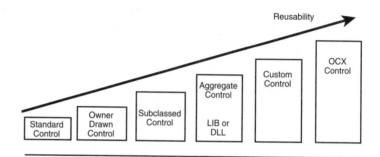

Owner-Drawn Controls

Owner-drawn controls offer one of the simplest types of customization over the standard Windows controls. If you only want to change the visual appearance of a standard control, an owner-drawn control is the way to do it. This is often the easiest way to offer advanced functions for your controls, and it requires very little code.

When you create a simple owner-drawn control using MFC, the functionality of the control is generally wrapped in a single class, derived from the basic control's class. For example, the list boxes created for InfoMan beginning on Day 7, "Basic Class Construction," were derived from the MFC CListBox class. Other basic Windows controls that can be owner-drawn are

- [ ] Menus
- [ ] Buttons
- [ ] List boxes
- [ ] Combo boxes

> **Note:** Programmers will often use an owner-drawn button to place a bit map on the button face. The MFC library includes a CBitmapButton class that simplifies this common use of owner-drawn buttons.

The MFC implementations of these controls provide the DrawItem member functions that can be used to handle drawing inside the control. You implement the DrawItem function and are

responsible for all of the visual aspects of the control, including the selection and focus states. The only parameter supplied in DrawItem is a pointer to a DRAWITEMSTRUCT. The following lists the contents of the DRAWITEMSTRUCT structure:

- ☐ CtlType Specifies the control type, which isn't very interesting if you are programming at the MFC level.

- ☐ CtlID Specifies the identifier unless a menu item is being drawn.

- ☐ itemID For menus, this is the menu ID. Otherwise it is the index for a combo box or list box. If the value is -1, the entire combo box or list box is receiving the focus.

- ☐ itemAction Specifies the type of drawing that should be performed on the control. For an example of using this field, look at the source code for the owner-drawn controls used in InfoMan. In the online help, you can find a list of possible values for this field.

- ☐ itemState This field contains the current state of the item being drawn. Again, for examples of using this field, see the source code for the owner-drawn controls in InfoMan.

- ☐ hwndItem This is the window handle for the control that is being drawn. Normally this field isn't needed for simple MFC-based, owner-drawn controls.

- ☐ hDC This is the handle to a device context that must be used to draw the control. If you are using MFC classes to draw your control, then you should use the CDC::FromHandle function to attach to this hDC. An example of using the hDC properly is shown in the CBmpPane source code in Listing 10.1. Do not, under any circumstances, delete this handle, because Windows will do this for you after you have finished drawing.

- ☐ rcItem This field is the RECT structure that is available for drawing your control. Unless you are drawing a menu item, your control will be clipped to this rectangle.

- ☐ itemData This is the data that is associated with the control. All controls can have user data associated with them; the message or function you use depends on the control type. For example, to associate a 32-bit value for an item when you are using the MFC CListBox class, the SetItemData function would be used.

Developer's Tip: Displaying the focus and selection state correctly for your control is an important part of the feedback supplied to the end user. Although these functions are not documented well in the SDK documentation, you can use the sample code provided for InfoMan's owner-drawn controls as a guide.

Although owner-drawn controls generally change only the appearance of the control, a lot of functionality can be added just by changing the visual parts of a standard control. For example, the File Manager directory tree is just an owner-drawn list box. You create the appearance of a nested directory structure by inserting and removing items from the list box, depending on the selections made in the control by the user.

In fact, there isn't a requirement that the new control must behave like the base control at all. For example, the button control is often used as a base for new control types. The CHeader class used as a list box's tab control on Day 9 is derived from CButton.

It's easy to create new owner-drawn controls with Visual C++ and the MFC classes. These new controls often can be easily reused, just by encapsulating them in a class derived from an existing MFC control class.

As an example, let's create a control that changes its appearance whenever the mouse passes over it. The new control will have two states, each corresponding to a different bit map. The CBmpPane class will be the simplest possible type of owner-drawn control. It will be derived from CButton and will handle just two functions: DrawItem and OnMouseMove. Use ClassWizard to create a class based on an existing class, as shown in Figure 10.2.

Figure 10.2.

Using ClassWizard to create a new class derived from CButton.

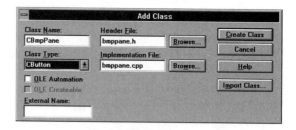

The majority of the code in the CBmpPane class can be found in the CBmpPane::DrawItem member function. Although there are a few lines of code that keep track of the mouse position and current control state, most of the code provided in Listing 10.1 consists of the DrawItem function. The constructors, message maps, and header file aren't shown, but the complete source for an example project that uses all of the classes discussed today can be found on the CD in the \CHAP10\CTRL directory.

Listing 10.1. A simple implementation of an owner-drawn control.

```
void CBmpPane::DrawItem(LPDRAWITEMSTRUCT lpdis)
{
    // Make sure the function was called with valid arguments.
    ASSERT( lpdis );
    CRect rc = &lpdis->rcItem;
    ASSERT( rc.Height() > 0 );
    //
    // If the item ID is LB_ERR, we are getting this DrawItem
```

```
        // call to set the focus for the entire control. We do
        // not handle this case in CBmpPane, since we don't draw
        // the focus rectangle.
        if( lpdis->itemID != LB_ERR )
        {
            CDC*        pdcTmp;
            CBrush      brGray;
            CBrush*     pbrOld;
            CDC         dcMem;
            CBitmap*    pbmpOld;

            // Test to make sure that we get a CDC*
            VERIFY( pdcTmp = CDC::FromHandle( lpdis->hDC ) );
            COLORREF    clrGray = GetSysColor( COLOR_BTNSHADOW );
            brGray.CreateSolidBrush( clrGray );
            pbrOld = pdcTmp->SelectObject( &brGray );
            pdcTmp->FillRect( &rc, &brGray );

            // In a real application, you would probably cache the
            // bitmap when the dialog box was constructed to save
            // time when drawing the bitmap.
            CBitmap bmp;
            if( m_fMouseOverhead )
            {
                VERIFY( bmp.LoadBitmap( m_nResCovered ) );
            }
            else
            {
                VERIFY( bmp.LoadBitmap( m_nResNormal ) );
            }

            dcMem.CreateCompatibleDC( pdcTmp );
            VERIFY( pbmpOld = dcMem.SelectObject( &bmp ) );

            pdcTmp->BitBlt( rc.left,
                            rc.top,
                            rc.Width(),
                            rc.Height(),
                            &dcMem,
                            0,
                            0,
                            SRCCOPY );
            // Restore original GDI objects
            dcMem.SelectObject( pbmpOld );
            pdcTmp->SelectObject( pbrOld );
        }
}

void CBmpPane::OnMouseMove(UINT nFlags, CPoint point)
{
    CRect   rc;
    GetClientRect( &rc );

    CButton::OnMouseMove(nFlags, point);
    if( rc.PtInRect( point ) )
    {
```

continues

Listing 10.1. continued

```
        if(m_fMouseOverhead == FALSE)
            InvalidateRect( &rc );
        m_fMouseOverhead = TRUE;
        SetCapture();
    }
    else
    {
        ReleaseCapture();
        m_fMouseOverhead = FALSE;
        InvalidateRect( &rc );
    }
}
```

Developer's Tip: The CBmpPane class is a simple control that illustrates an important design method. The code that handles the state of the control is completely separate from the code that handles its visual appearance.

When the mouse passes over the control, the state of the control is changed, and the control's rectangle is invalidated. This eventually triggers a request for the control to be redrawn by DrawItem, which uses the control's state to select a bit map.

The CBmpPane control normally contains a smiley face unless the mouse passes over it. Figure 10.3 shows a CBmpPane control when the mouse passes over it.

Figure 10.3.

A shot of the CBmpPane control when it is under a mouse.

Although the code from Listing 10.1 is simple and a little contrived, it shows that you can use an owner-drawn control in ways that are quite different from the base control. The CBmpPane control is derived from the CButton class, but from the user's point of view it's just a bit-map holder that changes its appearance when the mouse passes over it. A few lines of code have changed it into a control that appears to act completely unlike a normal button.

The class is also an example of a control that is reusable as a single class. It is very easy for another programmer to read the documentation for this class, include the class header, and reuse the control in another project.

Subclassing Controls

If you must have a control that "almost" works like one of the standard Windows controls but implements some special behavior, you should investigate subclassing. This is another method that you can use to easily leverage the functionality that exists in the standard Windows controls. By using the MFC support for dynamic subclassing, you can create your own classes that can be reused just like the previous example with owner-drawn controls.

Subclassing a control gives you a chance to intercept or modify messages from a control, before the control's window procedure receives the messages. When you subclass a window (remember, controls are just specialized windows), your message procedure is inserted between the control and its normal message procedure, as shown in Figure 10.4.

Figure 10.4.
When you subclass a control, your code gets the first shot at its messages.

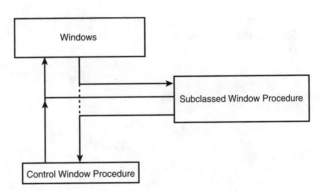

Think of subclassing as a mandatory detour for your control's messages. Once you have control of the message, you have three options:

☐ You can pass the message along unchanged.

☐ You can modify the message so that the control's window procedure sees a slightly different message.

☐ You can eat the message completely, and optionally take some action of your own.

Can you make a real mess of things by subclassing improperly? Sure you can, but that's part of the fun of Windows programming using the API. Luckily, the MFC classes make subclassing much safer than when you are working with the standard SDK using C. The MFC classes derived from CWnd implement a SubclassDlgItem function that handles all of the subclassing details for you.

An example of control subclassing is an edit control that allows only numbers as input. Implementing an edit control that rejected anything except numbers would be impossible without subclassing. One method might be to allow any sequence of numbers to be entered into the control, and reject any input that contained letters. This isn't a very good solution from the user's point of view, because the information must be entered completely before it is validated.

A better solution is to test every character entered into the edit control, and provide immediate feedback to the user. If the character is allowed, pass the character on to the edit control. If the character is not allowed, reject the character and provide some feedback to the user.

By subclassing a standard edit control, it's easy to create a reusable class that accepts only numbers, and provides feedback as each character is typed. The CNumericEdit class is based on the MFC CEdit class. Listing 10.2 contains the interesting details from CNumericEdit. The complete source and header file for CNumericEdit can be found in the \CHAP10\CTRL directory.

Listing 10.2. Partial listing of the CNumericEdit class.

```
CNumericEdit::CNumericEdit()
{
}

CNumericEdit::~CNumericEdit()
{
}

BEGIN_MESSAGE_MAP(CNumericEdit, CEdit)
    //{{AFX_MSG_MAP(CNumericEdit)
    ON_WM_CHAR()
    //}}AFX_MSG_MAP
END_MESSAGE_MAP()

// Reject any input except numbers, which will be sent on to the
// default window procedure.
void CNumericEdit::OnChar(UINT nChar, UINT nRepCnt, UINT nFlags)
{
    // Don't forget to allow backspace through to the message proc.
    if( (nChar >= '0' && nChar <= '9')||(nChar == VK_BACK) )
        CEdit::OnChar(nChar, nRepCnt, nFlags);
    else
        MessageBeep( MB_ICONASTERISK );
}
```

Although the CNumericEdit class consists of just a few lines of code, it demonstrates the three basic actions that you can take when subclassing a control:

☐ If any message except WM_CHAR is received, it is passed unchanged to the control's message procedure.

☐ If the WM_CHAR message is received with a numeric character, the processing of the message is sent to the default window procedure.

☐ If WM_CHAR arrives with a character that isn't allowed, the message is eaten, and the edit control's message procedure will never see it.

The CNumericEdit class is another example of a control that is reusable as a single class. Using this class as a starting point, it's easy to create several reusable classes that could discriminate between characters, numbers, or you could even create a "picture" control that allows the type of input to be specified on a character-by-character basis.

Controls that are contained in a dialog box should be subclassed during the dialog box's OnInitDialog member function. Listing 10.3 contains the code from the CNumEdit dialog box found in the CTRL sample.

Listing 10.3. Subclassing the dialog box's edit control during OnInitDialog.

```
BOOL CNumEditDlg::OnInitDialog()
{
    CDialog::OnInitDialog();

    m_editNumeric.SubclassDlgItem( IDC_NUMBERSONLY, this );
    return TRUE;
}
```

Aggregate Controls

Sometimes you need a more complicated control for part of your user interface. For example, on Day 9 a list box controlled by a moveable header control was used to display contact information. A diagram of the relationships between classes involved is shown in Figure 10.5.

Figure 10.5.
The classes used for InfoMan's Contact Manager tabbed list box.

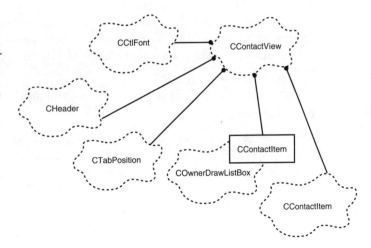

Individually, each of these classes is reusable in other contexts. The owner-drawn list box, the header control, and the self-creating font in CCtlFont are all examples of general and reusable classes.

However, in order to reuse these classes to create a similar control in another project, you need to know a lot about each class. For example, to re-create the existing control, the user needs to include at least four include files, as shown in Listing 10.4.

Listing 10.4. A partial list of the include directives for CContView.cpp.

```
/////////////////////////////////////////////////////////////
// CContactView
// contview.cpp : Implementation filefor the CContactView class.
//
#include "stdafx.h"
#include "Info.h"
#include "tablist.h"
#include "contact.h"
#include "header.h"
#include "owndrlst.h"
#include "contdoc.h"
#include "contview.h"
```

This certainly makes it more difficult to reuse the control, and although it's easily corrected by creating a single header file, there are more complexities that pop up because of the number of classes used by the control. Although the classes are reusable, the way in which they are being used is closely coupled to the application.

The user of this control also needs to know a great deal about the relationships between the control's classes. Information about the internal details of a control is almost always an unneeded complexity. This sort of detail is a good example of information that should be hidden whenever possible. Ideally, the user of a control should have to worry only about a single interface.

If you decide that your control should be used as a single component, consider creating an aggregate control. You build aggregate controls by bundling several different classes together to form more complex controls.

The user of the control can include a single class header file, TABLIST.H for example, whenever the new control is used. To make the class even easier to use, the code for the control can be precompiled into a static library (LIB) or dynamic link library (DLL) and added to the project. A class diagram of the new control is shown in Figure 10.6.

Figure 10.6.
A class diagram for a tabbed list box with a simpler interface.

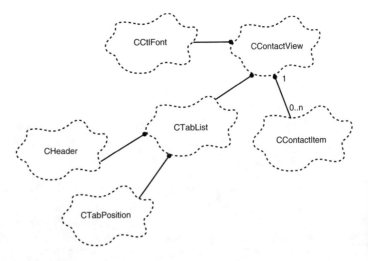

Building and Testing a Static Library Version

On Day 9 you learned the steps involved in creating a static library. To review, you need to

☐ Create a new project that creates a static library
☐ Copy your classes into the new project directory
☐ Add the classes to the project

In addition, for the tabbed list box example, all of the header files were placed into one file, named TABLIST.H. Other than the preceding steps, there aren't many changes required when you move a set of working classes into a static library.

> **Note:** There are two projects on the CD that are used for the static-library version of the tabbed list box. The project that builds the static library can be found in the \CHAP10\TABLIST\STATIC directory.
>
> The project that builds an application that uses the static library can be found in the \CHAP10\TABLIST\TSTSTAT directory. This project already contains a compiled static library for the tab control.

One change that was made in the CHeader class involved the loading and setting of the cursor resource used to mark the dividing point at each tab mark. It was necessary to change the code so that it used the semi-undocumented AFX function AfxFindResourceHandle. This function runs down the list of loaded DLLs and finds the instance that contains the resource for which you are searching. Without the changes in Listing 10.5, the cursor couldn't be loaded.

Listing 10.5. Using the AfxFindResourceHandle function.

```
void CHeader::OnLButtonDown(UINT nFlags, CPoint point)
{
    if( m_nCapturedDivision > -1 )
    {
        m_fDragging = TRUE;
        SetCapture();
        HCURSOR    hCurSplit;
        //
        // Search for the instance handle that actually contains
        // the cursor resource we're looking for. This function
        // uses the FindResource function internally; look there
        // for more info on the parameters.
        HINSTANCE  hInst = AfxFindResourceHandle(
                        MAKEINTRESOURCE(AFX_IDC_HSPLITBAR),
                        RT_GROUP_CURSOR );
        hCurSplit = ::LoadCursor(
                        hInst,
                        MAKEINTRESOURCE(AFX_IDC_HSPLITBAR) );
        if( hCurSplit )
        {
            ::SetCursor( hCurSplit );
        }
    }
}
```

Using a static library is appropriate when the control isn't shared with other applications and doesn't need release marking. If you need one of these features, consider using a DLL.

Building a Dynamic Link Library (DLL) Version

Another way to package your control components is to create DLLs that are linked with your application at runtime. In Win32, every DLL is mapped into the calling application's process address space, even if several different applications or multiple instances of the same application link to it. This makes DLLs much more robust than in 16-bit Windows, where DLLs are global resources.

Using DLLs for common libraries was introduced on Day 9. To review, the DLL is not part of your application's EXE; rather, it is loaded at runtime. If the DLL is already loaded, the operating

system simply maps the already loaded DLL into your address space, and your application uses the DLL as if it were a part of your application. There are some exceptions to this, which will be covered later.

By default, all MFC applications built with AppWizard use the MFC library DLL. The best (and easiest) way to create a DLL that adds MFC-based controls to your MFC application is to create an Extension DLL. Your DLL will actually become an "extension" of the MFC DLL. Extension DLLs make it very easy to pass MFC objects, such as controls, between the application and the DLL; in fact, AppWizard can do most of the work for you.

> **Note:** As with the static library, there are also two projects on the CD that are used for the DLL version of the tabbed list box. The project that builds the static library can be found in the \CHAP10\TABLIST\XDLL directory.
>
> The project that builds an application that uses the DLL can be found in the \CHAP10\TABLIST\TSTDLL directory. This project already contains a DLL and export library for the tab control.

10

The first requirement before using an Extension DLL is to make sure that both the application and DLL use the shared MFC DLL, instead of the static library version, at runtime. If your application uses the static library version, you won't be able to use this method. If you use AppWizard to create your DLL, choose MFC AppWizard (dll) as the project type, as shown in Figure 10.7.

Figure 10.7.
Using AppWizard to create an Extension DLL.

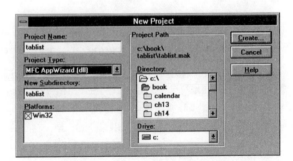

When the project is created, AppWizard will create all of the Extension DLL initialization code for you. It most cases, you won't have to touch this code unless you need to perform some start-up initialization in your DLL. Listing 10.6 is the Extension DLL code provided by AppWizard for the skeleton project.

Listing 10.6. The Extension DLL code created by AppWizard.

```
static AFX_EXTENSION_MODULE tablistDLL = { NULL, NULL };

extern "C" int APIENTRY
DllMain(HINSTANCE hInstance, DWORD dwReason, LPVOID lpReserved)
{
    if (dwReason == DLL_PROCESS_ATTACH)
    {
        TRACE0("TABLIST.DLL Initializing!\n");

        // Extension DLL one-time initialization
        AfxInitExtensionModule(tablistDLL, hInstance);

        // Insert this DLL into the resource chain
        new CDynLinkLibrary(tablistDLL);
    }
    else if (dwReason == DLL_PROCESS_DETACH)
    {
        TRACE0("TABLIST.DLL Terminating!\n");
    }
    return 1;    // ok
}
```

Note: If you would like to see another, larger example of building a general-purpose Extension DLL, look at the DLLHUSK sample program that is distributed with Visual C++. You can find this application in the \SAMPLES\MFC\DLLHUSK subdirectory under your compiler directory.

Unlike encapsulating your control in a static library, in a DLL you must explicitly export any symbols that should be publicly visible. There are three ways to export symbols from a DLL:

☐ **Export at a class level.** In the class declaration, immediately after the class keyword, type AFX_EXT_DATA to declare the entire class as being exported. This is the method used in the CTabList DLL sample.

☐ **Export individual symbols.** If you don't want to define an entire class, or if you have other symbols to be exported, use the AFX_EXT_DATA qualifier for those declarations also.

☐ **Export individual symbols in a DEF file.** This is the most efficient, and most difficult, method. This is also the approach used for the shared MFC DLL. This method requires you to know the decorated name for each C++ symbol, and isn't recommended for the faint-hearted. However, because the symbols are exported by ordinal, meaning that they are exported by number instead of name, they are much more efficient.

> **Developer's Tip:** If you would like to use your DLL with applications other than MFC-based Visual C++ projects, consider wrapping the exported C++ member functions with C functions so that they are visible to non-Visual C++ programs. The C functions must be declared as using a C interface instead of a C++ interface. This will enable your DLL to be used by a wider range of compilers, and even other languages.

If you export all of your symbols using AFX_EXT_DATA, a large number of error messages will be generated by the compiler. For example, the CHeader class is derived from CButton, but because CButton is not globally exported, a warning is generated. You can silence these warnings by using #pragma directives. Listing 10.7 is an abbreviated copy of the TABLIST.H used to build the DLL version of the tabbed list box, including the pragma and export information.

Listing 10.7. An abbreviated version of TABLIST.H used in the DLL version of CTabList.

```
#pragma warning(disable: 4275)
#pragma warning(disable: 4251)

// CTabPosition class
// Interface of the CTabPosition class.
//
class AFX_EXT_CLASS CTabPosition : public CArray<int,int>
{
    // Interface declarations here...
};

/////////////////////////////////////////////////////////////////
// Interface of the CHeader class.
class AFX_EXT_CLASS CHeader : public CButton
{
// Interface declarations here...
};
/////////////////////////////////////////////////////////////////
// Interface of the CTabList class.
//
class AFX_EXT_CLASS CTabList : public CListBox
{
// Construction
// Interface declarations here...
};
#endif //INFOMAN_TABLIST
```

After the DLL is compiled, the TABLIST.H and TABLIST.LIB files must be added to any projects for which you want to use the CTabList class as a DLL. Remember to add version information to any DLLs that are used in your application.

Developer's Tip: Make sure that you use debug versions of your DLLs and static libraries for your debug-mode application, and release mode libraries and DLLs for release builds. If you are working with a large team, where many people are building components for your application, you may want to create a naming convention such as the one used by the shared MFC DLL.

This can be useful if several applications are using a control DLL, and only one application needs a debug version. It's much simpler in these cases if the release and debug versions have different names.

Custom Controls

Custom controls offer a great deal of flexibility. In fact, before the MFC classes and Visual C++ made it easy to create aggregate controls, it was fairly common to have to create custom controls to offer any sort of specialized control. Using a custom control, it is possible to create completely new control types that don't need to be based on existing Windows classes.

Custom controls are built as DLLs, and use a well-defined interface that supports the old DLGEDIT dialog editor. DLGEDIT is still included with the Win32 SDK. Unfortunately, the resource tools in Visual C++ don't offer the same support for custom controls that was once provided with DLGEDIT.

If you have access to the Win32 SDK, or if you are creating a totally new type of control that should be implemented as a custom control, check out the Microscroll example. This sample program can be found in the \SAMPLES\WIN32\MUSCRL32 subdirectory under your compiler's directory.

OLE Custom Controls (OCXs)

Applications built for 16-bit versions of Windows often used Visual Basic Controls (VBXs) to provide extra functionality not offered by the standard set of Windows controls. These custom controls were originally offered for Visual Basic, but they proved so popular that C++ compilers started offering support for them as well.

Unfortunately, the VBX architecture is closely tied to the 16-bit version of Windows. There is no way to create a 32-bit VBX, which is a bit of a problem if you have applications that rely on VBXs and you're trying to port them to Win32. Among your options are porting your control to a class or to DLL, using some the techniques described in the section, "Aggregate Controls."

The newest type of custom control is the OLE custom control (OCX). These controls are portable to both 16-bit and 32-bit versions of Windows, and even to non-Intel architectures such as MIPS or DEC Alpha machines running Windows NT.

OCX controls are OLE objects supporting a special set of interfaces that define them to be OLE custom controls. In OLE-speak, the OCX is an *in-process server*. This means, among other things, that it is implemented as a DLL. The control is embedded in an OCX container that communicates with the control through OLE interfaces, as shown in Figure 10.8.

Figure 10.8.
Communication between the OCX control and OCX container.

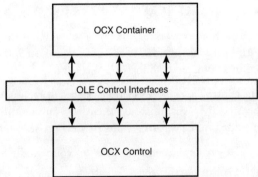

Visual C++ 2.0 includes the OLE Control Development Kit, enabling you to create MFC-based OCXs using a ControlWizard, which works very much like the AppWizard used to create MFC-based applications. The ControlWizard is shown in Figure 10.9.

Figure 10.9.
Using ControlWizard to create an OLE custom control.

Because there isn't any built-in support for creating OCX containers using MFC, it's difficult for you to add OCX controls to your application at the present time. For an example of the process required to create an OCX container, see the February 1995 edition of the *Microsoft Systems Journal.* In the article, "Putting Your OLE Controls to Work with Microsoft Access, Visual Basic, and C++," Joshua Trupin builds an OCX container. Otherwise, you can wait with the rest of us for a set of OCX control classes and built-in support for the OCX interfaces. I won't go into any detail about creating OCX controls, but there is a large section in Books On-Line that includes a tutorial on creating OCXs.

Modification Notes

If you are modifying an existing project, you may need to reuse an existing set of controls. These controls may be included in the current project and used in a different context, or they may be used in a completely different project.

If the controls are currently implemented in a reusable way—as custom controls, for example—then it will be easy to reuse them in your modified project. However, if the controls are embedded in the existing dialog or view classes, you have two options:

- [ ] Re-create the controls "as is" in your modified project
- [ ] Create reusable controls based on the existing controls

In the long run, you will be much better off if you can create a reusable control. It won't take more time than copying the code to the modified project, and in return you will have a reusable component for future projects.

Debugging the Process

If you are porting an existing project to Win32, you might have a problem if you depend on VBX controls. Although ControlWizard will help you port an existing VBX to an OCX, there is no support for OCXs in MFC applications at the present time.

Currently, your only option is to replace the 16-bit VBX with another type of control that is supported under Win32. This generally won't be too much of a problem if you have access to the VBX source code.

Error Reporting
and Metrics

Today you will learn about error reporting and metrics. You need to use error or problem reports, so you should learn to see them as tools rather than as bad news. By using techniques covered today, you can see error and problem reports as ways to help you create a better product.

An important objective of the software-development process is quality improvement. Collecting measurements for your projects is a good way to help yourself improve quality-wise. You develop metrics using measurements from a project, and use them when you are planning for the future, as well as checking a project's progress. Like anything else, metrics vary in their usefulness. You'll learn some good metrics, some bad metrics, and common pitfalls to avoid when performing software measurements.

Today there's not really much code, except for a few examples used to illustrate problems or measurements. You've finished the primary coding on InfoMan, and from now on you're just verifying, testing, and debugging.

Using Software Metrics

A *metric* is the result from a measurement that has been collected on some part of the development process. Most large software projects spend a significant amount of time and energy collecting statistics about their software process. Their motivation is quality improvement. Some examples of metrics include the following:

- ☐ Lines of code produced by a programmer per month
- ☐ Reported errors after release per line of new code
- ☐ Cups of coffee consumed per line of code produced

Note: This list is neither an offer to buy nor an offer to sell any of these metrics. At least one of these metrics is imaginary and, as discussed next, there are issues involved in selecting metrics that can help you measure your project.

A large project with hundreds of programmers has obvious reasons for using measurements to improve its software quality. These projects have big budgets and complicated designs, and usually a great deal of money is at stake. You may not realize it, but even if you're working alone, you can improve your quality by using some of the same methods that a large project might employ.

There is no single "best metric." Software metrics come in all shapes and sizes, just as software projects, problems, and people do. There are a lot of measurements that are available to choose from, and some will be more useful to you than others.

Textbook Tip: If you're working with a team, you should introduce software-quality measurements carefully. The most important thing to remember about collecting any sort of quality measurement is to separate the statistics from job performance reviews. Team members should not be worried about the negative impact that honest quality reports may have.

Consider baseball, for instance. It's not unusual for the third baseman or shortstop to have the highest number of errors on the team. The fact that they have the most opportunities for errors is not reflected in a simple quality measurement that counts only their total number of errors.

Continuous Improvement

A good way to approach software quality is to use the idea of continuous improvement, as practiced in total quality management, or TQM. With continuous improvement, everyone contributes to increasing the quality of the product, and with that contribution comes responsibility for the improvement. The basic idea behind continuous improvement is that every process and work flow can be improved somehow, and all tasks can be done better, more reliably, or faster. Performing quality measurements and collecting metrics are the first steps in the process of continuous improvement.

The key to improving your software quality, whether you work alone or on a team, is continuous improvement. It would be nice to be able to create the perfect software-development environment just by snapping your fingers. A slow, steady pace will be successful; unfortunately, it's not possible to travel from software fiasco to software Valhalla in one step.

The first step in your improvement process should be to assess your current status. After you determine your strengths and weaknesses, you can develop an improvement plan. There is a saying that applies to software processes in general: "If you don't know where you're going, all paths will take you there."

A similar saying that could apply to software quality improvement is, "If you don't know where you are, a road map won't help."

With those quotes in mind, your first measurements should focus on an assessment of your current work. These measurements should also be weighted toward quality measurements, instead of measurements that focus only on productivity. Some useful types of measurements and metrics are covered later (beginning in the section, "Collecting Metrics Wisely"), but some examples of good initial measurements include the following:

☐ Error rates reported after the product is released

☐ Time spent on "rework"

☐ Percentage of code changed after testing begins

Problems with Measuring a Software Process

Keep in mind that when you measure a software process, its behavior tends to change. Because programmers are people, they have a natural desire to at least look as though they're doing a good job. It's natural for anyone, even a person working alone, to want any job-related statistics to reflect well on their work. If a person feels that statistics collected about his or her work might not be flattering, that person will tend to change his or her work methods in order to be happier with the statistics reported from the measurements.

You should be careful to perform measurements in a general and nonintrusive way in order to minimize this side effect. For example, instead of recording the comments-to-code ratio for all of the source modules, it is better to make several general-purpose measurements at the same time using automated tools, if possible.

Textbook Tip: Automated measurements are especially important if you're working alone. If you are constantly stopping your development work to perform a measurement, the measurement will not be very effective, and you will have an incentive to delay or avoid measurements altogether.

For InfoMan, which is being developed as a single-programmer project, the only measurement that must be done continuously is tracking the time spent on rework (the time spent related to repeating a task). This isn't really intrusive, because it amounts to filling out a time sheet. All of the other measurements can be collected after the project has been completed.

If you were to measure the ratio of comments to code, that ratio would definitely increase. There would be a natural tendency for any programmer to increase that number, even if they weren't specifically told that their comment ratio was too low. However, if your goal was to improve the quality of the comments, you might be disappointed in the quality of the new comments. Because you are implying that quantity is preferred over quality by measuring only the number of commented lines, more lines of comments will almost certainly be generated. There is no reason to believe that the added comments will add any value to the code; they will just make the source-code files larger.

As an example, say that you work on a project on which you must record comment measurements. Listing 11.1 is a function that is used by InfoMan to add a new contact item in one of the lists of information maintained by InfoMan. The function is relatively easy to follow, and the comments follow the guidelines from the InfoMan coding standard developed on Day 5, "Coding Standards and Work Methods." Very little information that's obvious in the code is repeated.

Listing 11.1. The comment-coding style used in InfoMan.

```
// OnAdd - Displays the CContactAddDlg, and adds the contact if
//         the user completes the operation. A pointer to the item is
//         added to the list box. The data belongs to the doc, which
//         must delete it when the document is released.
void CContactView::OnAdd()
{
    try
    {
        CAddContactDlg  dlg;

        int nDlgReturn = dlg.DoModal();
        if( nDlgReturn == IDOK )
        {
            CContactItem* pItem;
            pItem = new CContactItem( dlg.m_szName,
                                      dlg.m_szAddress,
                                      dlg.m_szCity,
                                      dlg.m_szState,
                                      dlg.m_szZip,
                                      dlg.m_szNotes,
                                      &m_tabPos );
            CContactDoc* pDoc = (CContactDoc*)GetDocument();
            int nItemIndex = pDoc->AddContact( pItem, this );
            m_listBox.InsertString( nItemIndex, (LPCSTR)pItem );
        }
    }
    catch( CRangeException )
    {
        AfxMessageBox( "Internal Database Error" );
    }
    catch( CMemoryException )
    {
        AfxMessageBox( "Memory error while adding contact" );
    }
}
```

Look at a different version of CContactView::OnAdd that increases the comments provided for the user. Listing 11.2 adds nothing to the version in Listing 11.1; in fact, it actually makes using the function more difficult. Because the comments provide a step-by-step narrative of what can be easily found in the code, useful information is hidden and hard to find.

Listing 11.2. A version of `CContactView::OnAdd` **with excessive comments.**

```cpp
// OnAdd - Displays the CContactAddDlg, and adds the contact if
//          the user completes the operation. A new CContactItem
//          instance is created, and added to the document. First a
//          pointer to the document is fetched, then AddContact() is
//          used to actually add the contact to the document. The
//          pointer to the item is added to the list box. The
//          data belongs to the doc, which must delete it when
//          the document is released. If an exception is caught, a
//          message box is displayed for the user.
void CContactView::OnAdd()
{
    try
    {
        CAddContactDlg  dlg;

        int nDlgReturn = dlg.DoModal();
        if( nDlgReturn == IDOK )
        {
            CContactItem* pItem;
            // Create a new item
            pItem = new CContactItem( dlg.m_szName,
                                      dlg.m_szAddress,
                                      dlg.m_szCity,
                                      dlg.m_szState,
                                      dlg.m_szZip,
                                      dlg.m_szNotes,
                                      &m_tabPos );
            // Get a pointer to the doc instance
            CContactDoc* pDoc = (CContactDoc*)GetDocument();
            int nItemIndex = pDoc->AddContact( pItem, this );
            m_listBox.InsertString( nItemIndex, (LPCSTR)pItem );
        }
    }
    // Catch Exceptions
    catch( CRangeException )
    {
        AfxMessageBox( "Internal Database Error" );
    }
    catch( CMemoryException )
    {
        AfxMessageBox( "Memory error while adding contact" );
    }
}
```

It is important to perform quality measurements and collect metrics as a first step toward improving software quality, but it is important not to introduce more problems that need to be solved. Some good measurements that can be collected from source modules are presented later today. These metrics are not usually very helpful by themselves, but they often help when combined with other metrics.

Some More Examples of Bad Measurements

Before you see some ways to use quality measurements to improve your software process, look at some more ways that they are often misused. There are a few common mistakes that are made by people or teams that are just starting to use quality measurements.

As stated earlier, metrics are often misused because they are used to measure a single facet of a complicated process. The following sections list two software measurements that are typically poorly collected or used. It is by no means a complete list, because people are very resourceful when it comes to impeding improvement.

All of the following cases share a common flaw: They use quality measurements as a way to improve a process instead of a way to collect data to be used in the improvement process. This often happens when a decision is made to start quality measurements without a clear goal in mind.

Misusing the Lines of Code (LOC) Metric

Perhaps the most widely misused metric comes from the lines-of-code, or LOC, measurement. Usually, one compilable line in the source file equals one LOC, meaning that lines consisting only of comments or braces don't count in the LOC measurement. Used alone, it can tell you absolutely nothing about the productivity of a programmer. Several well-written classes that are fully reusable will look just as productive as one very long subroutine that is not even usable once. The LOC in a module is useful as a part of other metrics, but don't mistake it for a measure of productivity.

The LOC measurement also has the dubious distinction of telling you absolutely nothing about the quality or complexity of a source module, while at the same time encouraging programmers to increase code complexity. All it does is measure the number of lines in the source file; it cannot tell you if those lines are useful or well-designed. As a further side effect, it discourages code reuse by giving programmers an incentive not to use common libraries.

Look at an example to point out how this metric can miss the big picture. Listing 11.3 is a contrived example of two different ways to change the font for all of the child windows in a dialog box. The first method is obvious, and works well enough. You will receive no problem reports about this chunk of code, unless you add another control.

Listing 11.3. A brute-force approach to changing the font used in a dialog box.

```
// Change the font for all controls to pFont.
void CMyDlg::SetFont( CFont* pFont );
{
```

continues

11

Listing 11.3. continued

```
        m_treeControl.SetFont( pFont );
        m_nameEdit.SetFont( pFont );
        m_addrEdit.SetFont( pFont );
        m_cityEdit.SetFont( pFont );
        m_stateEdit.SetFont( pFont );
        m_zipEdit.SetFont( pFont );
        m_okButton.SetFont( pFont );
        m_cancelButton.SetFont( pFont );
        m_helpButton.SetFont( pFont );
}
```

The second version is provided in Listing 11.4. This function can be called for any CWnd object. It is totally reusable, and will work no matter how many controls are added. However, code like this typically takes longer to write than the code in Listing 11.3. The benefit, of course, is that the general function can be used forever, while the brute-force version can be used only once.

Listing 11.4. A general function to change the font for all controls in a dialog box.

```
// Iterate over the child controls, and set the font to
// pFont.
void SetControlFonts( CWnd* pWnd, CFont* pFont )
{
    CWnd* pChild = pWnd->GetWindow( GW_CHILD );
    CWnd* pFirst = pChild;
    while( pChild )
    {
        pChild->SetFont( pFont );
        pChild = pChild->GetWindow( GW_HWNDNEXT );
        if( pChild == pFirst )
            break;
    }
}
```

The last thing you want to do is discourage the coding style used in Listing 11.4. A simple metric such as LOC per day completely misses a more important element: reusability. LOC per day or per programmer is not useful except when estimating the amount of time required to complete a project; however, if you could measure code reuse, that would be a useful metric. Collecting measurements for this sort of metric is covered in the section, "Code Reuse."

Measuring Error Reports

Another simple metric that is misused is the error-report metric. Error, fault, and problem reporting is covered later today; for now, take as a given that a report of an error should not reflect on an individual programmer or module. It is important to track the number of errors, but in terms of individual or even team performance this is only part of the picture.

For example, software that's used for mission-critical applications is usually subjected to a higher standard than normal desktop software. Developers who are working on these systems may appear to be less productive, but a great deal of their work may involve building super-robustness into their assignment.

It is important to the entire quality process that people see reports or feedback about any part of the project as a chance to improve the product quality, not as a negative thing. In fact, later you'll call these reports "incident reports," just to take away the negative, bad-news connotation.

A similar metric that can actually help you improve the quality of the products you create is to track the number of reported faults that occur after the product is released. By collecting other metrics, such as code complexity, or changed lines, you can see where additional attention might be needed during the testing or design phases. Remember, you can use this information even if you are a programmer working alone.

Collecting Metrics Wisely

You can collect good metrics only when you perform measurements as one part of an overall improvement program. An improvement program works just as well for single-person organizations as it does for large ones. In fact, because you have fewer people to sell on the idea of process and quality improvement, it may work better.

Avoiding Measurement Side Effects

It can be difficult to accurately measure a software process if it's not using some sort of formal, repeatable development process. If every project is developed in a different way, measurements will be difficult to compare between different projects. As you learned earlier, measuring a process has a tendency to change or skew the results so that the measurement is successful. If you are using a formal process to develop your software, this interference will be minimized.

For example, if source-code reviews are required for all modules included in your project, many metrics that otherwise encourage bad coding practices will have a smaller negative impact. If code-coverage testing is performed by an independent testing group, the incentive for programmers to write easily tested code will be reduced.

The best way to avoid measurement side effects is to collect data generally and automatically, whenever possible. If you need the LOC measurement for a source module, that information is available from the source profiler. It's fairly easy to write a tool to count the number of comments in a source module. You can calculate module reuse by using reports from a configuration-management tool. All of these approaches are unobtrusive and will reduce measurement side effects.

Examples of Good Metrics and Measurement Plans

Of course, if all measurements and metrics were doomed to fail, you wouldn't bother to implement them. There are a number of good measurements that you can use to help you improve the quality of your project. All of the measurements and metrics presented next have specific uses, and will require very little extra work to collect.

Code Reuse

Code reuse, expressed as a percentage of old code used for new functionality, is one of the first metrics that you should utilize to improve the quality of your source code. Collect this metric by determining the number of lines added for a module and calculating the percentage of that code that was originally developed for use elsewhere.

If you aren't reusing modules, or if you would like to increase the amount of code reused in your projects, look for a barrier that is preventing you from achieving your goal. Some possible reuse barriers include the following:

- [ ] **Designs that emphasize solving a particular problem, instead of providing a general framework.** A large part of any design should be general enough for reuse. If it's not, reconsider your design methods.

- [ ] **Coding styles that cause too much coupling between modules.** If a module depends strongly on other modules, it won't be reusable without those modules.

- [ ] **Poor quality that prevents reuse.** If a module doesn't work well the first time, it probably won't be reused.

Errors Reported after Release

The number of problems reported after a product is released is an important metric. This measurement goes to the heart of your quality-improvement process—think of it as your "quality bottom line." After you determine this metric for one release, you can use it to track your improvement through future deliveries. If you can reduce the number of reported errors without reducing your number of customers, your quality has probably improved. If the number of reported errors increases, your quality-improvement program may be in trouble.

You can collect the number of reported errors from incident reports, which are covered later today. There are two interesting measurements that you can collect, along with the actual quantity of faults:

- [ ] **The part of the development cycle that introduced the fault.** Not all problems are introduced as coding errors. If you have made a system or module design error, you can use this information to help improve that area in the future.

☐ **The first phase of the development cycle that could have caught the problem.**
This information will help you identify which development phase could have provided feedback into the process, and could be improved.

Code Churn

The *code-churn* metric is based on the number of lines of code that have been added, modified, or removed. This metric is useful when you are trying to determine the risk that a module or group of functions will contain faults. The idea behind this metric is that source code that doesn't change is less likely to have faults discovered in it, whereas source code with a large number of changes is more likely to contain errors. During the early stages of a test phase, you can use this information to allocate more time to modules with a large number of changes.

> **Textbook Tip:** The information about lines added, moved, and deleted is available from almost all configuration management tools. This is a metric that you will use during a project to help in the development process to assess risk, unlike most other metrics that are used to assess quality. However, code churn can be used in quality improvement. After a project has been completed, you can look for modules that had high error rates; if these modules also had a high churn rate, more regression testing may be needed. Regression testing is used to make sure that changes haven't introduced new faults into the application.

Fault Intensity

Fault intensity is the number of new problems reported for a module over a fixed period of time. Generally speaking, the fault intensity should always be declining. If the fault intensity is increasing, it could be a problem with the code quality or design and a sign that more regression testing is needed.

For example, there are almost always a large number of problems reported after a product enters a new test phase. This is expected, because each test phase will execute different tests than the previous phase. Figure 11.1 shows a typical fault rate graph, where the fault rate increases slightly when a new test phase is entered, although the tendency is toward lower fault rates.

As more tests from a test phase are executed, faults that are corrected early in the phase should help improve quality later in the test phase. However, if the fault intensity increases, it could be a sign that corrections introduced to fix early problems are causing new problems and reducing the code quality.

Figure 11.1.
A typical fault-rate graph.

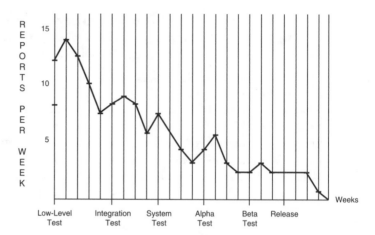

Changes and Errors Happen

On every software project that lasts any significant length of time, something will probably be changed. The most obvious changes happen because of reported errors or problems, but changes also happen when specifications change or are clarified. The nature of software design is that it is subject to modification as it is being built. It's very unusual to find any sort of program that has been specified, designed, built, tested, and delivered without some modification having been done to the original requirements.

This is not something that's unique to software. Buildings, bridges, ships, and almost anything else that's specified and built to order sometimes needs to be changed as it is being built. Understand that you must plan for change. You must be prepared to update your specifications, designs, test plans, and source code, because chances are excellent that someone is going to change their mind. Unfortunately, this often happens after the project is well underway.

Incident Reports

An *incident report* is used to give feedback about some activity in the development process. Because feedback can be required at any time during the development cycle, some organizations use the term "task report" or "problem report," or even "fault report." Using names like "task" and "incident" is becoming more popular because you can avoid the negative feelings that are associated with the word "problem."

 Note: The incident report form used for InfoMan can be found in the \CHAP11\DOCS directory on the disk that accompanies the book. As with all of the other documents, it's available in Microsoft Word and plain-text formats.

No matter what you call them, it's important to focus on using an incident report as a tool, just as metrics were used as a tool earlier. In order for reporting to be successful, it must be seen as a positive experience for both the reporter and the person or team that answers the report. Table 11.1 shows how the users of an incident reporting system might mold their attitudes to reflect the way the reports are presented.

Table 11.1. Attitudes toward quality reports may reflect their use.

Reports Used as Improvement Tools	Reports as Negative Feedback
An opportunity to improve quality	An indicator of a bad product
A key part of development	More worthless paperwork
Feedback from users	A complaint from users
Documentation improvement needed	Not a fault, read the manual

Using Incident Reports

You should use incident reports to give feedback to any part of the organization. Often, a large number of incident reports will actually be requests for new functions. You will use these reports when you are deciding on new functionality to be added for future releases. Table 11.2 shows an example of different types of incidents routed to different parts of an organization.

Table 11.2. Examples of incident reports and the responsible phase.

Report Type	Responsible Phase
New requirements	System design
More tests needed	Test design
Unclear requirements	System design
Broken functionality	Code construction
Poor documentation	Documentation

The example in Table 11.2 may be different from your project. For example, you may think that a problem with broken functionality might be due to a low-level design problem. Each development team should decide on the actual routing process. Also, if you're working alone or with a small team, all of the issues in Table 11.2 may be the responsibility of a single person.

Designing an Incident Report

The actual design of the incident report will vary a great deal from one development organization to another. It's a good idea to try to keep the design stable for at least one project, unless serious problems are found with the report design.

There are a number of options available for the actual implementation of an incident-report system. Figure 11.2 shows an incident report stored using the Windows CardFile program.

Figure 11.2.

Using CardFile to store incident reports.

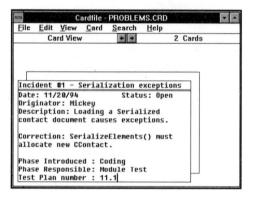

Using individual cards in CardFile is about as low-tech as is feasible. There are several commercially available programs that can be used to track incident reports. It also is possible to write a simple tracking tool yourself. If you're a programmer who is working alone, it's possible to keep hard copies of incident reports, though it will be difficult to generate information from a stack of hard copy.

The information that's kept in an incident report should always contain the following information:

☐ The name of the originator. Often, you will need to contact the originator. Providing a standard location on the incident report may seem obvious, but a large number of users may not realize it unless you remind them.

☐ The time and date of the report. Depending on the severity of the problem, you may want to guarantee a response in a certain time frame. Even if you don't make a formal guarantee, the time required to resolve an incident is a useful metric.

☐ A serial number for the report. It's not possible to do any sort of tracking unless you can identify each individual report.

☐ A description of the incident and a method to duplicate the problem.

- [ ] A space to record the resolution. This field should always be filled out with as much information about the solution as is practical. This information can prove valuable if similar reports are received in the future.

- [ ] The current status of the report. This information should be updated whenever the report is answered, closed, rejected, or undergoes some other change that your organization has defined.

The preceding list should be considered a minimum for any incident report. The following information can be useful, but it may not apply for every situation:

- [ ] The phase that introduced a problem or incident. This information is useful for metrics used for improvement purposes.

- [ ] The phase that had the first opportunity to correct the incident. This is also a useful improvement metric.

The Reporting Process

Different projects will have different requirements for incident reporting and tracking. However, the main goal of incident tracking is to provide feedback to different parts of the development process. The tracking process should encourage people to give feedback, and it should enable you to easily retrieve information about individual reports.

When it comes to reporting systems, one size doesn't fit all. There is a big difference between the tracking systems used by a developer working alone and the systems used by an organization with hundreds of developers.

Modification Notes

If you're modifying an existing project, there may be some metrics already available from previous projects. Even if the measurements seem unreasonable, consider using those same measurements for your current project. If there is an existing process for handling incident or problem reports, check to make sure that it can give you the information needed to track incidents and monitor your quality. If not, modify the tracking process to provide the information you need.

If no metrics are available for previous projects, you should try to construct your own. This is not as difficult as it might seem at first, though the resulting metrics will not be as accurate as they might have been had they been produced as part of the previous project. If source code, time sheets, and incident reports are available, you can do rough versions of many of the measurements discussed earlier.

Debugging the Process

If you have problems collecting data for your quality measurements, one reason could be that other members of the development team don't recognize the usefulness of the measurements. An important part of the measurement process is educating every member of the team about the need for software-quality improvement and for measurements to assess and improve your software quality.

Module Testing
and Integration

Today you will learn a part of the development process that's often overlooked: integrating the components for your project. A poorly executed integration of your project can cause significant problems later, and an integration that is done properly can help form a strong base for the test phases that follow.

You'll learn four different styles of integrations, and look at when each might be more or less useful than the others. You'll also learn the planning that's required for a good integration.

The last topic today is integration testing. At the end of the day you will learn how to plan, execute, and keep records as part of integration testing.

You can find sample code and documents from today in the \CHAP12\ directory on the CD-ROM that accompanies this book.

The Integration Process

A Windows program is almost always a collection of several small components that must work together to form a complete system. Even medium-sized programs are often made up of hundreds of modules. Unlike smaller modules or systems that are designed to work in a DOS-style environment, a Windows program must cooperate with the operating system so that other programs, even those not developed by you, work properly.

The actual integration process is made up of several steps:

- ☐ Combining some or all of the source modules
- ☐ Testing the module interfaces against the system design
- ☐ Resolving problems and errors
- ☐ Repeating the process as necessary

As discussed in the next section, the focus during the integration process is on the interfaces between modules. Before you begin the actual integration, you must complete the following tasks:

- ☐ Module (low-level) testing
- ☐ Integration planning
- ☐ Integration-test planning

The low-level testing of your modules should be completed already. Integration planning and integration-test planning will be covered in the next few sections. After the integration and test planning are completed, the actual integration process can begin.

Black-Box Versus White-Box Testing

As covered on Day 7, "Basic Class Construction," you should do low-level testing for all classes and source modules included in your project. The low-level tests performed on these modules are known as *white-box* tests.

The test designer who designs and executes white-box tests must have a great deal of knowledge about the inner workings of the module. This sort of testing is useful when you want to test an implementation's internal integrity. In your case, you used white-box tests in order to get maximum code coverage at a low level. Because the white-box tests passed successfully, you can be confident that the modules work reliably. However, you cannot be sure that the interfaces between the modules have been implemented correctly.

During the integration process you test the interfaces between the modules to make sure that the modules are working as designed. You do not need to understand how the modules have been designed or implemented. This idea is illustrated in Figure 12.1.

Figure 12.1.
During integration the interfaces are tested, not the internal parts of the modules.

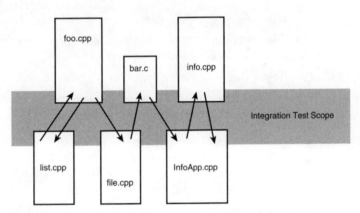

Each module is treated as a magic box that receives input and provides an output. When you are planning the tests to be performed on the integrated modules, the design documents, not the source code, should be your source of information. This restriction may be relaxed to include the class headers, depending on your own design objectives. Because you don't consider the actual implementation of the modules during the test planning or testing, it's called black-box testing.

Textbook Tip: When organizations are large enough, and if the project is a mission-critical system, black-box testing is often done by a separate, independent group. An independent test and verification team may be a luxury you

can't afford, particularly if you're a team of one. If so, you should use the same techniques that an independent team would use. Focus on the interfaces as they are designed, rather than on the underlying code.

Understanding Integration Phases

Generally speaking, during integration you aren't too interested in verifying that your program works correctly with other Windows programs. This doesn't mean that you turn your back on faults discovered during integration, but typically tests and processes during functional and system testing are tuned to discover those errors. These topics are covered on Day 17, "Functional Testing," and Day 18, "System-Level and Alpha Testing."

There are at least four different integration methods:

- **Big-bang integration**, where all the modules are integrated and tested at once
- **Top-down integration**, where the main control modules are integrated, and then new modules are added and tested in several phases
- **Bottom-up integration**, where the low-level functions are integrated first
- **Iterative integration**, where new functionality is added in an iterative process as it is designed and constructed, with a formal test phase after all modules have been added

Each of these methods has strong points as well as drawbacks. Some methods are more suited for particular types of projects or organizations. In fact, most projects will use some mixture of these techniques, though there is generally one preferred method. The choice of the best integration method is up to you, as always.

Each of these integration methods is discussed in detail in the following four sections. After deciding on the method that you'll use to integrate all of your source modules, you will need to create an integration plan and an integration test plan.

Using Big-Bang Integration

The *big-bang*, or *all-at-once*, integration method involves collecting all of your modules and attempting to combine them into a properly working executable in a single integration phase. This method of integrating the different parts of a project is most often used by developers working alone who aren't aware of more sophisticated methods. This method works only for the smallest projects.

Figure 12.2 is an example of big-bang integration. All of the modules used on a project are designed and constructed. After low-level testing, the modules are linked together and tested as a single unit.

Figure 12.2.
An example of using big-bang integration.

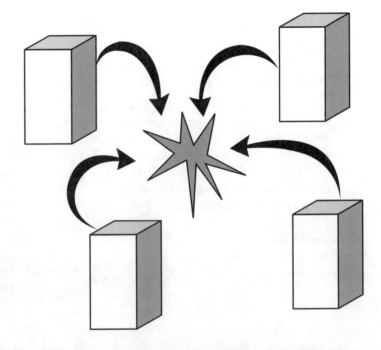

 **Showstopper:** Big-bang integration may look like a great time-saver, especially for large projects, but don't be fooled! All of the other integration methods are better suited for large-system integration. The purpose of using one of the structured techniques is to avoid problems later in the verification process. Only by testing properly at the integration level can you lay a strong foundation for the testing to follow.

12

The problem with this type of integration is that it becomes very difficult to handle problems if the project contains more than a handful of modules. Errors that occur after all of the modules have been integrated can be difficult to trace, because there is no trusted unit of core modules that are known to work properly. This can create frustrating delays while these faults are resolved.

Another problem is that the number of interfaces that must be tested will be quite large during the initial tests. This leads to the "It seems to work" syndrome, where the integration tests are given a low priority or skipped altogether. This approach will certainly work for small projects; however, it will fail for larger or more complex ones.

Using Top-Down Integration

With *top-down* integration the control, or base, part of the program is developed and integrated first, followed by other modules that add functionality to the system. Typically, the integration process follows several phases, with each phase integrating the next lower level of the project.

This technique is most often used for projects that have been designed and constructed using structured programming techniques, because the central modules are usually available first when structured programming is used. Figure 12.3 shows the steps involved in using top-down integration. The main control loop or central part of the program is integrated first, followed by the lower-level modules. With Windows programs, the WinMain and main window callback procedures are considered the central part of the program. Lower-level modules are added one at a time to the integrated part of the project.

Figure 12.3.

An example of using top-down integration.

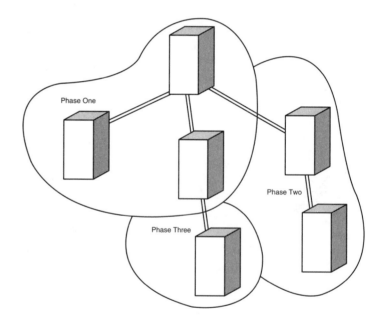

An advantage of top-down integration is that it enables the central or main part of the program to be integrated and tested first. This can be useful if the system has to be demonstrated occasionally or if the user interface needs to be tested separately from the rest of the program.

Program stubs are used with top-down integration to take the place of modules that haven't been integrated yet. A *stub* is a small function that simulates the work that will be performed by a function that hasn't been integrated yet. These stubs should not be very complicated because they exist primarily to provide data that will be used to test the interfaces between other modules.

Listing 12.1 is an example of a stub that is used to simulate input from a user. Note that there are no dialog boxes or other user-interface elements in the stub. Think of a stub as a sleight-of-hand trick that makes the rest of the program think that data has been entered by the user. More information on writing test stubs, drivers, and harnesses is provided later today.

Listing 12.1. A test stub that is used to simulate data entry by a user.

```
// Test stub for GetLogin(). Returns a non-zero value, and
// a user name with password. The password is returned in
// clear-text.
int GetLogin( CString* pszName, CString* pszPassword )
{
    *pszName = "foo";
    *pszPassword = "foopass";
    // Just in case someone is testing for TRUE instead of
    // testing for non-zero ;-0
    return 42;
}
```

Showstopper: When you perform the integration test, don't modify the code that has already been integrated. It's easy to forget and leave the modification in place. The purpose of the integration phase is to add the modules as they have been constructed. Otherwise, you should repeat the module tests.

If you must have a complicated stub that's based on a module from your project, make sure that the stub is used only for testing, and not as part of the project.

12

Using Bottom-Up Integration

Bottom-up integration involves integrating modules into the system starting with lowest-level modules first. This method is the opposite of top-down integration, because the central part of the program is integrated last. As with top-down integration, this method is usually employed for projects that were built using structured methods.

A benefit of using bottom-up integration is that the most complex modules are generally integrated first. This can help you complete the high-risk parts of the project early. Figure 12.4 shows an example of integrating from the bottom up.

Figure 12.4.
An example of using bottom-up integration.

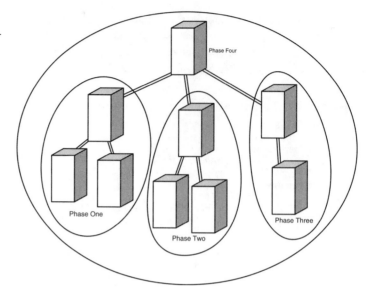

When you are testing a low-level module you use drivers to simulate the main program. You used drivers to test individual classes on Day 7. For many projects it may be easier to create a single test driver than a stub for every module. An example of a driver that tests several modules is shown in Listing 12.2.

Listing 12.2. A test driver used to test several modules at the same time.

```
void CTestApp::OnTest()
{
    CString szName;
    CString szPassword;
    CString szResult;
    int     nResult;

    //Test the GetLoginName Module
    nResult = GetLoginName( &szName, &szPassword );
    if( nResult == FALSE )
        szResult = "Result from GetLoginName was FALSE";
    else
        szResult = "OnTest: Name = " + szName + ". PW = " +
                    szPassword;
    AfxMessageBox( szResult );

    //Test the encryption module
    CString szEncrypted;
    nResult = EncryptString( &szPassword, &szEncrypted );
    if( nResult == FALSE )
        szResult = "Result from EncryptString was FALSE";
```

```
    else
        szResult = "OnTest: PW = " + szPassword +
                   ". Encrypted to " + szEncrypted;
    AfxMessageBox( szResult );

    //Test call to password database
    nResult = TestPassword( &szName, &szEncrypted );
    if( nResult == FALSE )
        szResult = "Result from TestPassword was FALSE";
    else
        szResult = "Result from TestPassword was TRUE";
    AfxMessageBox( szResult );
}
```

A major drawback to using bottom-up integration is that you are managing several different integration trees early in the project. Coordinating the integration between these different integration trees can be difficult, because each integration tree is a separate test application. Also, progress can appear to be slow from outside the project when compared to top-down integration, because there is no program available for demonstration.

Using Iterative Integration

Another approach for integrating your project is to design and construct your project by using *iteration*; that is, designing, constructing, and integrating a few modules at a time. After all of the iterations are completed, you perform a final, formal integration test of the project.

Figure 12.5 is an example of integration by iteration. During each iteration, you test new modules as you add them to the project. Each development cycle creates a system that has more features than the previous cycle.

Figure 12.5.

An example of using iterative integration.

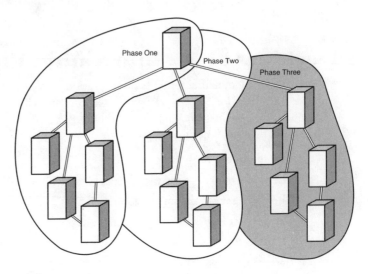

The iteration process breaks the integration and development cycle into several pieces to help you avoid problems that might arise during large integrations. This method is encouraged by using the C++ language and the MFC class library to design and build your application with small classes that have minimal interfaces and dependencies. The Visual C++ compiler helps by allowing you to place the code from each iteration into a separate group in the project tree.

The amount of testing you need to do between iterations depends on the project. If your project adds functionality to existing modules during each iteration, more testing is needed for each iteration. On the other hand, if each iteration results in new functionality that is separated from the older parts of the project, then you can save a formal test until the end of the integration process.

In the InfoMan example project, there are four main parts of the system that correspond to the iterations performed during the construction phases:

- [ ] The main skeleton MFC application
- [ ] Task management
- [ ] Contact management
- [ ] Calendar management

Integrating these different parts of a project like InfoMan is relatively painless because there is very little coupling between these different iterations. Because there is so little opportunity for one iteration to affect the existing project, InfoMan's formal integration testing can be done after all of the modules are integrated.

When you are integrating using iteration, the actual integrations use a mixture of top-down and bottom-up techniques, adding the new modules to the existing project. For small and medium-sized projects, it's possible to delay a formal integration test until all of the modules are integrated.

Deciding on an Integration Plan

After you review the different types of integrations listed in the previous sections, you should decide on a plan for the integration of your project. The decision about which method or methods to use to integrate your project shouldn't be made lightly. The following are some of the factors that you'll need to consider:

- [ ] The amount of integration required
- [ ] The complexity of individual interfaces to be integrated
- [ ] The experience of the integration team
- [ ] The amount of risk involved in the project

Projects that have a handful of small modules can use the big-bang integration method, probably with very little difficulty. Integrations for these small projects may be done with a minimum of formal planning or testing. On these smaller projects, any problems are likely to be inexpensive to fix, and the amount of risk to the development process is usually very small.

As projects become more complicated, the integration plan becomes more important. Any problems during integration will affect the development cycle if they aren't controlled by careful integration. As a general rule, integrating using iteration is a good method to use for medium-to-large Windows projects. The method scales up to a large size very nicely, and most difficult integration problems can be discovered early in the process.

The purpose of the integration plan is to spell out the process that will be used to perform the actual integration. The integration test plan should include the items on the following checklist:

☐ The number of integration phases that will be executed

☐ The modules included in each integration phase

☐ Start and stop criteria for the integration phases

☐ A reference to the integration-test document

Testing for Correctness

Integration testing is the first structured testing that you will do for your project. (Module testing doesn't count because it's closely related to code production.) The major focus of the integration test phase is ensuring that the integrated modules work together properly. If this is your first large-scale Windows project, this isn't always as easy as you might think.

An important part of the testing process is placing yourself into "testing mode." If you're like most people, while designing or coding a project you have a positive frame of mind. Everything will work as planned, all of the bugs will be fixed, and so on. This positive attitude is an important part of developing, especially in a team environment. After all, nobody likes to work under deadline pressure with someone who has a negative personality.

Unfortunately, that positive, good-things-will-happen outlook will work to your detriment during the testing process. In order to slip into testing mode, you have to take off your developer's hat and put on the one that says "tough to please." This doesn't mean that you have to be impossible to live with while testing, it just means that you should be a little bit harder to please while testing.

E.W. Dijkstra, a pioneer in software engineering, said, "Program testing can be used to show the presence of bugs, but never to show their absence." A good principle to use while testing is that you're trying to prove that the program works as intended. In order to discover as many faults as possible, use a structured testing approach.

12

Each phase of the testing and verification process will be used to verify that the program works properly at a different level. Table 12.1 lists the different test phases and the area that each phase addresses.

Table 12.1. Development phases verified by various test phases.

Test Phase	Development Phase Verified
Low-level or module tests	Coding and low-level design
Integration tests	High-level design, interface coding
Functional tests	High-level design, functional specification
System test, alpha tests	Requirements, functional specification
Beta tests	Requirements

You can use Table 12.1 as a guide to assist you with the test-planning process. Keep in mind, however, that the phases listed are the ones most exercised for each test phase. Of course, coding errors will be discovered in every test phase. Likewise, it's not unusual to find problems with the functional specification or requirements during integration testing.

Integration Testing

Like all test phases, integration testing is split into two separate parts: planning the tests and executing them. When you plan your integration tests, you must decide which interfaces should be tested and what test procedures should be used to test the interfaces. When you plan the actual execution of the integration tests, you must carry out the tests included in the test plan and record the results.

Planning Your Integration Tests

When you are planning your integration tests, it is very important that you determine the scope of the planned tests. Although the primary focus of the integration tests is on the module interfaces, you do not need to test every interface. Class libraries that are designed for reuse may have many interfaces that aren't used on this project; these interfaces don't need to be tested.

Otherwise, every interface exposed outside of a module should be tested as part of the integration tests. There are a few common-sense exceptions to this rule:

- ☐ Interfaces used within a module
- ☐ Constructors
- ☐ Conversion functions

You should have tested these interfaces during the low-level tests as discussed in Day 8, "Instrumenting Code and Debugging." The purpose of integration testing is not to get good test coverage because that's already been done. Nor is it necessary to have realistic test cases; those will be executed later. This is strictly a test of the module interfaces.

The high-level design that was produced on Day 2, "System Design," is your best reference for information about the interfaces between modules. After the integration has been completed, you can also use the Visual C++ browser to examine the Call Graph for the modules that have been integrated. Figure 12.6 shows the Visual C++ browser used to display the Call Graph for the CContactItem::Draw function.

Figure 12.6.
Using Visual C++'s browser to examine a Call Graph.

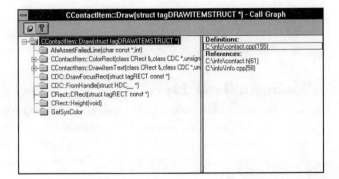

 **Textbook Tip:** You should not have to rely on the browser to find new interfaces, because the module interfaces described in your system-design documents should be kept up-to-date. If you do find an interface that isn't documented, make sure to update the system design as soon as possible.

12

Executing Integration Tests

There are two different approaches to executing the actual integration tests. One way is to use test drivers and stubs, as you did for the low-level testing. The other method is to set breakpoints in your source code using the Visual C++ debugger and trace the program's execution. When the breakpoint is reached, the Visual C++ debugger halts your application, enabling you to inspect variables and the status of the application at the breakpoint.

Using Drivers, Stubs, and Test Harnesses

Test drivers, stubs, and harnesses are all source programs and modules that are written to help test another program. In earlier parts of the book, you've used both test drivers and stubs for low-level testing. Earlier today, you saw some simple examples of both test drivers and stubs.

These three types of test modules have some things in common, as well as some fundamental differences. Each of these modules

☐ Is a temporary software module

☐ Is used to exercise part of the project being tested

☐ Is used to simulate part of the system that will be included later

The differences in these test modules lie in the way that they are used. Each type of test module has a specific role to play during the integration test.

Using a Test Driver

A *test driver* is used to exercise the modules of code that are being tested. Think of the test driver as "controlling" the tested objects. Each test driver may test several low-level modules at the same time. For example, in Figure 12.7 the GetLogin module is simulated by a driver in order to test the integration of three different modules. The source for GetLogin was provided in Listing 12.2.

Figure 12.7.
A single test driver verifies the interfaces with multiple modules.

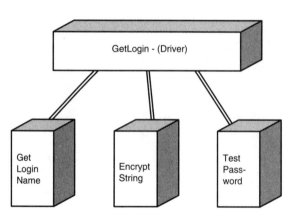

As you can see from the diagram, a test driver is used to simulate the top of a program. The only time that you should put a lot of effort into a test driver is when it can be reused. Most of the time, test drivers will be used for a single project.

Using a Test Stub

Like test drivers, test stubs are also used to exercise part of the system under test, but they do it in a completely different way. Stubs are used when part of the system that performs processing or input isn't integrated yet. The four modules in Figure 12.8, for example, are being integrated top-down, with the modules in the center of the figure currently being integrated. In order for the modules to be integrated, you must use stubs to simulate processing and data from the modules that aren't integrated yet.

Figure 12.8.
Using test stubs during a top-down integration.

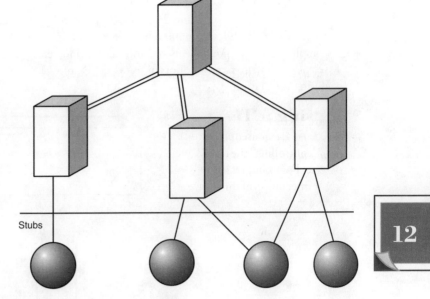

Stubs are usually needed to return a known value or simulate processing on data passed into the stub. Whenever possible, you should try to use stubs that perform the same function every time they're called; however, sometimes this isn't practical. Listing 12.3 is an example of a test stub that will return a different string every time it's called.

Listing 12.3. A test stub that returns a different string each time it's called.

```
LPCSTR GetLoginID()
{
    static int nLogin = 0;
    static LPCSTR lpszLoginArray[5] = { "Joe",
                                        "Harry",
                                        "Sally",
                                        "Tony",
                                        "Alice" };
```

Listing 12.3. continued

```
    if( nLogin > 4 )
        nLogin = 0;
    else
        nLogin++;
    return lpszLoginArray[nLogin];
}
```

Using Test Harnesses

A *test harness* is a combination driver and stub. You use a test harness when the modules being tested need to have a driver and one or more stubs in order to be tested. Because they're more complicated, they should be used as little as possible; remember, the objective here is to execute tests, not to write large amounts of test code. Figure 12.9 is an example of a test harness used during integration.

Figure 12.9.

Test harnesses control the input and output for a module.

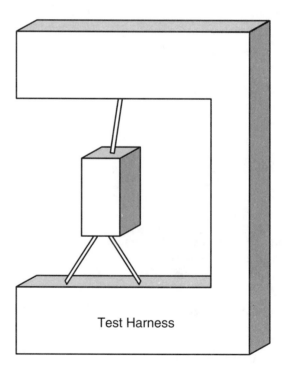

Test Harness

A test harness is used most often when the data provided from a low-level module must be synchronized with the test driver. If this synchronization isn't needed, it's much better to write separate test drivers and stubs.

Using the Debugger for Integration Testing

When you're integrating your project, you'll sometimes need to test an interface that doesn't need a driver or stub. In this situation you shouldn't add the code needed to verify a result and pop up a dialog box. Instead, you can set a breakpoint and use the debugger to test that interface.

Setting breakpoints with the debugger enables you to set up several tests at the same time. Until a breakpoint is tripped, there's no overhead involved in setting it. When the breakpoint is tripped, the debugger will bring you right to the breakpoint. Figure 12.10 shows the integrated debugger in Visual C++ being used for integration testing.

Figure 12.10.
Setting breakpoints to test a module interface.

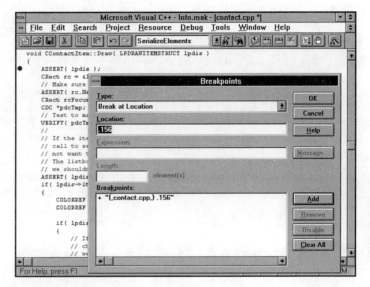

Once you're in the debugger, you have full access to all variables through the Watch and Locals windows. You also have access to the Call stack window if you need to verify the call path.

Using the integrated debugger is a good choice when

- [ ] You would have to modify the source code
- [ ] You're testing a complex interface
- [ ] You have to test with a wide range of values

Documenting Test Results

The results from your integration tests and other measurements should be recorded for use later. As discussed on Day 11, "Error Reporting and Metrics," you will use these measurements to create some metrics about your development process. This is a procedure that will be repeated for all of the testing done for your project.

Keep in mind that the purpose behind keeping these measurements is to help you improve your development process and your end product. After you've completed your project, you can look at your test results and plan for ways to improve all of your development phases.

At a minimum, your test results should have the following items:

- ☐ A record of every test attempt
- ☐ The result of each test attempt
- ☐ If the test failed, the action taken to resolve the fault

Modification Notes

If you're integrating changes into an existing project you have two options, depending on the type of modifications being done. If the changes are localized into new modules and can be integrated by themselves, then you should do so. After the new modules have been integrated, you can integrate the new modules into the existing project.

If the modifications to the existing project are spread out among different modules in the existing project, the integration may be more difficult. In this case, it's better to integrate in functional groups, just as if the entire project was new.

In either case, integration is just as important when you are modifying an existing project as when you are developing new ones. Resist the urge to try big-bang integration unless the changes are very small.

Debugging the Process

A common problem you might encounter when assembling the different parts of your project is deciding on an integration method. Remember, it's not necessary for you to stick to a single integration philosophy for the entire project. If some of the modules are easily integrated top-down and others are more easily integrated bottom-up, go for it. It's much easier to deal with several integration styles than to deal with integrations that aren't working.

Another concern is the amount of overhead spent on integration and integration test planning. If you're accustomed to working alone on smaller projects, this may seem like a great deal of overhead. However, you'll get this time back by having a more robust base for your test phases that follow. If you're really concerned about the amount of overhead, cut it to the minimum for one project, and see how much it saves you in quality costs later.

Documentation

Part III is four days long. All aspects of documentation are covered, including end-user as well as design documentation. The topics covered in this section include the following:

- ☐ Documentation formats
- ☐ Planning document reviews
- ☐ Changing control for documents
- ☐ Planning for documentation updates
- ☐ Developing online help

13

The Design-Documentation Archive

Today you'll learn the documentation archive and how to plan your documentation. The documentation archive is the central location where all of your documents are stored. You'll learn how to organize and plan your documentation, as well as learn how documentation fits in with the rest of the development process. Today you will see how the documentation for a Visual C++ project is organized.

Document Life Cycles

So far, most of this book has covered the design and construction of an application from the programming point of view. Starting today, you'll learn about some documentation and online help issues and how these two functions fit in with the rest of the development process.

Like the software modules that you produced earlier in the book, each piece of documentation will have a life cycle. These life cycles are intertwined with each other. You create some software from documents generated during the design phases, and create documentation based on the software. Figure 13.1 shows the relationship between the software and documentation.

Figure 13.1.
The relationship between the software and documentation created for a project.

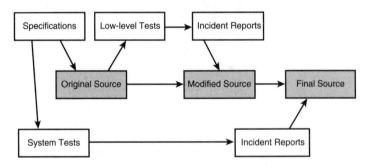

As a software project matures, the documentation that you develop with it also matures. Although you are aware of the evolution that source code goes through as it is developed, it's also important to understand the changes that the documentation goes through as it is developed.

A simplified version of the software-development life cycle is shown in Figure 13.2. Development phases are shown in the center of the figure and the documentation produced during each phase is shown above and below it. Here, documentation that is meant for end users is placed above the development line. Documents that are used internally as part of the development process are placed below the line.

There are three main phases in the life of a document:

☐ Definition

☐ Design

☐ Production

Figure 13.2.
Documentation produced during the development life cycle.

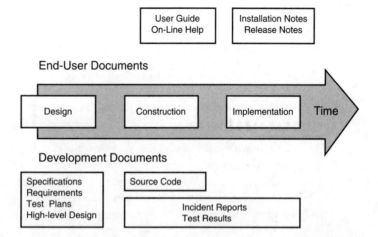

Today you will learn the design and definition of your documents. The actual production of the individual documents is covered as they are needed. For example, you learned how to produce some design documents already. The production of end-user documentation is covered on Day 15, "Developing End-User Documentation."

Types of Documents

When you are creating a document library, one of the first things you need to do is define some basic categories for documents that you will use for your project. These basic categories will form the basis of your documentation archive, which can be a three-ring binder or a formal document-storage system. Figure 13.3 shows the different document categories that might be used on your project.

Figure 13.3.
The different document categories for a software project.

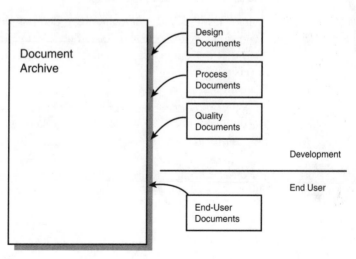

13

Documents fall into two basic categories: documents meant for end users, and the documents created as part of the development process. Even though these two types of documents are meant for different audiences, today you'll see that they have a lot in common.

The end-user category includes all of the documents that are normally delivered to a user of your program. You should keep the end user in mind when you create and review documents that are meant for the end user of your product. These documents should be separated from the development documents at least mentally, if not physically.

Documents that are created as part of the development life cycle are used for various tasks, such as recording the design of a module or listing the test cases that will be executed. All of these documents exist so that you can keep a record of the project's development. These documents exist because it is difficult for a single person to remember all of the project's issues, problems, and commitments—even for small to medium-sized systems.

The documentation that is used for the development of your project can be divided into three types:

☐ **Design documents.** These are the documents that are used for the requirements, specifications, and design of the project.

☐ **Process documents.** Process documents contain information about the preferred way to handle some part of the development process. The coding guidelines developed on Day 5, "Coding Standards and Work Methods," are process documents. Templates and example documents are also considered part of the process documentation.

☐ **Quality documents.** Review notices, meeting minutes, and incident reports are all examples of quality documents.

Defining Documents

The first step in creating good documentation is defining the documents that will be created. It is important to define the exact contents of the documentation set for your project as soon as possible, so that you can develop it along with the rest of your project.

Note: Don't make the mistake of waiting until the last minute to start planning your documentation for the end user. It can be tempting to wait until the product is nearly finished before you start to write the documents, but that will not leave any time for the document reviews. Reviewing documents is covered in detail on Day 14, "Reviewing Documentation."

Treat the documents as part of the development cycle and schedule their creation. Use the functional test, system test, and beta trials to verify your documentation, otherwise your customers will be forced to use documentation that hasn't benefited from being used during your testing process.

The user documentation for a small program that you or a few of your friends use will probably be very straightforward. In fact, you may simply convert your user manual into a help file and distribute your documentation as online help. Creating help files is discussed on Day 16, "Online Help."

More complicated projects may need to have several different types of end-user documentation. You may need to create separate installation, tutorial, user, and reference guides. Only you can decide which types of documentation are appropriate.

Textbook Tip: You should strive to keep your end-user documentation as simple as possible, while keeping it complete. Studies have shown that only a small percentage of users ever read the documentation. More and more large companies are spending more time on their interfaces and online help, and de-emphasizing their documentation. A good example of this is Visual C++, where almost all of the documentation is provided online.

A similar issue exists for the design documentation. If you are writing a very simple program, with a very narrowly defined lifetime, your development documentation can be simplified. However, if you are working on a project that may evolve over a number of years and may involve several teams of programmers, your documentation must be more detailed.

The key to deciding how much documentation a project should have is flexibility. For every project, you should decide which documents will be produced, reviewed, and released. You're in the driver's seat, but you should start planning as soon as possible so that you make your decisions based on your requirements, rather than on the amount of time left in your schedule.

When you consider adding a document to your project, consider the following factors:

☐ The cost of the new document. Each document that is added to a project adds extra overhead. The document has to be written, reviewed, updated, cataloged, archived, and, sooner or later, read. These costs should be avoided if at all possible.

☐ The new document's scope. Every document should have a clearly defined purpose. The amount of specialization for each document depends on the project, but you should never have documents that overlap in their contents.

13

☐ The lifetime of the new document. The lifetime of a document will specify when it is created and how long it is expected to be current. For example, the user manual will definitely change for every release, but there will always be a user manual. However, some design documents belong to a single release, rather than the entire project.

☐ How is the new document created? What part of the development cycle generates this document? What parts of the development cycle need this document to be changed?

Creating a Master Document List

After you have considered each of these points, define the documents that are needed for your project. This information should be kept as a master document list for your project. For every document that is included in your document list you should also indicate, or leave space for, the following information:

☐ The person responsible for the document

☐ The current document version

☐ The description of the document

☐ The location of the document directions

You can eliminate the current document-version information if you can specify the location where the latest version will always be stored. For example, if you have a formal storage archive, the location of the document in the archive is enough information. In fact, it's better to leave that information out if you can, because you can avoid updating this document whenever a revision changes.

Designing Your Documents

Once you have decided to include a document in your project, the next step is to design a format for the document. It's usually a bad idea to let the individual document authors create their own formats. Consistency is one important quality that good documentation has. If you skip the document design, that consistency will be lost and your documents will be less usable.

The steps involved in designing your documents don't need to be complicated or expensive to use. Once again, the key is to be flexible. If you've got a small project and you're working alone, your instructions may be very simple. Larger projects that have many different document authors should have more formal instructions and guidelines. In general, the steps involved in designing a document are the same for large and small projects:

☐ Decide on the focus of the document

☐ Decide on the general content of the document

☐ Create a format, using templates if available

If the document will be written several times during the project, you may want to create a sample document that can be used as a guideline. If the document is used only once, it may make sense for you to skip this step.

For a document-design example, consider the installation guide for your program. Don't panic if you aren't quite sure how some details of the installation will be handled. Remember, you aren't writing any documents now; you're just at the planning stage. The following list is an example of the focus, content, and format of an installation guide. Consider including a list like this one with your sample document instructions.

- ☐ **Focus.** The focus of the document is the installation of the project. The target reader is a new user of the system.

- ☐ **Content.** Instructions for installing the program on the user's system, as well as resolving any installation problems that might be expected.

- ☐ **Format.** Follows the format of other user documents. There is an introductory section titled "Scope," followed by a glossary section. Installation steps are laid out in a task-oriented sequence. The last section contains any error messages that the user might encounter from the setup program.

After you're satisfied with the design of your document, you should update your document list, store it, and update your master-document list. Suggestions for storing documents are discussed later today in the section, "Storing Your Documents."

Document Ownership

One of the most important issues concerning a document is ownership. Every document should be owned by a person (or a group, if you're working in teams). Each document should also "belong" to an identifiable part of the development cycle.

Document ownership helps when you need to track and update your documents. Tracking and updating is discussed later, but the basic idea is to establish some method to identify which documents need to be included, created, or updated at any point in the development process. For example, the development documents that were created for functional-test planning belong to the functional-test phase.

If any part of your project is modified, it's easy to update your documents if they belong to a certain part of the development cycle. If a new function is added, for example, it's clear that documents owned by the requirements, specification, and function test phases may need to be updated.

Different Types of Ownership

There are several possible types of document ownership. When a document is being written or updated, the author has ownership of that document. It is reasonable for the author to expect that no one else will modify the document on which they are working. This type of ownership should be limited to the time that the author is actually working on the document. Once the document is approved, another author may take control of the document to modify it.

Responsibility for the class of the document is another type of ownership. You may have a designated team member who is responsible for all of the test documents. This person doesn't author each test spec and test instruction, but they are responsible for the document instructions and sample documents. They may also participate in document reviews and resolve issues about proper use of the documents.

The last type of ownership is process ownership, which means the document "belongs" to some part of the development process. If some part of the process changes, or if the project changes during that phase of the development cycle, then the document should be updated. Figure 13.4 is an example of these three types of ownership for a test-plan document.

Figure 13.4.
The functional test plan has
three owners.

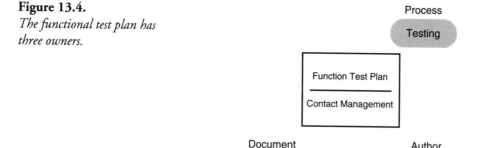

You may define ownership slightly differently in your project. For example, the team member responsible for test documentation may actually design and write all of the documentation. The important point to remember is that you need to define document ownership for each of your documents so that you can manage your documents more efficiently.

Storing Your Documents

A document archive is just like a library. In its simplest form, it may be a three-ring binder containing hard copies of your documents, along with the documents backed up on floppy disk. Large projects may store their documents in a specialized document-retrieval system. Either way, the document archive is simply a place where you store your documents.

The document archive may be separate from your version control system, but if you are using some kind of configuration management the documentation should be a part of it. Your documents are just as important as your source code, and need at least as much control as you use for other parts of your project.

Documents have a life span similar to the source code used to develop your program. It begins as a new document and is created, reviewed, stored, and updated as needed. Figure 13.5 shows a sample state diagram for the life cycle of a document.

Figure 13.5.
An example state diagram
for documents.

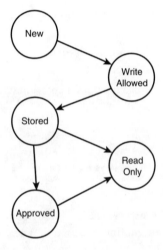

Note that it is not possible to reach every state from every other state. The most obvious restriction is that two people should not be allowed to modify the same section of a document simultaneously. Using configuration management for your documents automatically enforces this restriction.

13

Tracking User Documentation

There are some unique issues that come up when you are planning documentation meant for the end user. Unlike the documents that are meant to be used during the development process, end-user documents are typically meant for users that may not be familiar with your product. This may mean that you must target the documentation toward a less sophisticated reader, or you may even need to explain the purpose of the product. The documents must also be available as soon as the product is released and must be completely accurate. This accuracy must include any screen shots or user-interface details.

Unlike development-process documents, user documents are reviewed by a wide range of people who are concerned with everything from the aesthetics of the document to its technical accuracy. Reviewing the end-user documentation is covered on Day 15.

All of these attributes of the user documentation make it very difficult to create without careful planning. If you have infinite resources, you can wait until just before the project is released and then use five hundred writers to create the perfect documentation set while your program disks are being duplicated. If you don't have that many writers waiting for your application to be ready, you should take these steps to get your documentation completed as soon as possible:

☐ Start planning and developing the documentation early. This is an important first step. In order to have your documentation well-reviewed, it's a good idea to have a preliminary draft available when testing begins. If you wait until late in the project to start your documentation, you will miss out on a great opportunity to test your documentation.

☐ Track the progress of the documentation. Keep on top of the documentation schedule. If some parts of the system are falling behind, reevaluate your schedule.

☐ Synchronize the documentation with the project plan. Make sure that the documentation schedule meshes with the project schedule. This topic is discussed in the next section.

Synchronization with the Development Process

If you have ever tried to develop documentation while you are developing a software project, you have probably run into a situation where the documentation didn't match the final product. This isn't at all unusual, but it is aggravating to a user. Generally, mismatches between documentation and software occur because of the following factors:

☐ **Inadequate reviews.** If the documents aren't reviewed well, errors in the documentation will slip through. During your planning, set aside sufficient review time. Reviewing end-user documentation is covered on Day 15.

☐ **The software has become a moving target.** If the system software is allowed to change late in the development process, you have to allow time to update your documentation. This is addressed in the section, "Freezing the Project," later today.

☐ **Extra anonymous functionality.** There have been many cases in which developers feel the need to make one final improvement as the product is about to ship. This is a variation of the moving-target problem, but it is unplanned.

Inadequate reviews are a problem that's difficult to solve. It's especially hard if you're working alone on a project, because you don't have a large pool of reviewers from which to choose. One way to help reduce your dependence on the review process is to start using your documentation as soon as possible. As discussed earlier, the sooner you begin to use the documentation, the earlier you can find problems.

As a general rule, try to have at least a draft of your user documentation ready for the beginning of your function testing. This will give you several different test phases in which the documentation can be reviewed as it is tested.

> **Textbook Tip:** There are two important points on the time line that you should consider when planning your documentation: the functionality freeze date and the user-interface freeze date.
>
> The functionality freeze date is the date when the project is declared functionally complete. Depending on the type of project that you are developing, this may be as early as when the requirements are drafted or as late as the start of functional testing. Before this date, you have to keep your documentation and schedule flexible.
>
> The user-interface freeze date usually occurs after the functionality freeze date. This is the date when the user interface is considered complete. You must set this date, otherwise you will never be able to rely on your descriptions of the user interface.

If you use an iterative development process, as was covered on Days 6 through 10, you may want to create a rough draft of the end-user documentation earlier. As you distribute the incremental releases of your program, your users can try out the documentation also.

As you update the project, changes in the project that affect the end-user documentation must be synchronized with the documentation. This is mainly an issue of communication between the documentation and the development teams. Figure 13.6 shows how your synchronization plan should work.

Figure 13.6.
Changes to the project functionality or appearance should be reflected in the documentation as soon as possible.

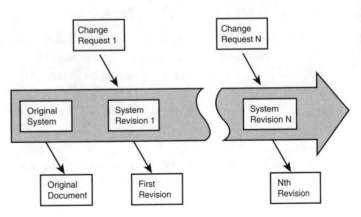

13

Freezing the Project

Unfortunately, if you start to develop your documentation early you'll have a problem synchronizing the project to the documentation. Every bug that is fixed, and every new feature that is added, may impact your documentation. The earlier your documentation is created, the more changes you will make to it during its lifetime. If any changes slip through, your documents will be out of date.

The way to avoid impacting the quality of your documentation is to set up freeze dates for your project. A *freeze date* is a period of time before a release when no changes are allowed to the functionality or user interface. If changes are received after the freeze date, but before the project is released, the modifications are added to the next release of the product. Figure 13.7 shows a sample time line for a project, with the freeze dates marked before each incremental release.

Figure 13.7.

A sample time line with freeze dates marked.

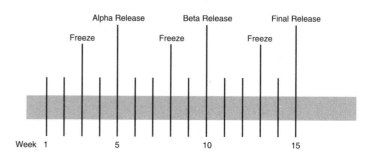

Early in a project, when you are getting feedback about the user interface, you may decide to postpone gathering screen shots or accept the fact that the screen shots may be inaccurate. Also, you may not think that it's necessary to have a freeze date before every test phase.

Modification Notes

If you are adding functionality to an existing project, you should try to follow the existing documentation structure if possible. Try to enhance what is already in place if necessary, especially for the end-user documentation. At all costs, avoid creating overlapping documentation that is almost like the existing documentation. It's much easier for end users to work with documents that have been integrated into the existing documentation.

If there is a formal definition for development documents already in place, it's much easier to use the existing documents than to create new ones. If the documentation has to be improved, try to plan an approach that enables the old and new documentation to coexist.

Debugging the Process

It's not unusual for documentation to be delayed due to other problems in the project. If parts of the user interface design are redesigned, or if there are a large number of other changes that require frequent updates to the documents, delays can be expected. Even minor changes to the look and feel of your application can cause significant changes in your documentation. For example, you may have screen shots of your application that need to be captured again, or new controls or dialog boxes that must be explained. If this happens to you, consider reducing the number of incremental releases of your documents, or accept the schedule delay. It is rarely possible to make up project delays by reducing the time allowed for creating the documentation.

13

14

Reviewing
Documentation

Today you'll learn about the document-review process. Much of what you will learn is related to end-user documents; however, the ideas from today can be used for any type of review. The primary subject today is the purpose behind document reviews and how you can optimize reviews to fit in with your development process. You will learn the benefits of several styles of reviews, because people with different development styles will prefer different review methods.

All facets of review planning are covered today, including selecting review teams, avoiding "groupthink," scheduling, and paperwork. Sample documents that you can use or modify for your own reviews are included on the disk that accompanies this book.

The Purpose of Document Reviews

The purpose of a documentation review is to improve the quality of your documentation by inviting other interested people to inspect it. Depending on the size of your project, this may involve a number of other programmers or other people involved in your project.

Documents are an important part of your project. To the end user of your program, the user manual and online help are one of the most visible parts of the program. When users have a question about an error message or advanced feature, they will turn to the user manual for help. By reviewing your documents with users and others involved in developing the project, you can make sure that the documentation will be helpful and accurate.

Documentation used during the development process should be reviewed for similar reasons. Any document produced during your project should be used sometime in the future (otherwise it shouldn't be created). Use these reviews to help make these documents useful and improve the quality of your design process.

The review process that is used for software projects comes in two basic types: formal review meetings and informal distribution of the documents for review.

Understanding the Review Process

When the time comes for an actual review, you should have a formal plan in place for performing the reviews. The review process can be broken down into the following main areas:

- [ ] Selecting the review team
- [ ] Scheduling the review
- [ ] Distributing the review documents
- [ ] Reviewing the document
- [ ] Revising the document
- [ ] Approving the document

Each of these areas will be covered in later sections. In real life, some of these phases may be repeated more than once. For example, if the document has a large number of changes, it may be reviewed again after it has been revised. If it still needs a large number of changes, it may be reviewed yet again after revision. Figure 14.1 shows some of the more common paths through a document-review cycle.

Figure 14.1.
The different parts of the document-review cycle.

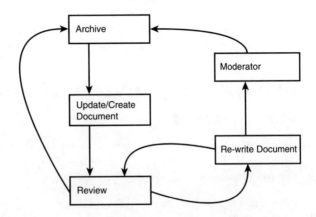

This may seem like a lot of trouble to go through just to check a few documents. The goal of the review process is to prevent errors from creeping into your final product. A little effort now soliciting reviews for your documentation will help prevent costly problems later.

Layout and Editing Reviews

If your development team is large enough, it is a good idea to have someone with an editing background review the documentation meant for an end user. This review should be done separately from any technical review of the document. Figure 14.2 shows an example of the review schedule for an end-user document.

Figure 14.2.
A typical schedule for an end-user document, with both format and technical reviews.

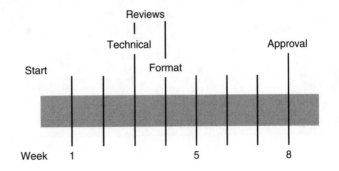

The format review should be attended by people who have an interest primarily in the presentation of the document, as opposed to strictly technical issues. The focus of this review should be to have a common look for all of your documents, and to make sure that the information is presented clearly. You can do this sort of review as a formal meeting, but it also works very well with an informal distribution of the documents, as discussed later.

When you are planning the extra reviews for end-user documents, remember to schedule enough time for two sets of reviews and two sets of rework. The actual process of creating and reviewing end user documents is covered in detail on Day 15, "Developing End-User Documentation."

The Formal Review Meeting Versus Distribution

There are basically two ways to handle reviews of your documents, and each method has its strong points and its drawbacks. The method that you pick for your project will depend on the size and complexity of the project.

Formal review meetings are often used for larger development projects, or when there is a higher-than-normal amount of risk involved in the project. Informal reviews are suitable for smaller projects or projects in which the work is routine. Both of these methods are covered next.

Using the Formal Review

The formal review consists of a traditional, formal review meeting. Medium- and large-sized projects will often use this sort of review for all of the documentation. In this type of review, the documents are distributed in advance of the meeting, giving the reviewers time to review the document separately. The review team meets together for the review, and any issues they identify are recorded and addressed in the meeting.

There are several advantages to using a formal review meeting:

- ☐ All of the reviewers are together at the same time.
- ☐ Formal review minutes can be taken for quality purposes.
- ☐ The review is scheduled at a fixed time.

Figure 14.3 is an example of the process involved in a normal review meeting. The document is developed, a review team is assembled, and the review takes place at a specified time. After the review, the document is approved, even though some changes may be required.

Figure 14.3.
The path taken by a document using a formal review.

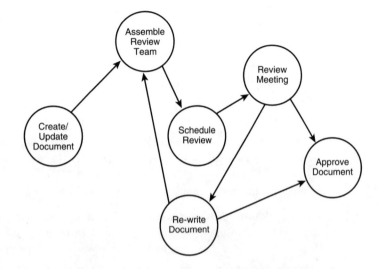

Using Less Formal Reviews by Distribution

If you are working alone or with a smaller team, it won't be easy for you to assemble review teams. In this case, you can distribute the document to be reviewed and ask for comments from the individual reviewers. The informal review has several advantages, especially on small projects or projects when you are working alone. Specifically, the advantages of an informal review include the following:

- ☐ Each reviewer can review the document when it is convenient for them.
- ☐ The review schedule can be more flexible.
- ☐ Small reviews incur less direct overhead.
- ☐ Reviewers can be in different locations.

These advantages don't come without a price, however. The biggest problem with distributed reviews is that they are informal. On large projects with interrelated schedules that depend on complete and accurate reviews, there may be problems with this type of review. Another problem is that the review team isn't brought together in a single location. It can be difficult to resolve issues that come up during the review if the author receives conflicting feedback about the document. Yet another problem is that the reviews may tend to drag out unless deadlines are placed on the review process.

If you can overcome these problems, the informal distributed review is a great way to review documents for small teams that are short on resources. Remember to set a definite deadline for the review feedback, and encourage communication among members of the review team.

Preparing for the Review

Documentation should always be reviewed by a team that is likely to find any faults that exist in the document. For end-user documentation, it's a good idea to include some potential users or people who have some knowledge about the potential users of your product. If you have a support organization that provides help to end-users of your product, it is a good source of feedback about documentation meant for the end user.

The role of a review team is to collectively ensure the quality of the document that is under review. Members do this by working as a team to find and resolve as many issues as possible with the document. Working together, however, may result in problems due to dealing with different personalities and rounding up cooperative team members.

When people interact in groups, conflicting and sometimes undesirable results may occur. Some people will agree to anything, while others will throw up roadblocks or bring their own agendas to a review. None of these qualities will improve your document review.

Assigning Roles to Team Members

A document review should be an orderly process that results in a higher quality, improved document. You can help this process by assigning specific roles to your review team. If each review team member has a specific role to play for a few hours, your chances of success will be improved.

If you decide to have formal reviews, you should outline the responsibilities that each review team member has during a review. The names and duties assumed during a review vary between organizations, but some common roles include the following:

- ☐ **Author.** The author doesn't do much during a review. In some organizations, the author is forbidden to do anything during the review. The author of a document rarely accompanies it to the end user's desk; preventing him or her from participating focuses the review on the document, rather than on any explanations offered by the author.

- ☐ **Moderator (or facilitator).** The moderator is responsible for keeping the meeting on track. The moderator decides which issues should be investigated outside of the review meeting, and resolves disputes that can't be decided by group consensus. Typically, the moderator is a senior or respected member of the review team.

- ☐ **Reader.** Some review teams will use a reader to walk through the document, guiding and prompting discussion. Do not, under any circumstances, allow the reader to actually read the document out loud. This is extremely slow and boring, and doesn't accomplish much, other than to put the review team to sleep. Everyone attending the review should have already read the document; the reader simply summarizes key sections of the document.

- ☐ **Secretary (or recorder).** This member makes a record of any faults or issues that are discovered during the review.
- ☐ **Peers (or reviewers).** These members identify issues and recommend changes to the document.

> **Note:** Avoid using the same team members for every review. If you're new to using formal reviews, you might think that keeping a single review team is a good idea. The problem is that the team may start to develop a sort of group personality and become less effective at finding faults.
>
> This is known as "groupthink," and it can lead to situations in which an entire review team makes decisions based on peer pressure, rather than on the members' individual views. It's much better to manage your review members so that they are always working with different peers.

When you select the individual team members, it's a good idea to pick a cross section of the entire development team if the team is large enough. You should try to get good review coverage for the entire document under review. This may mean that you will have to split the document into several separate reviews.

Using Reviews as a Learning Tool

One constant problem in software development is finding a way to share information among different parts of a development team. There are a lot of reasons for this, but it often boils down to a lack of communication. A review is one way to help share information among different groups of developers. It is also relatively inexpensive because this sort of information sharing is a side effect from the review.

Some teams find that newer members of a development team can use a review as a learning process. This is a good idea because the research involved in the review can help the learning process, especially on complicated projects or subsystems. Keep in mind that you still need complete coverage of the reviewed document, and less experienced team members may need some assistance.

You can enjoy both of these benefits whether you use formal review meetings or distribute your documents informally. The important point here is that by exposing your development team to new areas of the project, they can grow and help improve your development team.

14

Review Checklist

As part of your planning process, the first tool that you can create for use during your reviews is the review checklist. This form is just a laundry list of items that have to be complete before you schedule the review.

> **Note:** Don't rush into your reviews before you are ready. If you're like many people, you may be running short of time close to the end of the project when many reviews are taking place. You may be tempted to send out review invitations early, which may seem like a good idea, but in reality you're liable to rush into the review, possibly before you are ready. Also, if any unplanned crisis erupts before the review, you may wind up rescheduling, which is a real waste of time.

Every team or project should have a review checklist. You can find a sample checklist for InfoMan in the \CHAP14\DOCS directory on the CD that accompanies this book. The checklist should not be extremely specific or detailed. The InfoMan checklist has a location in which you can record the name of the reviewed document, and four tasks that should be completed before a review is held.

- ☐ The document must be stored in the archive.
- ☐ The key roles must be identified.
- ☐ The review team must be identified.
- ☐ The meeting must be scheduled.

If you distribute the document for review instead of having a formal review meeting, the last item in this list should refer to setting a deadline for review comments to be returned. If the review is held as a formal review meeting, allow plenty of time for the review to take place before the meeting. Otherwise, the review will be slowed down while the review team actually reads the document, and the review quality will suffer.

Review Invitations

After the checklist items have been completed, you're ready to send out the invitations for the actual review. The review invitations are only slightly more complicated than the review checklist. A sample review invitation can be found on the disk in the \CHAP14\DOCS directory. At a minimum, the invitation should contain the following items:

- ☐ The time and place of the review

- [ ] The other members of the review team
- [ ] The role each team member is to perform
- [ ] A description of the document to be reviewed

Each member of the review team should be specifically invited to the review meeting. This helps avoid miscommunication and allows you to get confirmation that each member will attend. It also helps to start the review in a controlled manner.

> **Developer's Tip:** The author should include a copy of the document along with the invitation if possible. This helps the reviewers in three ways:
>
> - [ ] They can physically see the review materials, which seems to help some reviewers.
> - [ ] They don't have to collect the materials themselves. This basically makes the reviewer's job easier when the documents are stored in an archive; but as a practical matter, this ensures that the reviewer has the document that needs to be reviewed.
> - [ ] The review team members will also be more likely to look over the review material in advance if it has been distributed to them.
>
> As the author, you will have the best access to the documents, so it should be easy for you to handle distribution. If you have access to e-mail, you may be able to distribute all of the documents electronically.

Optimizing Your Reviews

Most people have a natural tendency to try to reduce the amount of time they spend in meetings. Holding review meetings that are widely attended by development team members can consume a lot of time, and runs counter to common sense. Close to the end of a project, a large number of review meetings can be a tough sale. Although there are a number of benefits to holding reviews, these benefits are mainly long-term. The short-term benefit of avoiding meetings that the project avoids overhead, and that can be a very attractive benefit late in the project.

Like any other part of the development process, review meetings can be improved. Any improvements that you can make to your review meetings will translate into more time available for design or construction, which is very attractive. There are two basic types of review improvements for which you should aim:

☐ **Review coverage.** Improvements in this area will cause review meetings that are more likely to detect any faults or deficiencies that are present in the document. Although this improvement area won't necessarily reduce the amount of time spent on reviews, it will reduce rework later.

☐ **Review efficiency.** Improvements in this area will actually reduce the amount of time spent on reviews. When you are trying to improve in this area, be careful not to reduce your review coverage, or any gains that you make may be wiped out by higher rework costs.

Collecting Meeting Measurements

Every review should have a set of review minutes. If you aren't familiar with review minutes, they're discussed in detail in the section, "Recording Review Feedback." Basically, the review minutes are a record of faults and issues raised during the review meeting.

As part of every review, you should plan to collect some measurements on the review itself. You will be well on your way to improving your review process if the secretary can take a few seconds to note the following information:

☐ The number of review-team members at the review

☐ The number of review-team members invited to the review

☐ The amount of time spent preparing for the review

☐ The time that the meeting actually started (not the time it was scheduled to start)

This information is very easy to collect at the start of the meeting, it's not very intrusive, and it can be very useful when you try to improve your meeting efficiency. Later today you will learn how to put this information to good use.

Reviewing Smaller Project Documentation

If you're a developer working alone, you may have some trouble assembling a different team of reviewers for every project. There are two problems that you will probably encounter when you try to round up a review team:

☐ **Lack of knowledgeable resources.** If you are working alone, there obviously isn't anyone else on your team. Therefore, any technical reviewers are likely to be friends or other programmers that have agreed to help you review your documents.

☐ **Lack of time.** Even if you work on a small team, there may not be enough time to schedule formal reviews for all of your documents.

If you run into these problems, you can still review your documents using informal reviews. This type of review doesn't use a formal review meeting, so it's ideal for situations when you have scheduling difficulties. Instead of the formal meeting, the review team members review each document and make comments separately.

There are two ways to distribute your document for an informal review: serially or in parallel. If you distribute the document serially, a single copy of the document is distributed. Each team member will review the document in turn until the document has been reviewed by everyone. Figure 14.4 shows this distribution method.

Figure 14.4.
Distributing a document serially allows several documents to be reviewed at once.

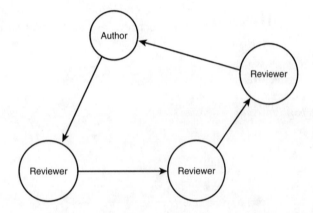

With this type of distribution, each reviewer can attach review notes to the document as it circulates, allowing later reviewers to see the input from other team members. Also, several documents can be reviewed at the same time because each reviewer can work on a separate document.

This method is well-suited for small review teams in which each member will concentrate on a completely different aspect of the document. For example, if the team is made up of a single technical reviewer, an editor, and a graphics designer, each of the team members can work independently of the other. Unfortunately, there are several problems with this approach:

☐ It can take a long time for a single document to be reviewed because it travels from one person to another. If you are running short on time, this may not be the best method for you.

☐ It can be difficult to quickly determine the status of a document being reviewed. If you use this method, you may have several documents out for review at the same time; tracking the status of these documents can become a headache.

14

 **Note:** It may seem like a good idea to circulate the document with a routing slip and allow each team member to pass it along to the next reviewer. This can be an enormous problem, especially if you're working on a tight schedule.

Make sure that the document is returned to the author after each review. That way the author always knows exactly where each document is and how many reviews need to be completed.

Another informal review method is to send out the documents in parallel, as shown in Figure 14.5. With this approach, each review-team member is given a copy of the document and a target date for completing the review.

Figure 14.5.
Distributing a document in parallel results in a faster review cycle.

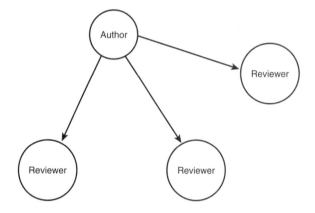

An advantage to this method is that each document-review cycle is shorter from the document's point of view. Unfortunately, it can be difficult to resolve conflicting review comments if two or more team members have different views about some part of the document.

Reviewing Documentation for Large Projects

On large projects, it's a good idea to use formal review meetings to review your documents. It generally isn't difficult to collect a review team, especially if review responsibility is rotated among the different team members. The benefits of reviewing your documents will outweigh the cost of the reviews.

If you want to improve your review process, there are a few ways that you can help reduce the amount of time spent in reviews. If you are already using document reviews but think they cost too much in terms of wasted time, try these simple improvements:

☐ Make sure that meetings start on time.

☐ Ensure that review team members have adequate preparation time.

☐ Make sure that your review team is knowledgeable.

If you aren't sure if you have these problems, you can find out by collecting quality measurements from your review meetings, as discussed earlier. Unlike some other software-quality measurements, statistics about your meetings will tell you immediately if you are wasting time in meetings. For example, if your meetings chronically start 15 minutes late, that's a lot of wasted time that can be recovered easily.

Recording Review Feedback

You can build many metrics from your document reviews. Metrics that are based on measurements early in the development cycle are especially useful for process improvement. The good news is that collecting these measurements does not have to be very costly. All that you need to do is record information from the meeting in a structured way.

An example of a review-minutes form used for InfoMan can be found in the \CHAP14\DOCS directory. The form is split into three sections:

☐ **General information about the review.** This section contains information about the time and date of the meeting, the role played by each reviewer, and the size of the reviewed document.

☐ **Meeting measurements.** This is information that can be used for process improvement, such as the time the meeting started, time spent for preparation, and the number of reviewers present.

☐ **Document measurements.** This is information about the reviewed document. This section has room to record faults or issues raised during the review, as well as information about correcting the fault.

During a formal review, the review minutes are filled in by the secretary. The moderator is responsible for ensuring that all issues raised during the meeting are resolved to everyone's satisfaction. If an issue can't be resolved during a meeting, the moderator should either suggest a solution or suggest that the issue be resolved outside the meeting.

If you are informally reviewing your documentation by distribution, as discussed earlier, you will need to assemble this information yourself, based on your reviewer's notes. You should supply a form that the reviewer can fill out with comments or issues about the document. You can find an example of one of these forms in the \CHAP14\DOCS directory.

14

After the Review

After the document has been reviewed, the author should make those corrections or updates needed to resolve problems or issues raised during the review.

Approving the Documents

Depending on the size of your development team, you may want to designate someone to formally approve all of your documents. A good victim for this task is the review moderator, because they should be aware of any issues that were brought up during the review. It's important to keep the actual "approval" of the document the duty of the review team. The final approval that's done (by the moderator, in this case) shows only that the document includes any changes recommended by the entire review team.

Reviewing Updated Documents

It's very likely that there will be changes to the project that result in changes to documents that have been approved. You should have some sort of plan in place for dealing with this situation. If you insist that no changes are likely to be made, you will probably have problems when the inevitable changes occur.

Showstopper: Even on large projects that have a lot of documentation, small changes in approved documentation can probably be handled very informally. This will save you time, and help you keep from getting bogged down with small changes. However, after you pass the freeze date for changes to the user interface and functionality, you should have another quick review of changed documents.

It's very easy for these small changes to sneak in and create a bug in your documentation at the last minute. Do yourself and the user a favor and run a quick review after all of the changes have been made.

Modification Notes

When reviewing the documentation for a project that is modifying an existing program, you need to take special steps to make sure that the documents fit in with the original project. Try to select team members that are familiar with the existing documentation and distribute the existing documentation along with the review documents.

Often when you are reviewing a new document, you will discover a problem in an existing document. These faults should be corrected, but if you are keeping quality measurement, make sure that these faults are not counted as part of the reviewed document.

Debugging the Process

Trying to build a consensus during a review can be difficult at times. If you attend reviews long enough, you may attend a review where an issue cannot be resolved. Rather than let the meeting hang on a single item, it's a good idea to assign a subset of the review team to resolve the problem after the formal review.

14

Developing
End-User
Documentation

Today you will learn how to create the end-user documentation for your application. Like the user interface, this part of the application comes in direct contact with the users, so it requires a little more planning than your internal design documentation.

Today you will learn the following topics:

☐ Targeting your documentation to a certain type of user

☐ Understanding the different needs of end users

☐ Reviewing your user guide

☐ Receiving feedback from the users

Planning Your End-User Documentation

Like most parts of the development cycle, creating your end-user documentation starts with a planning stage. There are three main steps to planning your end-user documentation:

☐ Defining your target audience

☐ Deciding on a user-guide type

☐ Organizing the topics for your user guide

You'll study each of these steps in turn. But first, take a look at a typical end user. Even though end users vary dramatically in almost every detail, they all share one common trait: they rarely read the documentation unless they're forced to. That's right; unfortunately, most users of your application won't read your documentation. If you don't believe this, look for a user's documentation during your next visit. Chances are you will find it under the desk or on a bookshelf far from the PC.

There are several reasons why users fail to use the documentation provided for them. In fact, entire books have been written on this subject. What it boils down to is that users of your application want to be productive. When they sit down to read a user's manual, they aren't actually using your program; therefore, they're not productive.

Studies have shown that most users will read the documentation only when they're faced with a problem that can't be solved in another way; they are basically forced into reading the documentation.

This impacts you as a developer in two ways: you must provide documentation that is helpful to the user during these times of stress; and your documentation should be easy to use, so that the user feels that time spent reading the documentation isn't wasted.

Defining a Target Audience for Your User Guide

15

One of your first priorities when you are planning your end-user documentation is to define the target audience for your documents. Who will be reading your documentation? The best documentation in the world won't help a novice user if it's written entirely for an expert. Likewise, if your end-user documentation is written for new users, experts may be frustrated by its slow pace.

Expert and novice users have different needs when it comes to documentation. You don't have to exclude one group entirely in favor of the other, but you should recognize that they bring different needs to your documentation. Later you'll learn some strategies for creating documents that are useful to both types of users.

Another thing to consider about your target audience is that novice users of your program may be experts in the area that your application targets, but new to your program. They may also become experts in using your application, but still novices in the target area. Figure 15.1 shows this idea as a matrix, where users are grouped according to both their knowledge of your program and the target area of the application.

Figure 15.1.

A matrix that shows two different measurements for end-user experience.

Knowledge of the Application

Low	High
Novice to Problem Area Novice to Application	Novice to Problem Area Understands Application
Understands Problem Area Novice to Application	Understands Problem Area Understands Application

Low

High

Knowledge of the Problem Area

As you organize your end-user documentation, your goal should be to help end users move into the box where they are experts at using your program and also experts in the application's problem area.

Ideally, all of the documentation produced for your application will be relevant to all of your users. However, your documents will be much easier to use if you understand the different needs for each part of your target audience.

Needs of Novice Users

A new user of your application may be unfamiliar with the problems addressed by your application, not just the application itself. Too much technical jargon tends to make a document difficult to read; for some novice users, too much unexplained jargon may make it impossible to read.

For example, if a tutorial for a word processor uses the term "gutter space" without explanation, most word-processing novices would immediately start looking for a definition of the term. (Those of you who are publishing experts can replace gutter space with "Bearer Capability," a telecommunications term typically left unexplained for new users.)

When novice users find a few new terms and learn their meaning, they may get a good feeling because they have learned something new. However, if your documentation forces the user to search for the definition of dozens of new words, a novice will become frustrated.

Instead of saying, "Remember to allow for gutter space when laying out your margins," try something like, "Remember to allow extra room on the inside margins of your pages, called *gutter space*, to allow for binding."

In most cases, it's a good idea to use less technical terms whenever you have a choice between two ways of expressing an idea. If you have to use a technical term, remember your novice users and give them an explanation in the text.

Needs of Advanced Users

Unlike novice users, advanced users know their way around the basic parts of your application and the problem domain. There are several features that you can add to your documentation that are useful primarily to more advanced users:

- ☐ **Advanced tips.** Notes or information that an experienced user might find helpful, but might be confusing or difficult for a new user.
- ☐ **Shortcuts.** Accelerator keys or quick ways of performing complicated actions. These steps may be too complex for new users.
- ☐ **Limitations.** These are the limits within which the application is designed to work.

Most of these topics can be added informally along with the more general parts of your documentation. Advanced tips and shortcuts can be handled informally as extra *sidebars* (such as the Developer's Tip boxes in this book) or as extra subtopics.

Documenting the limitations of your application isn't something that immediately springs to mind when you're writing your documentation. However, it is a problem for an advanced user who reaches an undocumented limitation.

For example, if an InfoMan user tries to store a large number of items in a contact file and the file-save operation fails, the user will probably report this as a fault. On the other hand, if there is a documented maximum size for the file, including attachments or notes, the user gains insight to the possible problem and may be able to solve it.

Textbook Tip: Include an index in early reviews of your documentation. One overlooked feature of good end-user documentation is an index. An index that has been set up properly can be a big time-saver for advanced users. An index that is just a sorted rehash of the table of contents is not very helpful.

When collecting entries for your index, start out by marking all of the subjects, topics, proper names, menu items, and functions. After you generate an index based on this list, include the index as part of the user-guide review. Remember, the purpose of the index is to help users look up a particular topic. If you review the index along with the rest of the document, you can collect feedback about your index.

Types of End-User Documentation

There are three basic types of end-user documents. It's possible that you might create one or all three types of documents for the users of your application. The three basic types are

☐ Task-oriented guides
☐ Reference manuals
☐ Tutorials

It's not unusual for a user guide to have elements of more than one of these document types. For example, the Visual C++ documentation contains examples of all three types, with individual guides sometimes separated into different tutorial, reference, and task-oriented sections.

If you can produce only a single type of user guide, you should create a task-oriented user guide. They are easy to write, and provide the most information to the new end user. In contrast, reference manuals are most useful to experienced users. You should use a reference guide to supplement other types of documentation because they don't work well by themselves.

Creating a Task-Oriented User Guide

Task-oriented user guides focus on different tasks that an end user can perform, rather than explaining each function of the application separately. The advantage of this approach is that the user does not need to read the entire manual in order to carry out the tasks covered in the user guide.

Using a task-oriented approach, you present the application to the user as a series of common tasks to be carried out. Similar tasks or activities can be grouped into sections, with shared tasks broken out separately. Figure 15.2 shows several different topics; each topic is composed of several tasks. Note that several of the tasks are shared between topics.

Figure 15.2.
A task-oriented guide contains a series of tasks, with some shared subtasks.

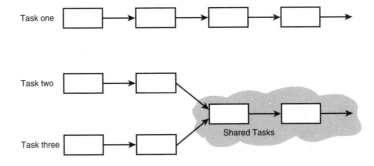

An Example of a Task

As an example of a task from a task-oriented user guide, consider the task of creating a new contact-management file in the InfoMan application. To refresh your memory, contact management enables a user to create a file that contains information about personal contacts, similar to a Rolodex.

One technique is to "storyboard" the individual steps required to carry out the task that is being described. Along with the description of each task, include a short description of problems or errors that the user might encounter. Each storyboard should be titled with a short slogan (see the following Developer's Tip box). For InfoMan, an example storyboard for creating a new contact file would include the following:

1. **File new.** Open the new document, which starts out as an untitled, empty contact list.
2. **Add contacts.** Add several contacts to the list. Adjust the width of the contact tabs as needed.
3. **Change views.** Change to the card view or split view.
4. **Save with new name.** Save the contact list using a new name.

Try different arrangements using the storyboard, and make corrections as needed so that you can get a good flow for each task. After the storyboard is completed, use it as a basis for writing the actual task descriptions.

Developer's Tip: Use the smallest storyboards that you can get away with. A good choice is 3×5 index cards, which can hold text on one side and a figure or sketch on the other. By keeping your storyboards small, you make them easier to handle and rearrange. If your office is large enough, you can actually pin up the pages on your wall and ask for input.

Finding Your Own Tasks

A good place to start collecting tasks for your user guide is the requirements specification, because it was probably written with specific tasks in mind. This is discussed in detail later, in the section titled "Using Design Documents as Input." Another good source of commonly used tasks comes from users. If you have a focus group, use it to help generate ideas about typical tasks that will be carried out.

Remember to be specific when you are defining your tasks. Tasks that are too general may not be useful for end users. They also tend to be too large, because the reader must spend a lot of time learning about different variations on the general task.

> **Textbook Tip:** Avoid too much cross-referencing in your user guide. When a cross reference is needed, refer the user to another task. However, try to keep the references to other tasks to a minimum. If readers have to jump back and forth too much between topics, they may become disoriented.
>
> Try to make your tasks as complete as possible, without duplicating information in too many places.

Creating a Tutorial

A tutorial is similar to a task-oriented user guide, except that the individual tasks are arranged to guide a new user through the process of using your application for the first time. Each task or topic that is presented builds on the preceding topics.

Figure 15.3 shows how a tutorial might be arranged. Topics that are covered early serve as a foundation for later material. For larger applications, it's a good idea to have several smaller tutorials instead of one large one.

Figure 15.3.
Tutorial topics are presented so that earlier topics can lay a foundation for later ones.

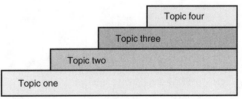

To be successful, a series of tutorials should start with simple tasks and work up to more difficult ones. For example, a series of tutorials for InfoMan might follow this pattern:

1. Open an example task-management file and browse the contents.
2. Create a new task-management file and store some new tasks. Save the tasks with a new filename.
3. Create a new file using the calendar manager, add some information, and save it.
4. Create a contact-management file, add some information, and print it.
5. Start up InfoMan from the File Manager by double-clicking a data file, using examples of all three files.

You should define the structure of your tutorial based on your target audience. Determine where a user of a tutorial is now, and where you want them to be at the end of the tutorial. These beginning and ending points are the key to a successful tutorial. Arrange the individual topics so that the tutorial has even steps between the beginning and ending levels.

Writing a Reference Manual

A reference manual by itself is not very useful for new users because it doesn't describe how tasks are done or offer any tutorials. However, when it is included with a task-oriented user guide or a tutorial, a reference manual can provide a great deal of help for more experienced users.

A typical reference manual is laid out in a hierarchical format, although there may be little physical connection between topics that are grouped together. Figure 15.4 shows how many reference manuals group their subjects. The Win32 Programmer's Reference is a good example of a reference guide.

Figure 15.4.

Reference manuals are arranged in a hierarchical format.

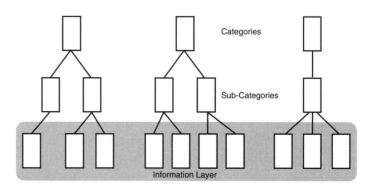

Some types of subjects work very well in reference guides. If a user has very little interaction with some feature of the system, a reference manual may be appropriate. If a large number of topics need to be indexed and accessed in a simple way, a reference manual can help cut down on the amount of documentation required by end users. Some other examples of information that is often placed into a reference manual include

- [ ] Error messages
- [ ] System capacities
- [ ] Fault handling instructions
- [ ] Technical support information

You should explain each subject in detail, possibly with an example when needed. A reference guide isn't meant to be read from cover to cover (at least not by mere mortals) so it doesn't have the same sort of readability requirements as tutorials or task-oriented guides. Each topic should stand on its own, with a minimum number of pointers to other subjects.

Including Screen Shots in Your Documentation

When you write your documentation, you may find it difficult to present your ideas to new users. One way to help present your topics more clearly is to include figures and screen shots with your documentation. For example, when you explain how different parts of the user interface interact with each other, a screen shot can be a great way to let the end user see exactly what to expect.

If you are using a word processor for your documentation, it may support the importing of graphics directly into your document. For example, Word for Windows and WordPerfect enable you to insert a wide variety of graphics formats directly into your document. Figure 15.5 shows an image being embedded into a Word for Windows document.

Figure 15.5.
Embedding a screen shot directly into a Word for Windows document.

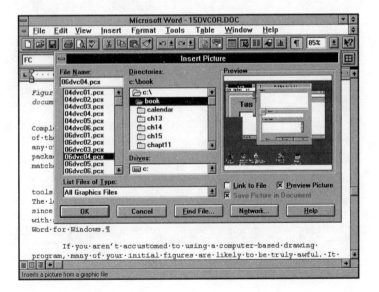

The screen shots used in this book were captured using Collage Complete for Windows. Collage Complete lets you easily select a region of the screen to be captured, and you can save the resulting image in any of the most common graphics formats. There are several similar packages available for Windows; you should be able to find one that matches your needs and budget.

If you're working on a tight budget, you can use some of the tools in your own garage to help you create figures and screen shots. The least expensive tool to use for creating figures is Paintbrush because it is included with Windows. Most good word processors also come with some kind of drawing utility; an MS-Draw applet is included with Word for Windows.

If you aren't accustomed to using a computer-based drawing program, many of your initial figures are likely to be truly awful. It takes a certain amount of practice before you can draw acceptable figures, especially if you don't have any art training. If you're artistically challenged but really need to have some artwork done, consider hiring someone to help with your graphics design.

Using Design Documents as Input

There are several types of design documents that can be used to help create your end-user documentation. The functional specification is a good starting point for most of your end-user documents because it was written with the end user in mind. However, make sure that the functional specification you use was kept current as the project progressed.

Most functional specifications are arranged according to the features provided by the application, so it's easy to convert a functional specification into the skeleton of a task-oriented user guide. An example functional specification for InfoMan can be found in the \CHAP2\DOCS directory on the CD that accompanies this book.

One problem that you will have as you work on your user guide is gathering information about operational details. Although all of the features in your application should be described in the functional specification, there will probably be very little low-level detail. You will have to collect this information from the system design and low-level designs.

Even after reading all of the documentation, you might still need to talk to other members of the development team to clarify any remaining issues about how the application works (this doesn't mean that you need to talk to yourself if you're working alone). Figure 15.6 shows some of the different inputs that you'll need for writing your documentation.

Although potential users of your application and other members of the development team are a good source of input, they can't replace the design documentation. You should use these design documents as your main source of information when writing your end-user documentation, at least for the first draft.

Figure 15.6.
There are a wide variety of inputs for your end-user documentation.

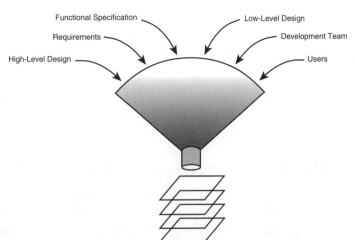

Reviewing User Documentation

The documentation that you supply with your application serves as a bridge between the application and the user. Earlier, you learned that users have a tendency to avoid reading your documentation. Your job is to try to convince them that the user guides for this application really are useful tools. The best way to do that is to get their feedback as soon as possible.

As you learned on Day 14, "Reviewing Documentation," it's a good idea to have some users review your documentation to ensure it meets their needs. You also should include others involved in the development process that have an interest in the end-user documentation.

One important thing to remember about the user documentation is that you need to work toward finishing the document. If your review team is made up of team members with several different backgrounds, you may wind up with an ever-improving document that never quite gets done. Make sure you establish target dates for the documentation to be finished, reviewed, and updated.

Updating User Documentation

As your project gets closer to its release date, the documentation must keep up with a changing product. There are two reasons why you should update your documentation:

☐ The documentation doesn't match the application.

☐ The application has changed and doesn't match the documentation.

You will probably discover cases in which the documentation doesn't match the application during review or through incident reports. When this happens, take some time to discover how

the error occurred. You may find that some design documentation needs to be updated or is ambiguous. Later, in the section, "Receiving Feedback from Incident Reports," you will learn more information about receiving feedback about the documentation.

If the application changes, you should update the documentation when other design documents are updated. On a larger team, where separate development team members are responsible for documentation, they should be notified when design documents are updated or when there are any functionality changes.

Problems with Feedback

One problem with feedback is trying to keep it current. If the application is changing, the documentation must also change. If you are trying to evaluate and react to user feedback at the same time, conflicts will occur. This can be a serious problem, because everyone may be wasting time testing or using the application with obsolete documentation. If inaccurate documentation is used, it can be difficult to determine if an application is at fault, or if the documentation has an error. Figure 15.7 shows three feedback loops that exist with an application and its documentation during development.

Figure 15.7.
Feedback loops in the documentation and development processes.

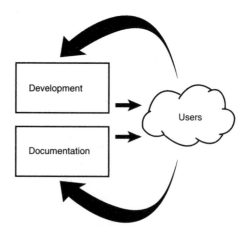

The best way to manage conflict that occurs because of these feedback loops is to restrict them as much as possible. In order to get the maximum benefit from your feedback, establish freeze dates as you learned on Day 13, "The Design-Documentation Archive." These freeze dates will allow you to synchronize your documentation with the product at specified intervals during the development cycle.

Receiving Feedback from Incident Reports

When you receive an incident report, you should always try to take steps to prevent similar problems in the future. This helps to turn a negative (the incident) into a positive (improvement). There are two types of feedback that will be reported with incident reports:

- [ ] **Accuracy reports.** These incident reports will help you identify places where the documentation doesn't match the released product. Hopefully, you will find all of these problems before the final release of your project. This is another reason to have documentation ready during the testing phases.

- [ ] **Usability reports.** These reports will deal with layout, content, and other problems with the document. You should consider this to be feedback about the quality of the document. When you receive one of these reports, consider getting detailed feedback about the problem directly from the user. After all, it's fairly difficult to find anyone who actually reads your documentation.

Modification Notes

Modifying an existing project can be very straightforward if the documentation structure is acceptable. The first step should be an inventory of the existing documentation where you note areas in the existing documents that must be updated. During the modification, handle reviews and updates as you would for a new project. Keep in mind that you may need to change documentation that refers to the modified part of the application.

For a final review, compare the old and the new documentation and check to make sure that nothing has been removed or changed incorrectly. Most word processors will generate documents with change bars that mark revised text and help make this step easier.

Debugging the Process

Sometimes it can be difficult to reach a consensus on end-user documents. The documentation is a very visible part of your application, so there may be a great deal of pressure to get it "just right." The problem with this approach is that you will eventually reach a point of diminishing returns and you will achieve little benefit by making future revisions.

You can avoid this problem by setting up some finishing criteria for the documentation. Setting an absolute final date for changes or establishing a final review date are two ways to get a review team to converge on a final document.

16

Online Help

Today you'll learn about online help. You will first learn hypertext documentation and how it differs from traditional hard-copy documents. After that, you'll learn how Microsoft uses hypertext in Windows Help, and how you can take advantage of it.

The following topics are also covered today:

☐ Adding context-sensitive help to your Visual C++ application

☐ Creating and editing Windows help source files

☐ Using third-party tools to create online help

Included on the CD that accompanies the book is a shareware tool called HELLLP!, an add-in for Microsoft Word for Windows that makes it much easier to write your help files. You'll use this tool to convert some existing documentation into online help.

Online Help Overview

It's almost impossible to find a Windows application today that doesn't supply online help. Although trivial applications may exist without an online help system, no serious programs are produced without it. In fact, online help is becoming so common that more and more applications are being sold without any hard-copy documentation at all.

The initial online help systems that were used with personal computers were just electronic versions of the hard-copy documentation. Searching and printing capabilities were poor, and the systems were not user-friendly. Starting with Windows 3.0, Microsoft has improved the WinHelp help engine so that it can be used to provide very high-quality hypertext-based help. With a small investment, you can learn to create excellent online help for the users of your application.

Understanding Hypertext Systems

A hypertext system is usually not arranged like a typical book; rather, hypertext systems enable information to be arranged into small "hypertext" pieces that are dynamically linked together to form a hypertext document. Users can find information much easier in hypertext documents, because the information can be arranged in any order (according to logical relationships in the document) instead of linearly. This enables a reader to browse through a document much easier than they can browse through printed books. Also, most hypertext systems offer sophisticated search facilities.

This is different from a hard-bound book, in which the topics have a fixed relationship with each other. Figure 16.1 shows how the topics in a book are usually arranged.

Figure 16.1.
The topics in a book are always laid out in a linear manner.

Hypertext systems don't have the restrictions that printed documents have. Because the pages don't have to be bound together, users can easily refer to information in another part of the document and immediately return to their original location. A single "page" in a hypertext document may be reached by many different routes; most of these routes will not be on adjacent pages. The same page may refer to several other pages, and so on throughout the document. Figure 16.2 shows an example of a hypertext document arrangement.

Figure 16.2.
Each page in a hypertext document can have links to many other pages.

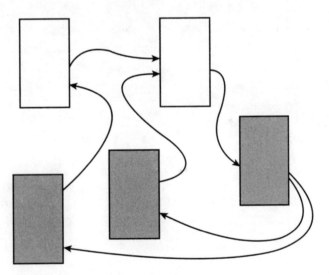

Components of Microsoft Help

Microsoft Help is a hypertext "engine" that is included with every copy of Windows. You can be sure that if your user is running your Windows-based application, there is a copy of WINHELP.EXE somewhere on the system. All that you, an application programmer, need to provide is a help file created for use with WinHelp. Figure 16.3 shows the relationship between your application, Windows, and your help file.

Figure 16.3.

WinHelp is launched by the application through Windows to provide help to the user.

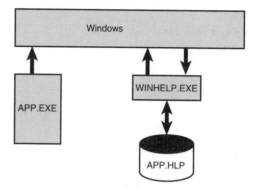

There are several ways for a user to invoke Windows help from your application. Your application can provide access to the help system in these ways:

☐ Direct selection from the main menu

☐ Context-sensitive help via the F1 key

☐ Context-sensitive help buttons in dialog boxes and message boxes

If you're unfamiliar with any of these help interfaces, don't worry; each will be covered in detail later today. In order to use any of these options you must add some code to your application. However, the amount of code you add is very small in relation to the amount of functionality you get in return.

Working with Rich Text Format Files

The source files used for your help program must be stored as Rich Text Format (RTF) files. The RTF format includes information about the document's format, along with the actual text. Most word processors, including Word for Windows and WordPerfect, support the creation of RTF files.

While you are writing your help text, the file will look just like any other document created with your word processor, except it is saved in a different format. RTF documents are portable between word processors made by different companies, so it's possible to create an RTF file with WordPerfect, and later edit it with Word for Windows.

One easy way to start writing your online help is to use your favorite word processor to create the first draft of your help document. After it's complete you can add the extra formatting needed for the Windows help compiler. Another approach that you'll use later today is to convert your existing end-user documentation into online help; that document can then be used as a starting point if you would like to create a more sophisticated online help system.

Tools for Creating Help Files

Until recently, sophisticated online help programs were found only on high-end consumer applications. One reason was that the extra formatting and management required for online help documents was difficult to justify for smaller applications. Fortunately for end users everywhere, there are now tools available to make this job much easier.

Strictly speaking, all of the tools that you need to create help files came with your Visual C++ compiler. You can find the help compiler, HC31.EXE, in your compiler's BIN subdirectory. To generate a help file, you will need to create the RTF source file and a project file, and then use the help compiler to generate the online help file.

If you are like most people and you aren't able to create RTF files by hand, you will also need a word processor that generates RTF-formatted documents. Figure 16.4 shows the tools and files used to create online help.

Figure 16.4.
The tools used to create Windows help files.

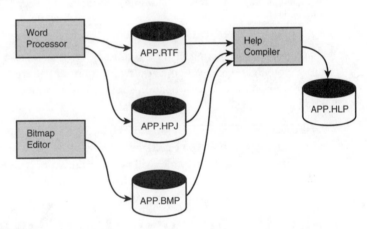

Most of the information about the structure of the help file is kept in the RTF file itself. You use the help project file (HPJ) to tell the help compiler how to compile the actual help file. The HPJ file includes information about the optional features and the names of the source files and bit maps included in the help file.

Information about keywords, jumps, pop-ups, and topic titles is actually embedded into the source file in the form of footnotes. Table 16.1 lists different tags used in Microsoft Help source files.

Table 16.1. Footnote tags used in Microsoft Help source files.

Tag	Mandatory?	Used For
#	Yes	Context string
$	If a keyword is assigned	Topic title

continues **277**

Table 16.1. continued

Tag	Mandatory?	Used For
K	No	Keyword list
+	No	Browse sequence

If you have never created an online help document before, and this seems like a lot of trouble, you're right. It's very tedious and error-prone work, and it's very easy to make a mistake. This is one reason why online help has not been used much for smaller applications. Listing 16.1 is an example of a footnote section you might use if you convert this paragraph into online help.

Listing 16.1 A sample Online Help footnote.

```
#Footnotes in On-Line Help
$Footnotes;Keywords;Topic Titles;Browse Sequence;Help Tags
+aboutHelp
```

You can avoid deciphering all of these codes by using a tool to create your help documents. Two different tools are covered in the next two sections. If you aren't using one of these tools to help create your online help, information about using RTF tags manually is documented in Books On-Line, in the *Win32 Tools User Guide*.

By the way, choosing a word processor can be a very emotional issue for many people, but most authoring tools are built to be used with Microsoft Word. You can use another word processor if you like, but creating help files will be more difficult because many of the tools available for Microsoft Word may not be available for other word processors.

Using the Microsoft Help Authoring Tools

Microsoft has released a set of unsupported tools called the Microsoft Help Authoring Tools. These files make it easier to use Microsoft Word to create online help files for your application by reducing the amount of work you have to do manually.

The help authoring tools are available in several places (see the following note). The following items are included in the package:

- ☐ An editor for managing your help project
- ☐ A set of Word for Windows document templates
- ☐ Some sample C code
- ☐ A sample RTF document containing help-file source files
- ☐ Documentation for all of the help authoring tools

Note: The Microsoft Help Authoring Tools are available in a variety of places.

If you are a member of the Microsoft Developer's Network, the help tools are on the Level I CD. Use the online searching feature, and search on "help authoring."

If you have access to file transfer (FTP) via the Internet, the help authoring tools are available by anonymous FTP from `ftp.microsoft.com`.

If you are a CompuServe subscriber, the package can be found in the WinSDK forum. Type `GO WINSDK` at any ! prompt.

Using the HELLLP! Package

Another package that is available for creating online help documents is HELLLP!. This shareware package adds functionality to Word for Windows that makes writing great online help practically painless. HELLLP! is an add-in for Word for Windows that completely automates the creation of online help.

An unregistered copy of HELLLP! is included on the CD that accompanies this book. To install it, follow these steps:

1. Copy the file HELLLP!.EXE to a directory on your hard disk.
2. Uncompress HELLLP!.EXE by typing `HELLLP!` at the DOS prompt.
3. Follow the remaining instructions in the NOTES.TXT file.

Note: The HELLLP! application is provided as a shareware package. You are entitled to use it for an evaluation period, after which you must either register it or stop using it.

After you register it you can receive updates and support from the author of the program. This package is worth far more than its registration fee, and I hope you will support the shareware concept by registering your copy.

The first time you create a file using a HELLLP! template you'll be asked for some information about your environment. You can change this information at any time by selecting Format, and then Change HELLLP! Setup from the main menu.

HELLLP! completely manages your help files for you, enabling you to compile and test help documents easily from inside Word for Windows. You'll almost never need to worry about macros, footnotes, or special RTF tags for parts of your help text, because HELLLP! will manage all of that for you. If you want to modify the footnotes or other help tags you still can, even if you're using HELLLP!.

Organizing Topics

The simplest way to organize your online help is linearly, just like hard-copy documentation. In fact, if you don't have a lot of extra resources, you can just convert your existing documentation created on Day 15, "Developing End-User Documentation," into help files.

The advantage of starting this way is that it is very easy for you as an author. You can copy your entire document into an RTF file and begin to create topics immediately. A very fast approach is to make every section a topic and make every chapter a collection of these topics. At the very top level, the table of contents contains a list of the chapters. Figure 16.5 shows an example of this method.

Figure 16.5.
A simple hierarchy for online help documents.

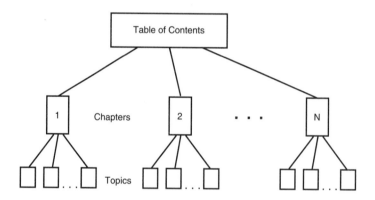

This type of document becomes a straightforward structure that's very easy to navigate. Even novice users won't have any trouble finding their way through this document.

The next few sections take an existing end-user document and convert it into an online help file. If your current end-user documentation is split into several files, convert your first file now; later you'll learn about using multiple help-source files to create a single online help file.

Copying an Existing File into a HELLLP! RTF File

The first step in converting your existing documentation into online help is to copy your existing document into a document that has been created using the HELLLP! template. Follow these six easy steps:

1. Open Word for Windows. If you are using version 6.0 or later, enable the Word 2.0 toolbar by selecting View, and then Toolbars from the main menu. Make sure the Word for Windows 2.0 option is selected.

2. Start a new file by selecting File, and then New from the main menu.

3. Choose HELLLP! as the document template. Figure 16.6 shows the template selection dialog box from Word for Windows 6.0.

16

Figure 16.6.
Selecting a HELLLP!
template in Word for
Windows.

4. The HELLLP! template will start loading, and ask you for some information about the project. If this is the first time the HELLLP! template has been used, you will be asked some questions about your environment.

5. After the template has loaded, it will insert default text into the new RTF document. Don't remove any of this text, because HELLLP! uses it internally when creating your help file.

6. Copy and paste the original document at the end of the new RTF file.

That's it. You've finished the first step in converting your end-user documents into online help. The next step is to convert each section of the document into a separate topic.

Developer's Tip: If you want to take advantage of the default MFC help source, now is the time to do it.

If you selected the help-support option when you built your application with AppWizard, there are already some help-source files ready to be added to your online help. The help-project file is located in your project directory. The RTF files and bit maps are located in the HLP subdirectory.

Follow these steps to add the MFC help-source files to a HELLLP! help project:

1. Make sure the HELLLP! project directory points to your project directory. If it doesn't, change it by selecting Format, and then Change HELLLP! Setup from the main menu.
2. Copy and paste the RTF files into your online help.
3. Change the extension for the existing help project file from HPJ to HPK. HPK is a file extension that tells HELLLP! to merge the existing project with the new one created by HELLLP!.
4. Edit the HPK file and remove the references to the RTF files copied in step 2, and remove any entries that are in the [Options] section.

Creating Individual Topics

The basic unit of help that is provided to the end user is the topic. Because you are the author, you get to decide the size and content of each topic. Each topic will need to have a topic title and a context string associated with it. If you can't come up with separate titles for all of your topics, either combine topics or use a placeholder for now.

Keep in mind that each topic will be seen by the user as an individual "page" of online help. Try to limit each topic to one or two pages if possible. If you have trouble creating bite-sized pieces of your help topics, just combine topics into more general "super topics." You'll work on shortening and optimizing topics later today.

Right now your document consists of one RTF file, with a single table of contents help topic. To convert your document into separate topics, follow these steps:

1. Go to the first line of the topic and press the "T" toolbar button. If the topic starts a new section of text and currently has a title, highlight the title first. A dialog box similar to the one in Figure 16.7 will appear, prompting you for the topic title. If the topic was highlighted, the title will be filled in for you. After you enter the topic title, press OK.

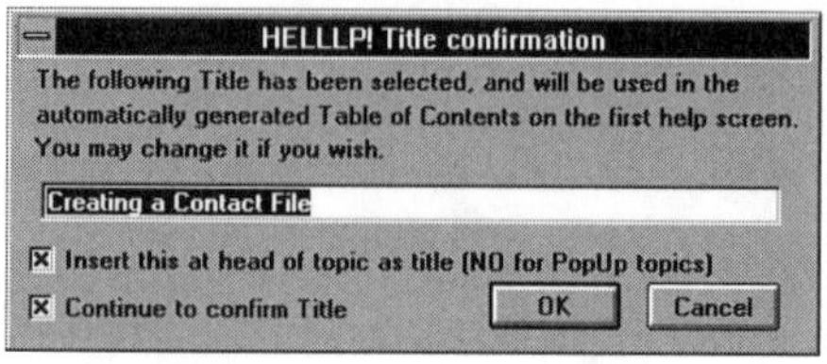

Figure 16.7.

Adding a help topic using HELLLP! and Word for Windows.

HELLLP! Title confirmation

The following Title has been selected, and will be used in the automatically generated Table of Contents on the first help screen. You may change it if you wish.

Creating a Contact File

[X] Insert this at head of topic as title (NO for PopUp topics)
[X] Continue to confirm Title   OK   Cancel

2. HELLLP! will present a list of possible keywords for this topic, as shown in Figure 16.8. Because the suggested keywords are based on the topic title, you will probably need to edit them. You'll learn about planning and modifying keywords later, so don't worry about adding all of your keywords now.

Figure 16.8.

Adding keywords for a new topic using HELLLP!.

3. HELLLP! will determine a unique context string for the topic and ask you to confirm it, as shown in Figure 16.9. If you have a different name planned for the context string, you can replace the suggested string. Because this string is never shown to an end user, you should almost always use the one suggested by HELLLP!; it's guaranteed to be unique. If this help topic will be used for a dialog box or view window, Visual C++ has a tool that will define a default context string. This string is the resource ID plus the letter H. If the resource ID for a dialog box is IDD_TASKDLG, the context string generated by Visual C++ will be HIDD_TASKDLG. You should use the context string that is based on the resource ID, because it simplifies integrating online help with your application later.

Figure 16.9.

Adding a context string for a new topic.

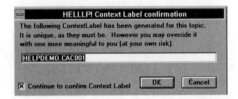

4. Repeat the preceding steps for the rest of your topics.

Notice that HELLLP! has added all of the footnotes used for generating online help discussed earlier. If you would like to see what your topic looks like in online help, press the arrow and circle symbol button on the toolbar. HELLLP! will start the help compiler, generate a help file with your topic included, and display it.

Don't delete any "extra" jump references yet!
After HELLLP! creates a topic, it places a jump reference to the new topic in the default table of contents. This jump reference will be used later when you assign your own jump and pop-up references. Eventually, you will learn where to move these extra jumps and how to hide them from your end users.

The problem with this approach is that you don't get much benefit from WinHelp's hypertext capabilities. The topics may be too complex or too long, and they may refer to other sections of the document, forcing the user to locate that section manually. In the next section you'll learn how to add basic hypertext functions to your online help.

Links, Jumps, and Pop-Ups

As you divide your help document into individual topics, you may notice that HELLLP! places a reference to each of them on the table of contents page. This is convenient for testing purposes, but not very user-friendly for online help. After the help system has been completed, the table of contents should contain references only to "top-level" topics. If too many topics are presented in the table of contents, it will be difficult for the user to find the desired topic.

In order to make your online help a little bit easier to use, you should arrange your topics in a hierarchy, establishing links between some of the related topics. There are three types of links that you can create in Windows Help:

- ☐ Jumps
- ☐ Pop-ups
- ☐ Browse sequences

A *jump* is used to move from one part of the hypertext document to another. This is the most common type of linkage in Windows Help, and it's usually found at the bottom of a topic's page, under a "See Also" heading.

Pop-ups cause a small box with the pop-up topic to be displayed on top of the current topic. A pop-up is best used for short definitions or explanations. Pop-ups generally do not have titles or links to other parts of the hypertext document.

A *browse sequence* is a collection of help topics that are arranged so that the user can select them in order by browsing forward or backward. The topics don't have to be physically sequential in your source document, just logically connected in some way.

Adding a Hypertext Jump

If you are using the HELLLP! templates for Word, adding a jump to another topic just requires a couple of mouse clicks. Before starting, make sure that your jump destination has been defined as a topic, and then follow these two steps:

1. Highlight the text that will be the jump "hot spot," then press the "J" button on the toolbar. HELLLP! will take over, and it becomes a completely automated process at this point.

2. HELLLP! will ask you to move the cursor to the destination topic in the table of contents, and press the "C" button on the toolbar. HELLLP! will then insert a jump from the hot spot to the destination.

That's all there is to it. If you want to test your links, just compile your help file from inside Word by pressing the arrow-and-circle toolbar button.

> **Developer's Tip:** At this point, you probably have dozens (at least) of jump references in your table of contents. Many of these references won't be in the final table of contents, and earlier you were warned against deleting them.
>
> After you have set up all of your jumps inside your help document, you can move the unneeded jump references to the hidden text page that HELLLP! created when your online help document was first started. This enables you to have a reference to all of your jumps and pop-ups for future use, while keeping unused ones hidden from readers of your online help.

Adding Pop-Ups to Your Online Help

Adding a pop-up topic reference is similar to adding a hypertext jump. Follow the steps for adding a jump, but use the "P" (pop-up) button on the toolbar instead of the "J" (jump) button.

Creating Browse Sequences

You use the "B" (browse) toolbar button to add browse sequences. To add or modify your browse sequences, highlight some text in your topic, and press the "B" button on the toolbar. A dialog box like the one in Figure 16.10 is displayed.

To add or replace the current topic in a browse sequence select the Add/Replace option. If the current topic is not in a browse sequence, you will be prompted for the sequence name and a browse sequence number. Default values will be provided for you, which you should accept in most cases. If you are building custom browsing sequences, you will want to override the suggested values.

Figure 16.10.

The Browse Sequences dialog box.

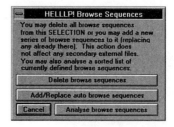

To remove the current topic from its browse sequence, select the Delete option. Because the topic is only in a single browse sequence, you won't be prompted for any input; HELLLP! will handle everything for you.

Taking Advantage of Hypertext

Now that you've converted your hard-copy documentation into online help, you should try to take advantage of Windows Help's more advanced features. Even though your online help is usable as is, you can make it more user friendly by tuning your document to take advantage of hypertext.

One of the things that you can do to make your user's life easier is to make your topics shorter. On a printed page, topics that stretch for a page or more are still readable. When displayed using Windows Help, these topics will stretch for several screen pages and be difficult to follow.

A hypertext system is most effective when users can see an entire topic on the screen. Try to split your topics so that they fit on a single screen, with links to other pages if needed. This will create a document that has more, smaller topics that each contain a "bite-sized" chunk of information. Figure 16.11 shows how the process of splitting topics works.

Figure 16.11.
Splitting long document pages into bite-sized hypertext chunks.

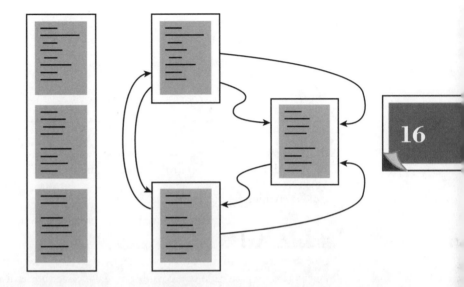

16

Linking Topics to Your Application

Earlier you learned that there are three ways to provide access to online help from your application. Each of these three methods requires some programming on your part, but because the MFC framework does some of the work for you, you need to do much less coding than you might expect.

Direct Access to Help Via the Main Menu

This is the simplest form of help support. The MFC Windows Help function assumes that the help file is located in the same directory as your EXE file. The help file must also have the same name as your EXE, with an extension of HLP.

All you have to do to enable this type of help support is to select the help support option when you build your project with AppWizard. The menu will be created for you, and all of the function calls will be provided by the framework.

Providing Help in Dialog Boxes

Providing help in a dialog box is only slightly more difficult than providing help from the main menu. All that you need to do is call one `CWinApp` public-member function and provide the context value of the appropriate help topic. For each of your dialog boxes, add a help button. Then map that button using ClassWizard to a function like the one shown in Listing 16.2.

Listing 16.2. The source code behind a dialog-box help button.

```
void CPasswordDlg::OnHelp()
{
    CWinApp* pApp = AfxGetApp();
    ASSERT( pApp );

    pApp->WinHelp( IDD_ADDTASK + 0x00020000 );
}
```

When the user presses the help button, `CPassword::OnHelp` is invoked, and it calls `CWinApp::WinHelp`. The `WinHelp` function will start the Windows help engine, displaying the help topic for this dialog box. Adding `0x00020000` to the dialog box's resource ID enables the help button to use the same context as if the user had pressed F1 while the dialog box was displayed. This is a very easy way to provide context-sensitive help for users of your application.

If you display AFX message boxes to the user, you should enable context-sensitive help for those dialog boxes by sending the help-context value along with the message. When the AFX framework detects an F1 keypress while a modal message box is displayed, it will use that context value when it calls Windows Help.

Providing Help with the F1 Key

Handling the F1 key is the most complicated of the three methods for providing help support for your application. In this case, you actually need to add code in several different places by hand. For your application, you will need to add about six lines of code.

To add F1 help to your views and dialog boxes, follow these steps:

1. First, define all of the help context strings that will be used for your views and dialog boxes using the recommendations from MFC Technical Note 28. If you would like to see an example of naming your topics according to this Technical Note, see the help source file for InfoMan, which can be found in the \CHAP16\INFO directory on the CD that accompanies this book.

2. Modify the MAKEHELP.BAT file that was created by AppWizard, and remove the line that calls the help compiler. The line to be removed should look something like this:

   ```
   call hc31 Info.hpj
   ```

3. Run the MAKEHELP batch file. This batch file will create a help-mapping file that will associate the numbers that are passed to `CWinApp::WinHelp` function, with the context strings that are used by the help file.

That's all you have to do. Now whenever a user presses F1 when this dialog box is active, the proper topic will be displayed.

Note: Actually, there is a fourth way to provide context-sensitive help for your application. The user can place the application into "help mode" by pressing the Shift and F1 keys at the same time. The current cursor is replaced by a "help" cursor, and the user can get help by clicking any part of the application. If you would like to support this type of help, you will need to respond to WM_HELPHITTEST, and return the proper context-sensitive help value. MFC Technical Note 28 has more information on this topic.

Modification Notes

When you modify an existing project, it's very important to keep the same help style as any existing help provided for the application. The best way to do this is to use any existing help-authoring tools that were used to create the existing online help.

If the existing help was created with help-authoring tools, the best approach is to use the existing RTF file as a guide, and copy as much as possible from any existing templates. You should almost never try to create a separate help file for the new portion of the application, because it would probably make the user confused in most cases.

Debugging the Process

If you don't have a word processor that generates RTF files, you are pretty much out of luck in this section. It's almost impossible to create online help by hand. The cost of word processors is falling rapidly, and if you want to write online help, you really need to pick one up.

If you use a word processor other than Word for Windows, contact the manufacturer for information about help authoring tools. More tools are becoming available for word processors other than Word; you can find a template for WordPerfect in the Windows SDK forum on CompuServe (type GO WINSDK).

Implementation

Part IV, the last part in the book, is five days long. The process of actually making the final preparations to release and support your application is covered in this section. The topics covered in this part of the book include the following:

- ☐ Functional and system-level testing
- ☐ Selecting and supporting alpha and beta test users
- ☐ Tracking and fixing any remaining bugs in your application
- ☐ Creating setup programs
- ☐ Supporting users after the application is released
- ☐ Planning updates and future releases

Functional Testing

Today you will learn about functional testing. This is the beginning of the formal testing of your application, and it's the first part of the development process that follows the test plans that you created on Day 3, "Test Planning."

Today you will learn different aspects of the functional testing, including the following:

☐ Independent versus team-based testing

☐ Automated testing

☐ Testing for regressions

☐ Controlling changes during functional testing

Along the way you will also discover a few faults in the InfoMan example application that was developed earlier in the book.

Functional Testing Overview

Functional testing is the first test phase that actually begins to verify that the system works as intended. Earlier test phases, such as the low-level and integration tests, were primarily used to verify that the system was working as it was designed. Starting today you'll test the system to make sure that it works as documented in the functional specifications.

On Day 3 you learned about validation and verification. You did verification earlier in the project, when you tested individual modules and performed integration tests. These tests were used to prove that the system was working as it was designed. Starting today, you'll begin what is often referred to as the *verification phase*, where you test the system against the functional specification and the real world.

Using the Functional Test Plan

The functional test plan was written on Day 3. You'll use this plan to help execute tests that will be carried out today. The test plan should have four items that will be used to prepare for the functional testing:

☐ Start and stop criteria

☐ Test descriptions

☐ Time estimates

☐ Test-environment description

Each of these items will be used later today when you perform the test cases. If anything is missing from this list, the test plan should be updated now, before the actual testing begins.

Textbook Tip: It's not unusual for changes and new functions to be added to your project during the development process. Make sure any changes that have been made to the functional specification are also included in the functional and system test plans.

If you have added or removed functions from your application, check your functional specification and test plans and make sure that

☐ No anonymous features are added to the project and/or are missing from the functional specification or test plans.

☐ Functions that have been removed from the project are not listed in the functional specification.

☐ All tests refer to functions listed in the functional specification.

Functional Testing is Part of the Big Picture

Before you begin executing the functional tests, consider how functional testing fits in with the entire testing process. Although some developers routinely test their applications by using several separate test phases, many do not. It's not uncommon for software developers to quickly finish a quick system-level test and immediately release the software package to beta test. In this case, the development team usually performs some informal testing while the product is beta tested by users. This is not the most efficient way to test your software for several reasons:

☐ Beta testers don't provide effective test coverage. On Day 19, "Beta Testing," you will learn the benefits of using beta testing. However, relying on beta testers to find faults in your application is doomed to failure. First of all, most beta users are not trained testers. They may or may not be familiar with your application, and they probably are not being paid to test your application. They help as a final acceptance check for your application, but they cannot be your primary testing method.

☐ Informal testing is not a reliable indicator of quality. Informal testing that is performed by testing semirandom functions is also unlikely to help improve your quality in the long run. This sort of testing seems like a good idea; after all, you don't waste time planning your tests. Unfortunately, beta testing is made up almost entirely of volunteer testers performing informal tests. Keep in mind that the time you spend planning and executing structured tests will help you predict the quality of your software.

☐ Test planning is very difficult. If you have a well-thought-out test plan, you can plan your equipment and resource requirements based on the plan. As time goes on, your experience in test planning will help you make those plans more accurate. Informal testing is very difficult to plan, because it is so unpredictable.

Note: An additional problem that can happen if beta testing is used too early in the testing process is that your reputation can be damaged. Even if you clearly state that an application is a beta release, users will still expect it to have most of its functionality. If your beta version has a large number of faults, the bad first impression of your product may be difficult to overcome.

It is much easier for you to improve the quality of your software if you have a planned, predictable testing process. Although you can't become a perfectly tuned testing organization overnight, by using structured testing and documenting your tests, you can start improving a little bit at a time. This is what continuous improvement is all about.

Textbook Tip: You can discover and correct every fault that is introduced into a software application. Experience has taught, however, that different types of testing will discover different types of faults.

No single type of testing can ensure perfect product quality, which is why most software today is tested in phases. The focus of each phase is to prove that the software is correct in a different way.

The functional-test phase will help you detect and correct any faults in the application that prevent individual functions from working properly. The individual functions are what you are really interested in testing right now. This doesn't mean that errors discovered in nontested areas of the application will be ignored; it just means that each test focuses on a particular function.

Before the functional-test phase, you tested each module thoroughly; you know that each of the modules works as it was designed. You should not have to worry that individual modules have internal coding errors, because that should have been detected during the low-level tests and integration tests.

After this test phase, you will test at the system level. You'll make sure that the system interacts with the operating system correctly, handles low-resource conditions well, and cooperates with any other applications that may be running. It doesn't make much sense to test those parts of

the system now, because you haven't verified that the entire system works correctly. Figure 17.1 shows some of the other test phases and how they relate to functional testing.

Figure 17.1.
The relationship between functional testing and other nearby test phases.

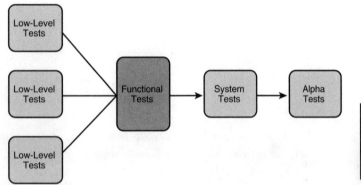

Different Strategies for Functional Testing

There are several different testing strategies for functional testing. No one strategy is the best for all users; the one that you choose won't necessarily be the best plan for someone else.

Don't let yourself get too wrapped up in a single set of testing methods. It's not unusual for some organizations, especially larger ones, to use a mixture of these different strategies for their testing. You should take their lead and use whatever techniques work best for you.

Independent Functional-Testing Teams

One of the first decisions that you should make about testing your application is the structure of your test teams. If you work alone, this decision has been made for you; but if you're working as part of a larger group, this is an important decision. There's no right or wrong decision; actually, there's quite a lot of debate about which method is best for most organizations.

Traditionally, larger organizations have used a separate, independent test group to test their products. This independent test group participates in design and requirements reviews, and is responsible for testing the product from functional test until release. The primary advantage of an independent test group is that it is separate from the design team. Figure 17.2 shows a typical design organization that uses independent testing.

Figure 17.2.

A typical design organization that uses independent testing.

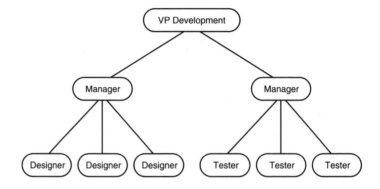

Ideally, the independent test group-reporting structure is separate from the development group right up to the highest levels. When the teams are truly independent, the development and test teams work separately, but with the same input. This helps promote a vigorous test of the product, and it helps to avoid "groupthink," which can also be a big barrier to adequate testing. Because the independent test team may create the test plans independently of the development group, the tests aren't contaminated by the application designers.

Independent testing is definitely justified for some types of software development. For instance, if you are building autopilot software, please do independent testing. To determine if you should use independent testing, ask yourself the following:

☐ Is the consequence of failure very high with my product?

☐ Is the extra expense and management structure justified by the failure risk?

☐ Is the organization capable of managing two software development trees—one for development, and a separate one for testing?

If you answered yes to any of these questions, you should consider independent testing. On the other hand, if you are like most people and answered no to all three questions, you can probably use a less expensive testing method.

Functional Testing Using the Development Team

Some organizations prefer to design and test in teams, with one single organization responsible for the entire development process. This helps to reduce conflict that can occur when two separate organizations are developing a single project. It also works better for small development groups that can't afford to have a completely separate test organization.

Each member of the team may be responsible for developing some part of the application, as well as testing a different part. If you have a choice, it's almost never a good idea for designers to test

their own code. Although it may seem inefficient, this actually has several benefits: designers get an opportunity to learn other parts of the application, and you get some of the benefits of independent testing. Figure 17.3 illustrates this type of testing.

Figure 17.3.

A typical design organiza-
tion that uses independent
tests.

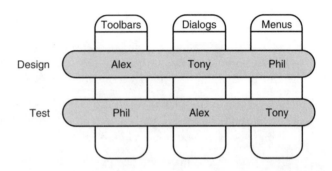

If you work alone, there won't be enough team members to go around for independent testing. One thing that you can do, however, is to consciously put yourself into a testing mood. Your testing personality should be different from your designer personality. Don't make excuses for the way an application works; your end users won't.

Showstopper: You should use self testing as a last resort. Although it may seem more efficient for developers to test their own functions, in reality many errors tend to be missed.

Look at it this way: the code is working as it was designed, because it has passed the low-level tests. Many of the errors that are caught during functional testing may be caused by design decisions. That's why it's much better to use a tester who has a fresh perspective, rather than the original designer.

If you are working alone and have no one else to help test your work, you have an excuse from this Showstopper.

Automated Versus Manual Testing

Whether you are testing independently, in teams, or by yourself, there are two basic ways to execute your test cases:

- ☐ Automated testing, using a test script
- ☐ Manual testing, where a tester exercises the application

Just like the debate over independent versus developer testing, there is no best method that works for every software project all of the time. Each of these methods has its strong points. If you can afford it, you should consider using both forms of testing for your application.

Manual Testing

If you use manual testing for your application, each test will be executed by a real, live tester, following the test instructions that were developed on Day 3. If a test needs to be executed again, then the tester will follow the test script and execute the test, again.

Test cases that are executed manually are relatively easy to plan. If your testers are familiar with the application, the actual instructions don't need to be extremely detailed. This ease of planning, however, creates several problems:

- ☐ Individual tests may vary, because the test instructions are always subject to interpretation.

- ☐ There may be a problem with interpreting test instructions, especially older instructions that don't apply or are being reused.

- ☐ Different results may be interpreted differently by several testers. This may lead to a problem with cognitive dissonance (see the following Textbook Tip box). Figure 17.4 is an example of a dialog box that is faulty, but might be missed because of cognitive dissonance.

Figure 17.4.
A faulty dialog box that can easily be passed as okay. (The icon is incorrect; a question mark icon should not be displayed for a warning or error message.)

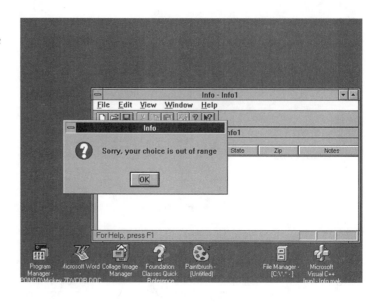

Textbook Tip: One of the problems with using manual testing is a problem known as *cognitive dissonance*. When people are presented with an object, they will often see exactly what they want, or expect, to see. When presented with a dialog box with a missing word or a dialog box with a reversed bit map, the tester may believe that he or she is seeing the proper results.

During manual testing some of your test cases may fail, often in subtle ways. Unfortunately, most people will eventually miss detecting some of these faults, especially if they are under time pressure.

17

Automated Testing

Another approach to testing is to use an automated testing tool. Automated tests are run from test scripts that are designed and created for each test. It generally costs more to execute your first series of automated tests versus running manual tests. However, after a test script has been proven correct, it can be easily reused with very little cost.

The primary benefits of automated testing are that the tests are reusable and are duplicated perfectly every time the test is executed. Also, the low cost of reusing a script makes automated testing perfect for tests that need to be run more than once. Automated testing tools never have problems recognizing faults, and they can run unattended, when you're not watching.

The major drawback for automated testing is the initial cost of the tool. If you're working alone and are not creating commercial applications, it may be hard for you to justify buying an automated testing tool. Also, you will need to learn how to program using the tool's scripting language.

By far the most popular tool is Microsoft Test (MS Test) for Windows. When you use MS Test you must use a form of Basic, known as Test Basic, to write test scripts that simulate a user interacting with your application. A sample test script fragment is shown in Listing 17.1.

Listing 17.1. A sample MS Test script that clicks the Cancel button if one exists.

```
'$DEFINE  W_CHECK
'$INCLUDE 'MSTEST.INC

If WButtonEnabled( "&Cancel" ) Then
    WButtonClick( "Cancel" )
Else
    Print "The Cancel button is missing"
End If
```

When you are programming your test routine, MS Test enables you to capture information from an interactive session and generate a script based on your input and your application's responses. You can use that script as a basis for more complicated test scripts.

At this point in a project, writing more code is probably one of the last things that you're looking forward to. Fortunately, MS Test enables you to capture a session of screen interactions and create a script that can be used to reproduce your key and mouse strokes.

Some parts of your application will be more suited for automation than others. For InfoMan, the testing was done manually so you didn't have to buy extra tools. However, if you are doing serious Windows development and you have tests that are executed more than once, you can easily justify the expense.

Executing Your Function Tests

No matter which method you decide to use to run your functional tests, sooner or later you need to stop planning and begin executing test cases. Before starting any of your test phases, including the functional test, it's a good idea to run through a checklist to make sure that you are really ready to start testing.

A Checklist Before You Start Testing

Before you begin the functional test, you should make sure that all of your functional-test entry criteria have been met, and that the application is ready for the start of functional testing. A sample checklist for a small application like InfoMan would include the following:

☐ Tested functions are code complete

☐ All high-priority incident reports from low-level testing are resolved

☐ Test instructions are complete

☐ Test stations are equipped with any needed equipment

All of these checklist items should be a part of your functional-test entry criteria. If you discover a missing item that should be on the checklist, you should add it to your entry criteria so that it's included for your next functional test.

Discovering Faults

There are two main classes of faults that you will find during your functional and system-level tests:

☐ Functional faults, where a test fails to give you the results that were expected

☐ Side-effect faults, where a test passes but a fault is discovered in another part of the system

The function test for InfoMan turned up two faults, both of which are associated with the contact-management part of InfoMan:

1. When the contact list view is displayed, the Delete button has the focus.
2. When the contact list view is displayed, empty fields are displayed as "..." instead of being displayed as empty.

Both of these problems are easily corrected, and are fixed in the release that will be used on Day 18, "System-Level and Alpha Testing."

Test Teams

If you are testing with a team, you may be able to work efficiently by dividing up work so that team members can specialize in some part of the functional test. There are three main activities during functional testing:

☐ Executing the test cases
☐ Isolating and resolving faults
☐ Planning and executing regression tests (which is covered in the next section)

Each of these activities can be carried out separately from the others. Figure 17.5 shows the relationships that exist between the different parts of functional testing.

Figure 17.5.
The relationships between different activities that are part of functional testing.

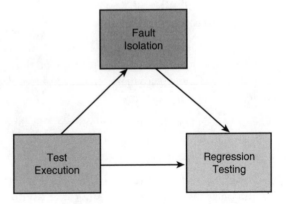

Initially, all of the tests are executed by all test team members. As test cases fail, some of the team members may be assigned to handle incident reports and isolate faults in the application. After faults have been resolved, more team members may be assigned to handle regression testing.

Regression Testing

As you test your application, you are probably going to find some faults. As you correct those faults, you run the risk of introducing new faults. One way to reduce the impact of these bug fixes is to test for regressions.

Understanding Regression Testing

At the end of your functional test, you may find yourself facing a problem. You have completed your functional testing and satisfied your stopping criteria. However, if you have made changes to the system after tests have been executed, you run the risk of introducing regressions. A *regression* is either a fault that occurs because of an attempt to fix a different problem, or a previously corrected problem that reappears.

The purpose of regression testing is to verify two different aspects of the system's quality:

☐ Faults that have been fixed stay fixed

☐ Things that have worked continue to work

After you have introduced changes to your application, you use regression tests to prove that the system continues to work as expected.

Choosing Regression Tests

Regression tests should be executed just like functional tests. This is because you are really testing a system function. After all, you're checking to make sure that a particular function is still working as expected.

Automated tests can be very handy for regression testing, because you can build a suite of test cases and reuse them whenever you want to run the regression tests. This reduces the cost of the regression testing and helps make it more attractive to you, which in the long run will make your product quality much better.

Whether or not you use automated testing, you should definitely collect a set of tests that will form the core of your regression test cases. These cases should represent a cross section of your application's functionality, and should be run after every major release.

Deciding what makes up a release is up to you. For small- and medium-sized projects, you might just run one phase of regression testing after your functional test.

Textbook Tip: The purpose of the regression testing is to quickly find any new faults introduced by corrections that you have made to the system. Your

> regression tests should not be slowed down by new test cases that have never been executed.
>
> Make sure that all of your test cases have worked at least once. Remember, if a test is new, it's not a regression test.

Performing Your Regression Tests

Your regression tests should be run just like a lightweight functional test. For InfoMan, the basic regression tests consist of 20 cases that are always tested after the project is tested and recompiled. The regression tests will be rerun at the end of the system, alpha, and beta tests. In addition, the tests will be run just before the final release.

Ending the Function Test

One of the hardest decisions to make when testing is deciding when to stop testing. There are many factors to think about when you are considering an end to your test phase. Different people may decide to stop testing at different times.

It is important for you to stop testing as soon as possible, but not too soon. Every test that you execute adds to the cost of your application; it also helps you improve the quality of your application. After all, that's why you're testing in the first place. However, more faults are found during the beginning of a new test phase than at the end. At some point, you should see the number of faults per test case begin to decline. If you don't see this curve at least flatten, you're in big trouble. Figure 17.6 is an example of the number of faults found per test case on an imaginary project.

Figure 17.6.
A failure-rate curve for a typical project during functional testing.

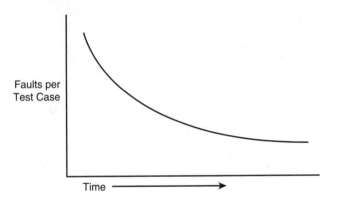

If you are working on a large project, the cost to detect and exterminate every possible bug increases at the end of each test phase. As fewer faults are detected per test, you receive fewer benefits, but your costs remain constant. Unless you are working on very small projects, or are working on a large, mission-critical application, it will not be practical to try to prove that there are no faults in your application.

The difficulty of discovering bugs is the reason that most commercial software contains a disclaimer against undiscovered errors causing consequential damages. Although you should not use a legal disclaimer as an excuse for shipping faulty products, the fact is that it's very difficult and extremely expensive to detect and eliminate every possible fault in a nontrivial software application.

Developer's Tip: Some development groups, including some very successful ones, monitor the reported fault rate during each of their test phases. When the fault rate drops to an acceptable level, the test phase is stopped and the project moves into the next phase.

By using metrics developed from previous projects, they feel that they can predict the best time to end a test phase. The important thing to remember here is that these groups plan their ending criteria.

Good Reasons to Stop Testing

There are both good and bad reasons to stop testing. The first and best reason to stop testing is meeting your exit criteria. If you meet the criteria, your functional test is over and you can begin working on your system-level testing.

The exit criteria for InfoMan were specified when the functional test plan was created on Day 3. To refresh your memory, the following were the exit criteria:

- ☐ All priority-one and -two tests completed
- ☐ At least 50 percent of priority-three tests completed

It may not seem like a reason, but rejecting the application is also considered a good reason to stop testing. If you are failing a large number of tests, it really doesn't make much sense to continue testing. It is much better for you to try to determine the reason for the large failure rate, and correct the problem.

On the other hand, if your exit criteria aren't met, your functional test isn't completed. It is almost never a good idea to change your exit criteria so that you can exit a functional test. If you

have too many outstanding faults, or too many test cases have failed, it's much better to continue testing and fixing faults.

Documentation for Functional Testing

There are several types of documents that will be used as part of the functional testing. The two most often used will be

- [ ] **Incident reports.** You should track incident reports for all of your functional tests. Any reports that can't be cleared during functional testing should be addressed in the next test phase.
- [ ] **Test-execution reports.** Tracking this information can help you determine which areas of the system may be more likely to have faults, or need other improvements.

In addition, you may want to perform some quality measurements on the fault rate and error intensity during the functional tests. Information on measurements and metrics was covered on Day 11, "Error Reporting and Metrics."

Modification Notes

If you are modifying an existing system, your functional testing should be restricted to the areas where you have made modifications. The purpose of functional tests should be to test only your new functionality.

However, it's a good idea to also add some regression test cases that can help make sure that your modifications aren't creating new errors. If the current project was tested using MS Test or another automated tool, you may be able to use an existing script for your regression test.

Debugging the Process

A common problem during functional testing is unclear test instructions. One way to avoid unclear or ambiguous instructions is to have the person who writes the test case execute the test during the functional test.

Unfortunately, the person that originally wrote the test instruction may not be available. If you're a developer working alone, you may not remember what the instruction was meant to do. If you can't decipher a test instruction, the best thing to do is to write a new one and replace the existing instruction. If this happens frequently, you may want to investigate automated testing, or better test plan reviews.

17

18

System-Level and
Alpha Testing

Now that you have successfully passed the function test, today you will learn two more test phases: system-level testing and a limited release of the application to test users, known as alpha testing. The *alpha test* is a prerun for the beta trial that will be run on Day 19, "Beta Testing." Preparing and running the alpha tests are covered today.

The system-level testing will be the last test phase that has formal, structured test cases. You'll learn how system-level testing differs from functional testing, and how you can use system-level testing to make your alpha and beta users happier. Along the way, you will also fix a couple of bugs discovered in InfoMan, and you'll build a setup program.

Creating a Setup Program

During the function test, you concentrated on making sure that each function worked correctly. Today you will look at the system as a whole package, including the application itself, the documentation, and the setup program.

All Windows applications should have a Windows-based setup program. There's nothing like using a DOS-based setup program as the first introduction to a new application. Supplying an easy-to-use setup program for your users is the first step to making them happy with your program.

It's important for you to start building your setup application now. If you wait until the product is about to be released, you run the risk of shipping a buggy installation program. By creating your setup program now, you will be able to try it out during the alpha, beta, and system-level testing.

What is Windows Setup?

There are several third-party setup packages that are available to help you create installation programs. Some of these are shareware; some cost hundreds of dollars. All of them perform the same basic task: installing your application on the user's PC and interacting with the user through a Windows application.

If you have the Win32 SDK, you have access to the Setup ToolKit provided by Microsoft. If you don't have the SDK, you can still create a Windows-based help program by using a third-party commercial or shareware-setup utility.

Showstopper: Whatever you do, don't try to write your own installation package. There are a lot of issues involved with writing a good setup package, and it's unlikely that you could write a new one in a short period of time.

These setup programs all work in much the same way:

☐ The setup program copies itself into a temporary directory on the user's PC.

☐ The program asks the user for installation information.

☐ The setup program copies the application from the distribution disks, and performs any Windows initializations that are required.

Some setup packages will make these steps easier for you as an application developer. Some of them also have bells and whistles that you can use to make your setup program easier for the user, or snazzier, depending on your outlook on setup programs. Figure 18.1 shows the relationship between the user's PC, the setup program, and your application.

Some setup packages also let you specify how the user can uninstall your application. Because many Windows applications modify startup files used by Windows and install files in the Windows system directory, it can be difficult to remove an application cleanly. More and more users are asking that Windows applications have uninstall utilities that are as easy to use as a setup program.

Figure 18.1.
The relationship between the setup program and the application.

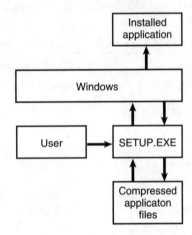

For InfoMan, the setup program was created using the Microsoft Setup ToolKit. This package is included in the Windows SDK. The steps you use for Microsoft Setup are also similar to most other forms of setup.

Using the Microsoft Setup ToolKit

For Win32, the Microsoft Setup ToolKit has a new interface that enables you to write your setup programs in the C programming language. This toolkit is documented in *Books On-Line*, but the steps required to create a setup program aren't really very clear, and there's only a single sample setup program in the SDK.

Creating a List of Application Files

The first step in creating your setup program is to make a list of the files that are needed to run your application. This includes all of the data files, DLLs, EXEs, HLP files, and anything else that needs to be copied to the user's hard disk.

Don't forget to include files that aren't installed in the user's directory, but are needed by your application, such as fonts, system DLLs, and other files. Recently, there have been problems with applications installing shared system files like CTL3D.DLL improperly. For example, most 16-bit Windows applications that have 3D effects use CTL3D.DLL to provide the 3D shading effect. If an application installs CTL3D.DLL in the wrong directory, or ignores the version control information and overwrites a newer version of the file, other applications that the user has installed may stop working correctly. Every redistributable file that is provided in the SDK has instructions that specify exactly how to install it, so make sure you know what your application needs, and where to install redistributable files.

InfoMan is a fairly small application, so it only has a few files to be installed. One file that it needs is MFC30.DLL. Because you are still using the debug of this file version until the beta tests, you will use MFC30D.DLL. Table 18.1 shows the list of files InfoMan needs to have installed.

Table 18.1. Files used by InfoMan and their default locations.

File	Default Location
INFO.EXE	C:\INFOMAN
INFO.HLP	C:\INFOMAN
RELNOTES.TXT	C:\INFOMAN
CTL3D32.DLL	C:\WINNT\SYSTEM
MFC30D.DLL	C:\WINNT\SYSTEM

For every file, also note whether it is a shared file and whether the installation should fail if the file cannot be copied. RELNOTES.TXT is a file that should not cause an entire installation to fail because it is just a text file that will contain late-breaking information for the user.

You should also group your files by their destinations, known as *sections*. Every file that is copied to the user's hard disk must belong to a section.

Planning the Setup Dialog Boxes

The next step in creating your setup program is to create a tree that shows the path that a user can take during your setup program. The first version of setup used by InfoMan is very simple, and there is very little interaction with the end user. Figure 18.2 shows the possible paths that a user might take through the first version of the InfoMan setup program.

Figure 18.2.

A tree that shows the possible paths through InfoMan's setup program.

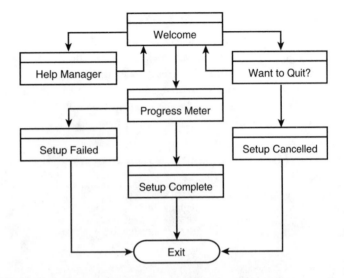

The file DIALOGS.RC supplied with the Setup ToolKit contains all of the standard setup dialog boxes displayed to the user. You can edit the dialog boxes in this file using the resource editor in Visual C++, as shown in Figure 18.3.

18

Figure 18.3.

Editing the setup dialog boxes using the Visual C++ resource editor.

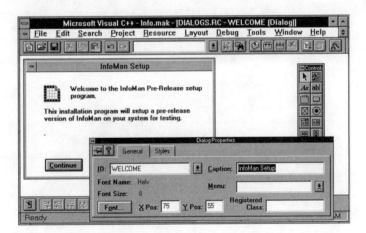

After you have edited the dialog boxes and other resources, build a new version of MSCUISTF.DLL and copy DLL, LIB, and EXP files into the setup source directory. MSCUISTF.DLL contains all of the user information and resources for the setup program. If you want to add wallpaper, billboards, or additional dialog boxes, add them to MSCUISTF.DLL.

Creating Your Setup Program

Your next step is to modify the SETUP.C program to install your application. The setup program used for InfoMan can be found on the CD, so you have two samples to compare. The first version of the InfoMan setup program doesn't have many of the features that are commonly part of a Windows setup program. The setup program used in the final version of InfoMan has more features, and will be discussed in Day 20, "Release." The WinMain function for the first InfoMan setup program is shown in Listing 18.1.

Listing 18.1. The WinMain function used by the first InfoMan setup program.

```
INT PASCAL WinMain( HANDLE hInstance,
                    HANDLE hPrevInstance,
                    LPSTR  szCmdLineArgs,
                    INT    nCmdShow)
{
    hInst = hInstance;

    if( InitSetupToolkit( szCmdLineArgs ) > 0 )
    {
        if( FInitRegDb() )
        {
            //Start setting up the application. This is
            //where you can create your wallpaper background
            SetTitle("InfoMan System and Alpha Test Setup");
            ReadInfFile( SzCatStr(szCurDir, "info.inf") );

            lstrcpy(szInstallPath, "C:\\INFOMAN\\");
            GetSymbolValue("STF_SRCDIR", szSrcDir, cchMax);

            WelcomeDialog();

            BuildLists();
            Install();
            TerminateRegDb();
        }
        EndSetupToolkit();
    }
    exit(0);
    return(0);
}
```

With the new Setup ToolKit, you have complete access to the Win32 API. If you have experience using the Win32 API functions directly, you will probably like this method better than the older Setup ToolKit, which used a form of Test Basic as its scripting language.

Creating Your Disk Images

After the setup program is completed, you need to build your distribution disks using the DSKLAYT utility. This program helps lay out your files and collect compression and other

options from you. It also creates an INF file, which will be used to create the actual distribution disks.

Before you use DSKLAYT, it's a good idea to copy the files needed by the Setup ToolKit, including the setup DLLs, into their own directory. Figure 18.4 shows DSKLAYT being used to build the INF files for InfoMan.

Figure 18.4.
Using DSKLAYT to configure your setup distribution disks.

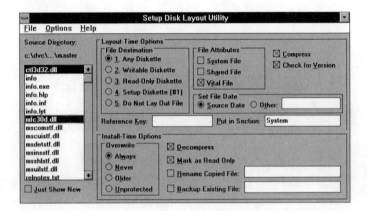

The next step is to use the DSKLAYT2 program to actually create your distribution disks. Think of the DSKLAYT and DSKLAYT2 utilities as the equivalent of a make command for your distribution disks.

That's all there is to creating a simple setup program. You will improve this program on Day 19.

System-Level Testing

System-level testing, or system testing, is the last structured test phase before the application is released. It actually looks a lot like functional testing, and many organizations run system-level tests as part of their functional testing.

Another name for this type of testing is acceptance testing, in which the application is tested at a high level to make sure that it works as expected. Whatever you choose to call it, you should run these tests before you release your application to alpha or beta tests.

Understanding the System Test

The *system test* is a short test phase in which you can verify that the system works correctly at a high level. This differs from functional testing, in which you tested a single function at a time. During the system test, you put the application into high-stress conditions and verify that the

application still works as expected. The application should also be tested to make sure that it cooperates well with the operating system and other applications.

The purpose of these system-level tests is to exercise the application under stress in a controlled environment. After the application is released, users will encounter these situations; if the application fails, the failures will be reported as faults. However, many of the situations may be difficult for the user to reproduce, so the fault information that is received is likely to be inaccurate or incomplete.

The tests that are executed during the system test were defined on Day 3, "Test Planning."

Goals for System Testing

The goals for system testing are to find all of the faults that prevent the application from working well at a high level. You have probably used Windows applications that didn't perform well under stress or worked poorly with other applications. Some of the faults that should be detected during system test include the following:

- ☐ Handling low-memory conditions
- ☐ Memory and resource leaks
- ☐ Faults that occur on minimum machines
- ☐ Faults caused by unexpected user input

The purpose of these tests is not to rerun all of your functional tests; ideally, none of these tests should be found in your functional tests.

Executing the System Test

Executing a system test should be very similar to executing your functional tests. You should run all of your tests from the test plans that were created on Day 3. If you discover faults, you should record them on incident reports. Also, you should record the results from the system tests in the same way you recorded your function tests.

There are some new areas to test during the system test. For this test phase, the documentation should be available—if not in a final form, it should at least be a very good draft. Also, the setup program should be ready so you can correct any problems discovered with the setup application.

If you are part of a large development organization that includes a support team, you may want to have that group participate in the system test. The advantage of using the support team is that they might have some real-world experience with support issues, and can probably help execute the system tests very effectively.

 **Developer's Tip:** A tool that can help you trace hard-to-find memory leaks and other errors is Bounds-Checker, available from Nu-Mega. Bounds-Checker launches your application and tracks all of the resource and memory allocated and used by it. If resources or memory are leaked or used improperly, an error message is displayed, usually with enough information to help you fix the problem on the spot.

Although this program isn't cheap, it's a bargain if you have some hard-to-find memory problems.

Preparing for Alpha Testing

Congratulations, you have finished all of the structured testing for your application. Now you begin the process of moving the application out into the real world. One problem with software testing is that it is very difficult to anticipate exactly what sort of demands the user is going to place on your software.

Understanding the Alpha Test

One way to get feedback from end users about your finished application is to run alpha and beta tests (also known as alpha and beta trials). During these test phases, you select users to help you verify that your application is both useful and bug-free.

An alpha test is an early version of the beta test. Running a beta test is covered on Day 19. An alpha test is generally limited to very few users and is used to verify that the application is suitable for use outside the development team or a small circle of friends. Beta testing involves a somewhat larger audience, and the final release will hopefully be used by millions of satisfied customers. Figure 18.5 shows how the number of users increases as you move through these phases.

The alpha and beta tests are different from any of your earlier tests because they are unstructured. You really don't have any control over what a user will do with your application once you've distributed it. Any errors that are discovered during alpha and beta tests must be counted as pure luck because there is no way to specify the tests that are to be executed.

18

Figure 18.5.
The number of users for an application increases through the test phases and release.

Pre-Release		◯ Development Team
Alpha		◯ Small group of test users
Beta		⬭ Expanded group of users
Final		⬭ Available to the world

Showstopper: The alpha test should be restricted to a small number of test users, and should be as short as possible. Your primary goal is usually to establish that the application is suitable for a wider beta test.

During the alpha test, you are still getting your procedures in place for supporting the end users, and you're still finishing up your documentation. If you have a large alpha test, you will need to support a large number of users for a product that is still being finished.

Hopefully, your alpha testers will use your application in their daily work. You can use the feedback about the program and the documentation to help make your beta test more successful.

Choosing an Alpha User

An ideal alpha test user is someone with close ties to the development team. It's important that the tester be able to help you track down faults in the application and be comfortable reinstalling or reconfiguring the application if needed.

The ideal alpha tester is also

- ☐ Committed to using the application
- ☐ Technically advanced
- ☐ More organized than a typical user

For these reasons, alpha tests are generally run with members of the development team. If you're working alone, you can draft family members or close friends as part of your alpha team.

A Checklist for Starting the Alpha Test

Before you start the alpha test, you should run through a checklist to make sure that you're really ready. Remember, this is the beginning of a whole new style of testing for your application; it's going out into the cold, cruel world, so take a few minutes to make sure that it's really ready.

The start criteria that you use will be tailored to your own project. For an application like InfoMan, the following items will be on the alpha checklist:

- [ ] All previous test phases have been successfully completed
- [ ] End-user documents are ready for distribution to alpha testers
- [ ] The alpha team is defined
- [ ] The support plan for the alpha team is defined

As with the start criteria that you defined for other test phases, the purpose of defining the requirements is to help your test run smoothly. The preceding list should be used as a starting point for defining your own test-entry criteria. Any special requirements that are needed for your application's alpha testing, such as special training for the test team, should be included in the start criteria.

Running the Alpha Test

Unlike the previous test phases, the alpha test doesn't involve a lot of testing by the developer. Most of the work that you'll be doing is distributing the application and supporting the alpha testers. When problems are reported, you'll need to verify that the problems exist and supply updates to the alpha users.

You should be prepared to supply several updates to your alpha testers, as well as provide support for any problems that they may find. It's important to use this phase to help get the wrinkles out of your support procedures.

Supplying the Application to Alpha Users

The first step in the alpha-testing process is to supply the application to the alpha-test users. This is more than just sending them a disk in the mail. You also need to send them the current documentation, a list of known errors, and information about product support.

You should try to make the package you send to the alpha-test users as complete as possible. Include an accurate setup program and any documentation that's ready to be used. Depending on your application, this may mean a great deal of coordination before the alpha version is released. However, it's much better to put in the extra work now, so the entire product can be tested during the alpha test.

18

Collecting Feedback from Alpha Users

The purpose of the alpha test is to get early feedback from some early users of your application. It is important to try to get that feedback as quickly and as accurately as possible. One of the criteria for selecting members of the alpha test team was their technical ability. Hopefully, that will translate into incident reports that are technically accurate.

One thing that you can do to help improve the quality of the reports from the field is to make it easy for your alpha testers to report problems. This probably means that you need to modify the incident reports that were used during the development process.

Anything that you can do to make reporting easier will increase the amount of feedback you receive. If users feel that reporting problems is more trouble than it's worth, you will receive fewer incident reports. Unfortunately, it won't be due to a lack of problems in your application. Those faults will still be there, waiting for a customer with the retail release to find it.

If some alpha testers aren't reporting any problems, don't assume that they're having no problems. They may be having problems and not reporting them, or they may not have installed the package yet. Hunt your testers down if necessary to get feedback about the alpha version of your program.

Distributing Updates

The alpha testers also should receive regular updates throughout the alpha test period. If you create new versions of the application, you should update all of your users. This also applies to bug lists or documentation that is updated.

It's important to keep the entire test team using the same release. If some users are running an older version of the application, they will be rediscovering problems that have already been corrected. Worse, they may not be finding faults in the new version of the application.

Showstopper: Don't let your alpha test team shrink out of sight. Remember, the purpose of the alpha test is to pave the way for the beta test that follows. If you allow the alpha testers to start using multiple versions of your application, the alpha test team will shrink, because only a subset of the original team is still using the latest software.

If you are planning to have a very short alpha-test phase, there may not need to be any updates. For example, a small program like InfoMan would plan for only a single alpha-test phase. However, you should still have a plan in place in case updates are needed. A quick, simple plan written now will go a long way if you need to send out an update to all of your alpha testers.

Testing the End-User Documentation

An important part of the alpha test is the end-user documentation. All along during the development process, you've been handing out partially functioning versions of the application to friends and coworkers. However, no one outside the development team has actually tried to use the end-user documentation.

It's important that all of the aspects of the application be tested. That's why a version setup program was created for the system and alpha tests. Do your best to try to get the alpha-test team to use the documentation.

Distributing Your End-User Documentation

The end-user documentation should be distributed to the alpha testers along with the application. At the very least, they should have access to the parts of the documentation that deal with installation and error handling, so that they can give you feedback about it.

There is still some time before the application is officially released, and many times the documents aren't completely ready. That's not unusual, and it's not a big problem, as long as some information is available. If parts of the end-user documentation are still in rough-draft form, or if some of the online help isn't quite finished, it is still worthwhile to get some feedback about the existing documentation.

> **Developer's Tip:** Any time you prepare to send out an unfinished product, you should make it very clear to the end user that you know it's incomplete. Especially in alpha and beta trials, you don't want to waste the tester's time with reports about incomplete documentation if you know it's not finished.

As you finish the documentation, you should distribute it as soon as possible to the alpha testers so that you can get some feedback before the beta begins.

Updating Your Documentation

Feedback about the documentation will usually be received along with reports about the rest of the application. It's important that the end-user documentation be as close to error-free as possible for the beta tests. For that reason, you should be ready to release documentation updates as quickly as possible.

The process of updating the end-user documents was covered on Day 15, "Developing End-User Documentation." Review the topics from that day that relate to the system and alpha tests.

Updates Due to Application Changes

After you enter the alpha-test period, changes to the application should cause very few changes to the documentation. However, it does happen, especially when serious usability problems are discovered.

When you need to change the documentation because the application has changed, the program and the documentation should be distributed together. Nothing will disrupt your testing more than having an application that doesn't match the documentation.

Even if it means a delay in releasing an update, wait for the documentation to be released before sending out a new version of your application that has user interface changes. Otherwise, you'll spend a great deal of time supporting a problem that could have been avoided. You will also miss the opportunity to have the new documentation reviewed during the alpha test.

Correcting Documentation Errors in General

The other source of feedback about the documentation is incident reports describing faults in the documentation. When you receive an incident report about the documentation, there are five steps that you should follow:

☐ Verify that the problem exists.

☐ Make sure the application is not at fault.

☐ Add the correction to the errata list.

☐ Add the correction to the end-user documentation.

☐ Correct the online help if necessary.

A lot of coordination is required at this stage to make sure that updates for the documentation are handled correctly. Corrections in the application and end-user documents can easily become unsynchronized. If they do, you will have to spend a lot of extra time supporting the alpha testers unnecessarily.

Developer's Tip: One way to release updated documentation inexpensively is to release it as a README file that is distributed with application updates. If there are a large number of changes, it may be more appropriate to create a full errata list that is formatted like the documentation.

This won't completely take the place of documentation updates because it's awkward for the end user. However, it is much easier and faster than printing updated documentation.

Documenting the System and Alpha Tests

The documentation for the system test will look a lot like the documentation created for the functional testing on Day 17, "Functional Testing." As a minimum, you should document:

- [ ] **Incident reports.** You should track incident reports for all of your tests. These reports will be useful when you design test cases for the next release.
- [ ] **Application changes.** Any changes made to the application should be noted.
- [ ] **Test-execution reports.** Tracking this information will help you see which test cases need to be updated in the future.

In addition to the system-test documentation, you should also document your alpha-testing activities. There are no formal tests executed during the alpha test, but you should track the incident reports and application changes.

Modification Notes

You should reuse existing tools whenever possible. If you are modifying an existing project, there may be some existing tools used to help exercise the application during system testing. For example, if you write financial software, there may be a collection of test data used to validate previous releases.

If the project that is being modified has used alpha and beta testers for earlier releases, there may be existing procedures for selecting alpha-test participants. In fact, there may be a pool of volunteers that have been used for alpha testing in the past.

Debugging the Process

One problem that often occurs during system and alpha testing is that you may fail to meet the exit criteria for the test phase. There are two possible reasons for failing to meet your preplanned criteria:

- [ ] The exit conditions are too difficult.
- [ ] The product isn't ready.

You won't be doing yourself any favors by moving the project into the next phase before it is ready. If the product is not ready to move into beta testing, it's almost always better to continue alpha testing.

Beta Testing

Today you'll learn about the process of beta testing your application. It is actually a lot like the alpha testing that you did on Day 18, "System-Level and Alpha Testing," although beta testing differs from alpha testing because it is usually distributed to a larger group of users. Usually, the beta test will have more participants than the alpha test.

The wider audience for the beta means that you will need to spend more time supporting the testers and distributing updates than during the alpha test. Today you'll learn different support options, as well as methods for receiving feedback.

After the beta is finished, your application will be ready for release (which is covered on Day 20, "Release"). Before you get to that point, you'll learn some ways to help you squeeze out any remaining bugs in your application.

Beta-Test Overview

During the alpha test for your application, which was covered on Day 18, you distributed your application to a small group of test users. Those users (hopefully) gave you some feedback about improving your application for the real release.

Textbook Tip: Don't use the same team for your alpha and beta tests if possible. The purpose of having two stages of acceptance testing is to allow the program to be evaluated by two separate types of users.

The alpha-test participants should be familiar with the product, and technically capable of helping you track down problems with the application.

The beta test should be more wide open, and match your target audience more closely than the alpha test. It is okay to include alpha-test participants in the beta, just be sure to also include some new users.

The Purpose of Beta Testing

The purpose of the beta test is to prove that your application runs under a wide range of conditions. One way to achieve this is to distribute the application to a group of potential users. These users then report any problems that they find, and you reward them with free copies of your application, T-shirts, and a release party.

Beta testing cannot take the place of functional or system-level testing. It works best when it is used as a tool to help you get a large number of users to try your application in their day-to-day work. The major benefit you receive from having your application beta tested is a little more

exposure to the real world. Figure 19.1 shows an example of how beta testing relates to some of the previous test phases.

Figure 19.1.
As the application moves closer to release, it is exposed to a little more of the real world in every new test phase.

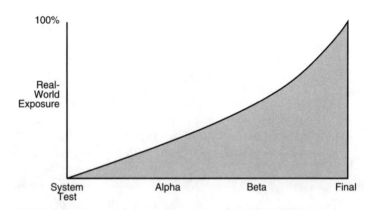

You should think of beta testing as a sort of acceptance test, instead of a real test phase like functional or regression testing. It is very difficult to substitute an unstructured test phase like the beta for the structured functional testing covered on Day 17, "Functional Testing." If your beta isn't close to bug-free and you start your beta testing anyway, you'll wind up with a buggy product and upset beta testers.

Beta testing is very good for discovering interaction problems between applications, or problems with certain hardware configurations. If you have run a good series of tests to this point, your beta test phase will probably be very short.

The Goals of Beta Testing

During beta testing, try to get as much feedback as possible in a short period of time. One of the most important things you can do to help your beta run smoothly is to improve any rough spots discovered during your alpha testing.

Remember, the alpha and beta tests are a bridge between the structured testing you do during the development cycle and the actual release of your application. Use the alpha trial as a proving ground for the beta, and you'll have a much more successful release.

Beta Test Entry Criteria

When you started the alpha test on Day 18, some of the support and documentation may not have been ready. That's okay, because the alpha-test users are generally technically oriented, and the alpha test is a very limited release. However, the beta test has more participants, and there is a wide range in the technical ability of the users. This places more demands on the support and documentation supplied for the beta. As discussed earlier, the product should be as stable as possible to cut down on the amount of support required.

The beta test is your last chance to try out your application on a group of real-world users before the general release. It is also your last chance to make sure that other parts of your release process are working correctly. Take the extra time needed to assess results from the alpha test and consider how your documentation, support, and fault-resolution activities can be improved.

If you had problems supporting the alpha users with updates, documentation, or bug fixes, you should address those areas before you begin the beta testing. You will get three different chances to put your product, including support, in place: the alpha, beta, and final releases. Figure 19.2 shows these releases as iterations, with the entire project improving between releases.

Figure 19.2.

The entire application, including support, should improve during the alpha and beta tests.

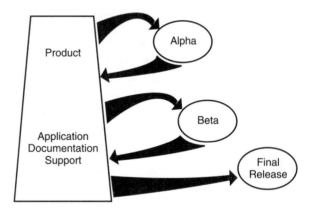

Planning Your Documentation for the Beta

The end-user documentation must be complete before the start of the beta test. This will give you a good test of the complete product, including the documentation, before it is released to the final users.

You should deliver your documentation in its final form if possible. If you're planning to offer online help as a standard feature, and the hard-copy, end-user documentation as an option, break your beta testers into groups that reflect the different options.

If the application is delivered in more than one configuration—for example, "light" and "professional" versions—make sure that the beta testers get the documentation that matches their version of the application. The idea here is to avoid discovering important information missing from one of your documentations after the final product is shipped.

Planning Your Beta Support

You should use the beta test to determine the support that you will provide after the release. Unlike the alpha test, you will probably need to provide more comprehensive support for your beta-test users. In fact, the amount of support that you can provide to the beta testers should determine the number of participants in the beta.

Showstopper: Support is a real problem for smaller development teams. Many times you may see a product offered for beta test with limited support, or even no support at all. This is not a good idea. You should make sure you give support to beta testers who have problems with your application, so that you can improve your product.

The primary goal for your beta test is not to just pass a few weeks while the user documentation is being printed. The real goal is to improve the product, and that means reaching out to your testers.

There are several support options that you can use for beta testing. Most users would love for you to provide full, 100-percent support until the application is released. Even if you are working alone, you should try to provide as much support as possible.

Of course, the amount of support that you provide also depends on the application that you're offering. If you are beta testing a small program like InfoMan, support via e-mail, with updates released at fixed intervals during the test period, is probably sufficient. On the other hand, if you're testing critical software, such as that used for a telecommunications network, the support offered during beta testing will be greater than the normal level.

The amount of support that is offered for your application can probably be split into three different levels:

- ☐ **Full support.** The product receives at least as much support as it would receive for a normal release. Some mission-critical applications may actually receive a higher level of support. Bug fixes may be addressed individually, so that the user suffers the minimum amount of down time. This type of support is very expensive for you to provide, but you will get the maximum benefit from your beta test if you offer full support to your testers.

- ☐ **Partial support.** The product receives less than full support. Reports of troubles may be handled via e-mail or a BBS. Updates to correct problems with the beta are sent on a scheduled basis. Very few, if any, faults are fixed immediately. This type of support is less expensive than full support. Because it creates more work for your testers, you

19

may not get the benefit from your beta test. You should offer this type of support if you need to test with a large number of beta testers, but can't afford to offer full support.

☐ **Unsupported.** If the product is unsupported, the user is expected to report problems via e-mail or BBS, but will not receive any sort of assistance setting up or using the application. Updates may or may not be supplied after the original beta distribution. This type of beta test is not very useful unless you use it as a marketing tool. You will receive very little feedback if you offer this type of support.

The amount of support that you plan to provide during the beta test should be somewhat related to the support planned for the official release. If the product is an unsupported freeware application, it would be unusual to offer full support during a beta test, if a beta test was even run at all. However, most applications do offer some level of support, even if it's an application that you distribute just among your friends. During the beta test, you're not just dealing with testers; you're dealing with potential customers, and support is a valuable part of your application.

Outstanding Faults

Usually, there will be a few faults left hanging around after your alpha test is completed. Because the alpha testers are still using your application, you may still be receiving some incident reports. Depending on the type of application being developed, it's probably okay to enter your beta test with a few minor outstanding faults from the alpha test.

However, you should not release a buggy beta version of your program to the beta testers. There is a difference between a few small cosmetic errors and faults that actually prevent full use of the application. The former is usually acceptable; the latter is not.

The goal of your beta test is to verify that no faults can be found in your application. The cleaner your application is when it enters the beta test, the easier this goal will be to reach.

Last-Minute Improvements

In general, you should avoid doing any changes during the beta. For all practical purposes, the project is now closed for new functionality. Note that this means changes to the program's functionality or user interface that would require user-documentation updates and a lot of regression testing.

However, there are a few cases in which you may need to make changes at the last minute. You should continue to fix any faults that have been reported, as during previous test phases.

Adding Last-Minute Changes

You should consider only a few changes to your application during the beta test. Any changes that are added will take away resources that could be assisting beta users and fixing problems, so choose your changes carefully.

One area that will be changed for InfoMan is the setup program. A new bit map will be used for the logo displayed during the application setup. This is the sort of change that really has very little functional impact on the application, but makes the program a little bit nicer to use.

To create a bit map for the application setup logo, use Paintbrush or another drawing program and create a two-color bit map that is white on black. Figure 19.3 shows the InfoMan logo inside Paintbrush.

Figure 19.3.
Creating a new logo for setup using Paintbrush.

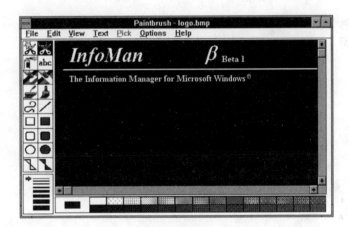

The area to the right of the InfoMan logo can be used to display the current program version. It says "Beta 1" now, but as one of the final stages in preparing for the final release, it will be changed to "Version 1.0."

You may also notice that the setup program that is used for the beta test is a little more user-friendly than the version used for the alpha testing. The new version asks the user for a destination directory for InfoMan's installation, instead of always using the C:\INFOMAN directory.

Prioritizing Changes

Changes that are added to the application late in the beta should be prioritized. Only changes that have an extremely high priority should be considered. Remember, any changes that are made to the application will need to be tested and documented. If the change doesn't fix a fault in the application, it may be better to wait until the next release of your application.

 Textbook Tip: The chances of introducing a new fault when correcting an existing fault or making a change has been calculated at up to 50 percent by some studies. Many of these faults are eventually corrected, of course, but the risk is still real.

When changes are made to your application late in the development cycle, it can be difficult to catch errors created by the modification. During the beta test, it can be almost impossible.

Learning to Say No

If you turn down requests for new functionality, you will probably need to defend your decision. The trick is to do it in such a way that the beta user knows that their feedback is valuable. One way to do that is to accept changes and feedback when you aren't close to your final release deadline. If users know that this is due to your concern about the product quality, you have a better chance of keeping them happy.

You should also let them know when the change will be added to a future release. The best way to make your users happy with a deferred request is to make sure that it's eventually added to the release.

Running the Beta Test

Running the beta test will be similar to the alpha test. However, because there will be more users, everything will get bigger. There will be more updates, more incident reports, and more requests for improvements for your application.

 Note: You're probably stretched to the breaking point now, trying to support the beta test while finishing up the alpha test. That's why so much emphasis was placed on functionally completing the application by the end of the system test.

Selecting Beta-Test Sites

Selecting beta users is a lot like finding users for the alpha test. However, you should try to find users with a wider range of backgrounds and hardware for your beta test.

One problem with using developers as your beta testers is that they will generally have more modern hardware than the typical user. Try to find users who are using the minimum Windows platform. That means users with old dot-matrix printers, monochrome or VGA displays, and very little RAM. You should also try to find a user to test your application on a laptop.

You should always try to find users that are running in environments different from your own. For example, look for users who run on a different type of network or users who are running different shell utilities, like Symantec's Norton Desktop.

If you know any users that run international versions of Windows, sign them up as beta testers. Many applications run into problems in an international setting.

> **Developer's Tip:** If you don't know any international users, you may want to try out your application using one of the international versions of Windows that are included in the Microsoft Developer Network (MSDN) Level 2 subscription package.
>
> Access to international versions of Windows is just one of the benefits to subscribing to MSDN Level 2, which also includes just about every SDK available for Windows development.

Supporting the Beta

19

As discussed earlier, the amount of support that you offer during the beta will depend on your application and your organization. You should definitely meet any support commitments that you made at the beginning of the beta. If you are offering full or partial support, you should acknowledge receipt of any support requests or incident reports as soon as possible. This will improve your level of support in two ways: duplicate reports will be reduced when you acknowledge receiving them; and testers will feel that you really are looking into their reports.

If you are working alone or in a small team, there are a few things that you can do to help make your support more efficient. One of the best things that you can do is to make your support as automated as possible. If you can spend time on beta test support as needed, rather than whenever a tester has a problem, you'll be much more efficient. A few ideas for providing better than average support:

☐ **Set up a BBS.** A bulletin-board system for beta support is an easy way to provide support to your beta testers. If most of your users have access to a modem, you can accept incident reports and provide bug fixes via your BBS. All you need is a phone number, a modem, and some BBS shareware.

- ☐ **Use e-mail for incident reports.** If you have an Internet address or an account with a major online provider (CIS, AOL, Delphi, Prodigy), you can provide support for most problems via e-mail.

- ☐ **Set up an FTP area.** If you and your beta testers have access to the Internet's File Transfer Protocol (FTP), you can set up an FTP location where testers can pick up new versions and drop off incident reports. This works only if your users have FTP access, so it may be only a partial solution unless you require your users to have access to FTP.

- ☐ **Create a WWW home page.** Providing information via the World Wide Web (WWW) is the hot ticket right now if you need access to a large number of people. If you have Internet access, you can provide a hypertext-based home page that works a lot like a combination BBS and online help system hooked up to the Internet.

All of these options have something in common. They offer convenience to you and your beta testers. You can update the BBS or WWW home page when it is convenient for you, and users can send e-mail or pick up the latest release via FTP when it's convenient for them.

You may not be able to use all of these options for your application; it depends on your beta participants, as well as your own resources. However, if you can provide support electronically, you will be much more efficient.

Supplying Updates to the Beta Testers

In most cases, there should be at least two beta distributions. The first release is the general beta, which will be used by all of the beta testers. There is almost always at least one release candidate—that is, a test release you believe is complete, and shipped just prior to the official release. Handling release candidates is discussed later today.

As was covered in the previous support section, there are several different ways to send updates to your beta testers. In general, you should try to send as many updates to as many testers as possible.

Collecting Feedback

On Day 18, you created a form that was used for feedback from the tester to the development team. You can continue to use that form, or you can develop a new one that is tailored to beta testers.

Just as in the alpha test, the form should encourage testers to provide as much information as possible. If you receive reports that don't have enough information to help isolate the problem, you will spend a lot of time collecting that information from the user.

Unlike the alpha testers, some of your beta testers may be relatively inexperienced when testing prerelease software. For their benefit, you should provide some examples of beta incident reports with information filled in properly. This will make their job easier, and give you better report information.

Automated Reporting Tools

Many companies have started providing automated reporting tools with their beta software. This software can make it easier for the user to report faults, and easier for you to use the reporting information at the same time. Figure 19.4 is a figure showing how these tools work.

Figure 19.4.
Using automated tools can make problem reporting easier.

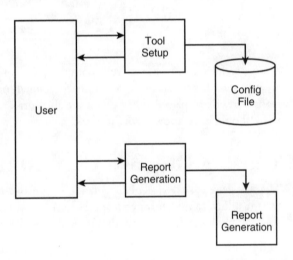

The first step is for the tool to collect information from the user when it is installed. Information about the user's name, address, registration, and hardware configuration is collected and stored in a database.

When the user has a problem that needs to be reported, the application is launched, and the user fills in a report interactively. This helps to ensure that the incident report is filled out as completely as possible.

Feedback Examples from InfoMan

During the InfoMan beta, two problems were reported by end users. One was reported about the setup program, and another was a fault in the actual application. The new setup banner that included a Greek beta symbol apparently confused a few of the beta testers. That has been removed, and Version 1.0 is now displayed instead. The new version of the setup screen is shown in Figure 19.5.

Figure 19.5.
Creating a new and less confusing logo using Paintbrush.

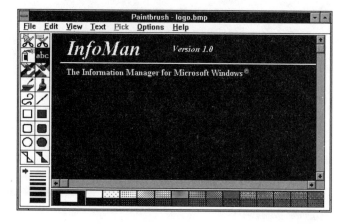

A more serious report was received about the behavior of InfoMan's child windows when they are minimized. Because no icons had been defined for the individual documents, the default icons were still displayed. The new release also corrects this problem. Because every document really should have its own icon, it would have been an embarrassing error to have released.

Creating Release Candidates

After you have corrected all of the outstanding problems reported from the beta test, you should create a release candidate for your application. A *release candidate* is a version of your application that will be shipped, providing that no faults are discovered in it.

At this point, the project should be moving very quickly, and you are probably not planning to do much testing. The release candidate will only be sent out for a last and final check before the actual release. Most development organizations ship release candidates to a small number of testers.

When you distribute the release candidate make sure that the testers who receive it know that immediate feedback is needed. This is one reason why the release candidate is sometimes shipped to a subset of the entire beta-test team. For the release candidate, turnaround time during testing is an important goal.

The number of release candidates required varies from project to project. If your release candidates have problems that prevent them from becoming the final release, you may have to create several release candidates. If no faults are discovered in the release candidate, your testing is complete, and you can begin the process of releasing your application. Figure 19.6 is a flowchart that shows the procedure for releasing updated betas and release candidates of your application.

Figure 19.6.
A flowchart showing how betas and release candidates are updated.

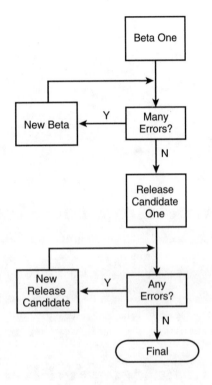

Exit Criteria

The exit criteria for the beta test should be straightforward. If you're happy with the application, the beta test is over. Unfortunately, different people will have different levels of satisfaction. If you are working with a team, it's much better to use formal exit criteria as you have used for other test phases.

The release criteria for the final release will be the tightest of all of your release criteria. The reason is simple: updating a released product is very difficult. If you thought it was difficult to release an update to your friends helping you perform beta testing, you probably don't want to release a bug fix to all of your application's users.

For your exit criteria, you should define a minimum amount of time for a release candidate to be released with no major faults detected. You also should define the number of outstanding faults, if any, you are willing to accept and still release your application.

Showstopper: You should not release your application with any faults that aren't considered cosmetic problems, or minor functional problems that are well-documented. If you release a program that has a problem, you may spend more time supporting the release than it would have taken to fix the problem originally.

Keep your users happy and your support costs down, and fix all of your reported faults if you can.

Documenting the Beta Test

The documentation created during the beta test will be very much like the alpha-test documentation. Primarily, your documentation should help you determine how many faults were found during the test period, and how many of these faults were eventually fixed.

If you like, you can also keep track of your beta-test users so that you can determine which ones really participated in the beta, and which ones were more passive. Several large development organizations do this so that they can improve the quality of their beta test team.

Tracking Deferred Requests Made During the Beta

Whenever an incident report is created, there's always a possibility that you won't be able to correct the problem in the current release. Sometimes this is due to the fact that the report is received very late in the test phase. Other times, the report may require too much work to be done too close to a scheduled release.

An incident report that is postponed until it can be addressed is called *deferred*. Prior to the beta test, deferred incident reports could just be handled during the next test phase. Unfortunately, there is no "next phase" after the beta test.

Any incident reports that can't be handled during the beta should be reviewed during the requirements and design phases for the next version of your application. Deferring an incident report until the next release should be done only for reports that request new functions to be added, not for faults.

Modification Notes

If you are modifying an existing project, you are probably using some of the existing users as beta-test participants. As these users are evaluating the modifications, they may discover faults with the existing product.

There are two ways to handle problems that are reported with the existing product:

☐ Create a new incident report for the existing product and have the team responsible for that product, sometimes called a "sustaining" team, correct the problem.

☐ Investigate the problem as part of the beta test, and supply the correction to existing users.

The method that you use depends on your project and the structure of your organization. It's usually a good idea to separate sustaining faults from new faults for tracking purposes, even though the user shouldn't have to make that determination.

Debugging the Process

The most common problem that comes up during a beta test concerns support. If you have trouble providing adequate support for your beta users, the effectiveness of the beta test phase will suffer. In the worst case, beta testers will become frustrated, and problems may go unreported. This is a very dangerous situation, because it will lead to unreliable information that may cause you to end the test phase too early.

If you are having problems, try to determine the cause of the extra support load. Some common causes of heavy support costs include the following:

☐ **Applications with lots of faults.** If your application has more faults than expected, you will have a heavier demand on your resources.

☐ **Documentation that is incomplete or faulty.** If the users can't use the documentation, they will either make mistakes or be unable to do their work. Either way, it means a call for support.

☐ **Untrained beta testers.** If your application requires training or other special knowledge in order to use it, make sure that your beta testers are trained.

☐ **Lack of support resources.** After you investigate all of these causes, you may find that you just need more help in the support area.

If you can identify one of these causes as the root of your support problems, you should correct the problem. Remember, it's much easier to keep a beta-test team happy than to fix a broken one.

Release

20

Today you'll learn about the actual process of releasing your application. This is only Day 20, and there's still another day left because there's still work to be done after your application is released.

Today the material is split into several sections. Because much of the release process depends on the application and the developer, some sections may not apply to you.

The topics covered today include the following:

☐ Running your final regression tests

☐ Using a prerelease checklist

☐ Marketing your application

☐ Planning your training and support

If you think that some of these topics don't apply to your application, take a look at the sections anyway; you may find a new way to market your program or provide more attractive support for your users.

An Overview of the Release Process

After the beta test has ended, it's time to start working on the actual release of your application. There are several final steps you must take to ensure that your product is launched in the best possible way.

There are several aspects to actually releasing your first Windows application. Depending on the size and complexity of your application and your own resources, the details of the actual release of the application will vary. However, all software releases eventually boil down to the following steps:

1. Make sure the software is ready.

2. Make sure you're ready.

3. Let people know about it.

4. Get rich and move to a tropical island.

In reality, items 1 and 2 from this list often happen together. As you are making the final tests on your application, you are also double-checking yourself and your organization. Figure 20.1 shows steps 1 and 2 being executed at the same time.

In larger organizations, all of the steps may be done together, with the announcements and other marketing and sales activities done by different groups within the organization. For example, there may be a dedicated marketing staff that handles the nontechnical part of the release process.

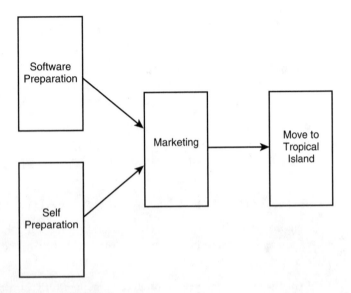

Figure 20.1.
The major steps involved in releasing a new application.

Software Preparation

Self Preparation

Marketing

Move to Tropical Island

Getting the Software Ready

Getting the software ready refers to the steps needed to move the application from the beta test into its final release form. For most small- and medium-sized projects, this step is very straightforward. There are a few common-sense steps that you should take to prevent last-minute faults from slipping into your application.

When you are preparing for the release of a large project, these steps become more complicated, and the risk involved with the release grows. However, the basic steps, which will be covered in detail later, are

☐ **Regression testing.** A final test of the application to make sure it hasn't developed a fault in its core functionality.

☐ **Building master disks.** Create the final set of release masters for your application.

☐ **Checking documentation.** Make sure that the documentation used during development is up-to-date.

Getting Yourself Ready

This step really refers to getting the entire organization or group ready, if more than one person is working on the project. This step is very simple if you are a single developer releasing a simple application. If your application is more elaborate, or if you are part of a larger organization, this step may be more complicated.

20

Marketing Your Application

Of all the different activities that make up the development of your project, marketing is the one that will vary the most between different applications. If you work as part of a large development team, there is probably an entire staff that handles this part of the development process.

If you're working alone as a single developer, you probably don't have a lot of resources to spare on marketing and selling your application. If you don't have a large budget set aside to hire marketing experts or run an advertising campaign, you should consider releasing your application as shareware, which is discussed in detail later.

Escaping to a Tropical Island

You probably will find this last step to be the most difficult. This step is probably best left up to you and your accountants, because there will probably be some limitation on the size of the island that you can escape to, at least at first.

In place of tropical retreats, most development groups substitute a "ship party," where everyone who worked on the release can celebrate the end of the project. Afterward, it will be time to start thinking about the next project or the next version of your application. Planning the next project is discussed on Day 21, "Collecting Feedback."

The Final Tests Before Shipping

The focus today is turning your last beta or release candidate into the final release of the application. The most important step in this process is the final regression test. In most cases, it's a good idea to perform a final round of regression testing before your application is shipped. The final version of the application should be able to pass your regression tests with flying colors.

Some people like to save a set of test cases for the final release, as a kind of extra check on the software's quality. These cases might be taken from earlier releases that had problems, or they may just be traditional prerelease checks that are done by that person or group before any release. Figure 20.2 shows how this looks in relation to the last few phases of your project.

The problem with this approach is that any possible problem uncovered by these tests is discovered much too late. On Day 17, "Functional Testing," you learned how to have a common base for your regression tests. If it is worthwhile to test for these faults, they should be a part of the functional-test cases, and possibly the regression tests. The purpose of structured testing is to find faults as early as possible during the release.

Figure 20.2.
Adding extra tests to a regression test prior to shipping.

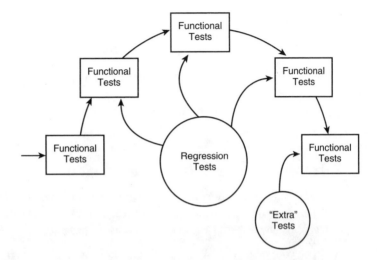

Developer's Tip: If you have been saving some test cases until the last minute, shame on you. The purpose of structured testing is to find as many faults as early as possible. Faults discovered late in the project are much more likely to cause regressions in the final release.

For the next version of your application, consider using these cases as part of your regression tests. That way these faults can be discovered earlier in the development cycle.

After you execute the regression-test cases, the development and testing phases of your application will be finished. If you discover some problems during your tests, make sure you read the next section, which discusses how to handle faults discovered during the release process.

Change Management at Release

As you prepare the software for its final release, you should take care to ensure that your application is as bug-free as possible. The final results from the beta test have been received, and the release candidate that you have sent out has received excellent feedback. The application has passed the final regression test with no errors. You have a green light, and you're ready to ship.

At this moment, just as you are getting ready to wrap up the project, it seems as if there is always one last change that needs to be made. Maybe it's fixing a display that doesn't look quite right, or changing the wording of an error message.

In anything but extraordinary circumstances, you should avoid making any changes to your application. You first started limiting changes on Day 17 as you were ending the functional tests. Now is the time to stop all changes, unless they correct a fault that severely impacts the application.

Closing the Change Door

In any well-crafted project, there is always a desire to make the application as perfect as possible. When this is translated into rigorous testing and attention to detail, your application will be well-received. Or at least, it won't crash because of programming errors.

When your desire to make the perfect application results in a large number of changes, you may have problems, especially at the end of the project. Every project will have different needs; some projects may require changes right up until release. However, if changes are allowed to continue this late in a project

☐ Your end-user documentation will be affected

☐ You will need to update design documents

☐ You will have to rerun regression tests, and probably generate a new release candidate

☐ The final release will be delayed

Showstopper: At the end of a project it's not unusual for people to have a small laundry list of things to do. Often, one of these things is to install a project-credit screen, or "Easter Egg." If this involves adding new code to your project, there's a good chance that you are introducing a fault into your application.

How impressed will your users be if your Easter Egg causes problems in low memory or certain types of video drivers? How happy will they be if your credit screen GPFs and causes them to lose some data that they haven't managed to save? Do yourself a favor and save all of your changes—even the fun ones—for the next release.

If you have been making continuous changes to your application's design, you have probably experienced the feeling of trying to hit a moving target. Late changes to applications are a major cause of problems. As more and more functionality is added late in a project, it is very difficult to ensure that the newest changes have been properly tested, as shown in Figure 20.3.

Figure 20.3.
Adding features to your application after testing begins may cause test-coverage problems.

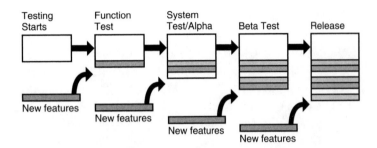

This discussion applies to changes that add functions to your application. Fixing bugs is a completely different problem that is the subject of the next section.

Fixing Faults Discovered After the Last Minute

After you decide that no new changes will be made to your application and that the release is absolutely complete, what happens if a new fault is discovered? A fault can't really be treated in the same way as a functional change, because every fault should be corrected before the application is released.

In the worst possible case, you have successfully completed all of the functional tests, alpha tests, beta tests, and release candidates. Then one new incident report is received just as you are ready to start duplicating disks (or worse, after you have duplicated the disks). Now what do you do?

The best answer is, "It depends." You basically have two options: you can stop the release and fix the fault, or you can fix the fault in a later release. There are a number of factors to consider when you are deciding between these two options, including:

☐ **The likelihood of the fault occurring.** If the fault occurs every time the application runs, you'll need to fix it, even if the fault is minor. If it almost never happens in everyday use and the fault is minor, you may be able to get away with documenting it as a known bug that will be fixed in the next release.

☐ **The severity of the fault.** If the fault has severe consequences, it may be a good idea to correct the fault, even if it rarely occurs. Fault severity is a relative term, and you'll have to decide what makes up a severe fault in your application.

☐ **The cost of correcting the fault.** This includes more than the cost of actually figuring out a solution to the fault. It also includes the extra testing that will be needed for the new version, and any release candidates that you will need to regenerate.

☐ **The time frame until the next planned release.** If you have a new release planned in a few weeks, you may be able to ship a few minor, documented faults. If the next release isn't for another year, the users of your application will prefer a bug-free release.

20

There should always be a healthy tension between your desire to add more features or weed out every last bug, and the need to get your product out the door, as shown in Figure 20.4. If you wait long enough, your product will be irrelevant when it's released. On the other hand, releasing a buggy or incomplete product will not help you in the long run.

Figure 20.4.
There are always forces that want the release delayed, and others that want it moved forward.

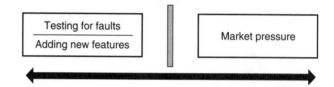

All of this talk about last-minute faults should remind you of the risk analysis that you did on Day 3, "Test Planning," and at other times. Any time that you have to decide between two options, consider the possible risks involved in each to help you decide on an appropriate choice.

Release Criteria

The release process is very critical to the success of your application. As you have been developing your project, every part of the development cycle has been followed by another that built on the previous phase. Usually, any problems that are discovered in the next phase can easily be corrected. However, the release of your application is the end of the road, and any new problems discovered will be found by real users of your application. That's what makes the release process so critical, and errors so costly.

The release criteria for your application should be almost the same as your exit criteria for the beta test. In addition, you may have some extra tasks that are carried out prior to release. The best way to make sure that your expectations for releasing applications are met consistently is to create a release checklist.

Creating a Release Checklist

It's a good idea to use a final-release checklist to make sure that you have completely addressed all of the issues that came up during your alpha and beta tests. The following list should be considered a minimum checklist for a relatively small application:

☐ **Documentation.** Are your internal and external documentation complete? Your internal development documentation will be used in the future when this application is modified. Take the time now to make sure it's correct.

☐ **Support.** Are you ready to support your application? In most cases this should be very easy to determine, especially if you're working alone.

□ **Open faults.** You should set a low threshold for the maximum number of minor open faults that can be reported for a shipping version of your application.

□ **Tools.** Are all of the tools you used to build the release tracked somehow? Unless this is a very small application, you should save all of the compilers, libraries, and other tools used to build the release. Ten years from now, you don't want to be desperately hunting down a copy of Visual C++ 2.0, when everyone else is using Visual C++ 10.0. Worse, you don't want to be looking for BillyBob's Bitmap Maker, last seen on some obscure BBS.

□ **Final-release masters.** If everything else is ready, it's time to build your final release disks. (This topic is covered in the next section.)

This list is just a guideline; you may want to add some more information for your application. If you're part of a larger organization, you may also need to make sure that training and marketing are ready for the product to be released.

Developer's Tip: The strength behind the release checklist, like all of the checklists discussed earlier, is that it is a living document. If this is your first application, your first list is likely to be fairly short. If you have any problems with this release, consider adding to your checklist.

In fact, in larger organizations you may actually have two separate releases for an application. A release to manufacturing (or something similar) is done by the development team; this is the green light to manufacture the disks and other material sent to end users. The commercial release is actually handled and coordinated through marketing or some other group.

Creating the Final-Release Disks

After you have decided on your absolute final release, it's time to create your master distribution disks. A few words of warning here, based partly on urban legends and partially from personal experience:

□ **Use fresh floppies.** Use brand new, unformatted floppies that you unwrap and format yourself. More than once, stories have circulated about applications shipped with extra files, or files that could just be undeleted. Even if those stories are pure fiction, why worry about it? Spend a few cents, and use brand new media for your masters.

□ **Test the installation.** After you create the master disks using your setup utility, test the installation package. There are actually cases where big (BIG) companies have shipped products with defective setup routines. Don't introduce your product to a new user by making it crash during the setup program. Do yourself a favor and take a few minutes to retest at least the setup portion of your application.

☐ **Scan for viruses.** After you install the package on a test machine, run a virus scan on the target machine. If you don't have virus protection enabled on your machines by default, you could be infected and not even know it. Don't become the software equivalent of Typhoid Mary. Get yourself some virus-scan software, and test your masters.

Documenting the Release

One of the best ways to reduce your support and maintenance costs is to make sure your documentation is in order before release. This applies to both internal and external documentation. *External documentation* is supplied to end users, and includes user guides, promotional materials, and training information. *Internal documentation* refers to everything else; primarily it is the documentation created while the application was being developed.

After the application is released it is too late to make sure that the documentation is ready. If you have been following along with your own project, your documentation should be complete at this point. You should just make a final check to ensure that all of your documents are in order.

Documents Used for Future Development

Before the application is released, make sure that all of your design, development, and testing documents are complete. This includes things such as your

☐ Functional specifications

☐ Module descriptions

☐ Test instructions and results

All of these documents were created as they were needed during the application's development. Make a quick check through all of your documentation and make sure that they are complete and up-to-date. There are two reasons to make sure that these documents are complete:

☐ You can re-create the release if you need to

☐ They can be used in the future if the application is modified

If your design documentation isn't available, both of these jobs will be much harder to perform.

End-User Release Documentation

Poor end-user documentation will create much higher support costs. This is true whether you're releasing an application to a few dozen of your friends or a few million customers of your word-processing package. Either way, helping users handle simple tasks over the telephone was not your prime objective when your project began.

Poor documentation also irritates your users. When your application is working well and they are using the application to handle everyday tasks, your users may never even crack the documentation. As you learned on Day 15, "Developing End-User Documentation," many users never read their documentation.

However, the first time they need to figure out an error message or understand an advanced use of your application, they'll look in the user manuals. If they can't get the information they need, they won't be very happy, and they may wind up calling you for support.

Selling Your Product

If you're a developer working in a large development organization, you probably have a sales and marketing staff that is responsible for selling your application. If so, then you probably don't need any help from this section of the book.

On the other hand, if you're a developer working alone, you may be wondering how to market your application. You probably don't have a lot of resources to put into marketing and selling your product, much less dealing with distributors, advertising, and market planning.

Distributing Your Application as Shareware

An alternative to selling your application through distributors is to release your application as shareware. Distributing your application as shareware allows you to reach a large number of potential users at a low cost.

Although marketing a shareware product is less expensive than traditional forms of marketing, there are still some costs involved. Successfully marketing your application as shareware requires more than just uploading your application to CompuServe and waiting for the registration fees to roll in.

The major selling point for shareware is that a user can "try before they buy." If you want to be successful when selling a shareware application, there are three items that need to be satisfied for your target audience:

- ☐ **Exposure.** Your product has to be available and noticed before a potential user will even read the description. If your application is only available on BBS or online services, you are limiting your potential customers.

- ☐ **Interest.** Your application should be available to your target audience, and it must serve some type of need. For example, the HELLLP! shareware package is available at many locations where a Windows programmer is likely to come across it. In addition, it serves a need in the Windows-programmer community.

20

☐ **Registration.** No matter how many people download your application and try it out, you have to convince them that it's worthwhile to register the application. Offering upgrades, hard-copy documentation, and extra support are some of the typical ways in which registration is encouraged.

If you can satisfy all of these requirements, you'll be on your way to successfully distributing your application as shareware.

Joining the ASP

The Association of Shareware Professionals (ASP) is an organization that helps shareware authors distribute their products. They set minimum standards for your application, and offer an ombudsman service to help resolve problems that occur between users and shareware developers.

Joining the ASP is easy, with only a few requirements:

☐ Your application must be nontrivial. This test means that a proficient programmer should need more than a day or two to develop a similar product.

☐ Your application must be fully functional, not a limited demo version. This fits in with the ASP's desire to have shareware seen as fully functional software that you can "try before you buy."

☐ Your application must meet standards for support and usability. Because the ASP is lending its seal of approval to your application, the association likes to promote products with no obvious bugs.

If you would like more information about the ASP, you can visit its CompuServe forum by typing GO SHAREWARE at any ! prompt.

Training and Support

Training and support are areas that vary a great deal among different types of applications. There are very few training requirements for an application like InfoMan, which is intended to be a simple end-user application. You may need to provide training and specialized support for applications that require the user to have certain skills.

Training

The type of training you provide varies with every application. As explained earlier, InfoMan will have no training other than the end-user documentation. However, if you are developing CAT scan software, you will probably need to offer training if you want your product to be successful.

There are two general categories of training that may be required for your application:

☐ **External training.** External training is offered to end users of your application. This may include training in areas that are, strictly speaking, outside the scope of your product. For example, if you develop spreadsheets, you may offer financial training, using your applications as a tool.

☐ **Internal training.** This category of training is provided for support, sales, and development members of your organization. Of course, they won't all receive exactly the same training, but the training would probably be more detailed than that offered externally. Generally, internal training focuses on supporting the user and the application, rather than on using the application.

 Textbook Tip: Training depends on the user, not the size of the project. End users of vertical applications, meant for a specialized market segment, may also need training.

The important thing to remember about your training is to use it as a tool. Planned properly, any training that you offer can reduce your support costs and make your application more attractive for your users.

End-User Support

There is a long history of applications that have failed because of poor end-user support. After a customer has purchased your application, the last thing they want to do is fight through your support process. Take the feedback that you have received during the alpha and beta tests and plan the type of support that will be offered to your end users. You should develop minimum standards for your support that can be tested after release to make sure that users are being supported well.

For example, a goal may be to answer all problem reports within 24 hours (or one week). If supporting the end user is a high priority, make your goals tighter. If you are a one-person development team, you may want looser support goals. Either way, try to develop concrete plans for your user support. Evaluating your support is covered on Day 21.

Having a Release Party

When it comes to your release party, you are on your own. Developing a Windows-based application is a lot of work, and you deserve to have a good time. Remember to invite everyone who participated in your alpha and beta tests, as well as anyone else who helped you during the

release. Don't stay out too late, though. There's still work to be done on Day 21, when you'll look at what you need to do after the release of your application.

Modification Notes

If you are modifying an existing project, you should probably use any release methods that are already in place, at least from the end user's point of view. It's okay to be more stringent on your release criteria internally, because it's easy to retrain engineers and programmers; retraining end users about new release methods is much harder.

Debugging the Process

If you run a set of final-release tests and discover a fault just before shipping, you have a problem. Unless the fault is extremely minor, you should create a new release candidate and send it out to a few users. If the new release candidate looks good, you can start the release process over again.

If the fault is extremely minor, you might be able to correct the problem and restart your release procedure. Bear in mind, however, that you are taking a risk, and more faults could have been introduced by the latest correction.

Collecting
Feedback

Today you'll learn about the things that should be done after your application is released. This includes collecting feedback from all parts of the design process, as well as from users of your program. You also should monitor your end-user support and start planning the next version of your application, or maybe even a completely new project.

You won't write any code today, and there's not even a time frame for some of the things you will learn. This chapter more or less covers the things that you should do during the lifetime of your application after it's released.

What Happens Next?

Your work isn't finished after the release. Now that the application is released, users of your application need support. Even if no faults are ever discovered by users of your application, there will be plenty of support questions. Interaction with other programs, questions from prospective users, and the occasional false-bug alert will keep you busy.

In addition to supporting the application, it's also the time to start thinking about the next release. If you removed planned features from your application during the design phase because of time constraints, you can start planning to add them into the next version.

Another important job you must do after you release the application is a self-evaluation. Now that the smoke has cleared, it's a good time to look back and try to find some areas to improve in your development process.

After the Project is Released

After your project has been released you should do several tasks right away. Although a lot of the work covered today may seem to be part of the next project, or unrelated to the application that was just launched, these tasks provide an ending to the project, which would be missing otherwise.

The main focus of all of the activities today is to provide feedback about your process of developing applications. This feedback will come from several places: end users, other development team members, even you. The important thing to remember is that it's all part of this project. Some of the activities that occur after an application is released are shown in Figure 21.1.

The following are the three main post-release activities:

- [ ] **The project wrap-up.** This is a document, and possibly a meeting where the project is reviewed. Places and activities that performed well, as well as areas of possible improvement, are identified.
- [ ] **Planning for future releases.** Plans for the next version of the application are started, as well as the investigation of other projects.

☐ **Providing end-user support.** This is an ongoing activity that will last for as long as the application has users. End-user support may begin today, but it will last much longer.

The activities on this list occur right after the end of the project and are not repeated. You'll learn each of these items in detail later today. On the other hand, providing support to end users is something that continues as long as your application has users.

Figure 21.1.
Activities after an
application is released.

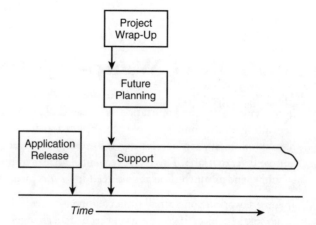

Millions of Happy Users

In most cases, your primary objective should be to keep your customers happy after the release of your application. Even if you have distributed the application to friends only, you still want to keep them happy, right?

Keeping end users happy means more than just fixing any faults that they report. It also means collecting other types of feedback and releasing updates to your application, hopefully with features requested by the application's users. You can encourage this type of feedback by asking your end users to send you ideas for new functionality, as well as reporting problems that they find with your application.

One unusual aspect of dealing with end users is that a happy user will tell a few friends about your application; word-of-mouth is a good way to pick up new users for your application. However, an unhappy user will do a much better job of spreading negative information about your product. Figure 21.2 shows a contrast between happy and unhappy users.

By encouraging users to participate in deciding which features are added to future versions of your application, you turn the feedback process into a positive experience for yourself and your users. Of course, you also will get a large number of useful suggestions about improving your product. You'll learn more on this topic later.

21

Figure 21.2.
Unhappy users spread the word more effectively than happy users.

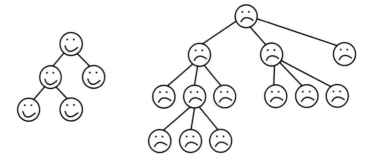

The Project Wrap-Up

The project wrap-up is a self evaluation of the development project, and is usually done immediately after the application is released. The project wrap-up can take several forms, depending on the complexity of your application and the size of the development team. If you have an informal wrap-up meeting, it's usually best to record the wrap-up as a document so that you can refer to it later. This is an excellent chance to improve your development process, so you should spend as much time as you need for a complete assessment.

If you are working on a small project alone, the project wrap-up will probably be an informal review of the project. If you have kept records of changes and incident reports, you can use them to refresh your memory. Larger teams should have some team members generate a project wrap-up report.

The project wrap-up is an important tool in improving your overall development quality, so make sure that it's given the priority it deserves. It's okay to make mistakes, especially if this is your first Windows application. However, it is not okay to keep making the same mistakes without learning from them.

Purpose of the Project Wrap-Up Meeting

If you are working as part of a team, it's a good idea to have a wrap-up meeting. The purpose of the wrap-up meeting is to begin to identify the parts of the project that worked well, and the parts that can be improved. Input from this meeting can be used to create the project wrap-up report.

It's important to have everyone involved in the development of your application participate in the meeting. If you have large teams, it may be better to have one member from each team at the meeting. The only way to get a good self-assessment is to make sure every part of the development process is represented, as shown in Figure 21.3.

Figure 21.3.
Every part of the development team should participate in the project wrap-up.

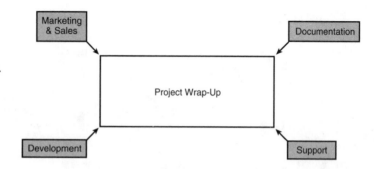

The goal of the meeting should be to improve your development process. If there were problems during the development of your application, you should try to identify ways to avoid those problems in future projects.

> **Developer's Tip:** If you work alone, planning the meeting will be easy, but you must evaluate yourself. Self-evaluations are always difficult, but it's important for you to perform this evaluation honestly if you want to improve.

Using Information from the Wrap-Up Meeting

If you have a productive project wrap-up meeting, you will probably walk away from it with lots of ideas for improving your development process. In most cases, you should pick a few improvements for your next project, and save the rest for future consideration.

It's much easier to concentrate on a few areas of improvement than to rewrite your development process for every new project. There are several reasons for this:

☐ **It's difficult to give feedback while changing.** It is difficult to evaluate different development projects if your development process is completely changed for each new release. Progress can be tracked more easily when you select a few areas for improvement.

☐ **There is a cost associated with change.** Every change that you make in your development process will cost you something. By making a few changes at a time, you can reduce the cost of improvement.

☐ **Evolution is easier than revolution.** If you constantly rework your development process, every project will start from scratch. By identifying a few areas for improvement in every project, you can manage this change and still get the benefits of previous experience.

On the other hand, if you didn't get much feedback at all from your wrap-up meeting, you should look harder. Any improvement is better than no improvement at all, and every development process can be improved, no matter who you are.

Feedback and the Development Process

In previous chapters you learned the need for, and benefit of, continuous improvement. Information that you receive from the project wrap-up meeting and report can be used to help improve the development process. In this section you will learn other sources of information that can help you improve, and how to use that information to make better Windows applications.

The development process itself will be a source for some of this information. Incident reports, measurements, and metrics are some of the tools created during the project that you can use for improvement now, before your next project begins.

Looking for Improvement Areas

The first place to look for improvement ideas is the project wrap-up. By targeting areas for improvement identified in the wrap-up, you can improve the development of your next project. Places where things didn't work smoothly or had high fault rates should be improved first.

Showstopper: Try to avoid adding bureaucracy into your development process. Sometimes there is a tendency among groups of people to wrap any problem in paperwork and procedures. When you find an area that needs improvement, consider removing existing procedures to streamline your process, as well as adding new procedures.

Features for New Releases

Ideas that couldn't be added to your application during the last development cycle should be considered now. For example, if you had a list of features that couldn't be added on Day 20, "Release," you can consider adding them now.

Developer's Tip: Before deciding on new features to be added to your application, you should analyze your application as well as all of the features that are candidates for the next release.

Later you will learn some ideas for prioritizing new features, as well as scheduling new releases of your application.

If you have any ideas for similar projects, now is the time to consider those as well. If you reuse new classes built for this project you can reduce the cost and development time of the new project. Figure 21.4 is an example of reusing classes for a new project.

Figure 21.4.
Using products from one development cycle for newer projects.

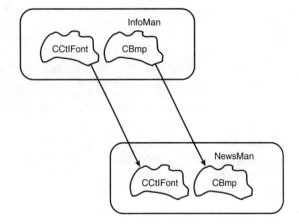

This is the best type of reuse, because it is completely free for the new project. This is a good indicator that the classes that are being developed are general and reusable. On Day 11, "Error Reporting and Metrics," you learned different types of software-quality measurements. Encouraging this type of reuse should be a goal of any measurements that you put in place.

Deferred Incident Reports

While you are planning new releases, remember that you need to plan releases for bug fixes as well. If you have incident reports that are currently being investigated or have been deferred to a bug-fix release, your first update should address these incident reports.

This initial update to correct outstanding problems should be planned as soon as possible. If you can correct faults before your end users notice them, you'll be way ahead of the game. This initial update should not contain new features, unless the lack of the feature is considered a bug. Figure 21.5 shows a release schedule for an application, with a bug-fix release scheduled soon after the primary release.

Figure 21.5.
Planning a bug-fix update after the main release.

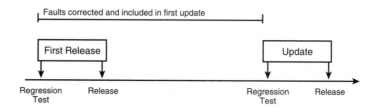

Except in unusual circumstances, you shouldn't plan new updates to fix minor bugs every time one is reported. This is costly in several ways, and doesn't significantly help the overall quality in the long run. Scheduling maintenance releases is covered in more detail later.

Accepting User-Problem Reports

In general, the sooner you discover a fault in your application, the better. During development, faults that are discovered and fixed early have a much smaller chance of causing problems after release, because they undergo more testing than faults discovered late in the process. Even after the application is released, you should strive to discover faults as soon as possible.

Faults that are quickly reported will be corrected before faults that aren't reported at all. Unreported faults still exist and still frustrate your users, but unless you know about them, you can't fix them. Your goal should be to get those incident reports as quickly as possible. The best possible scenario is to be notified whenever a user discovers a fault. That way, you can be sure that you know every time a user has a problem with your application, enabling you to turn around a solution as soon as possible.

The forms (or bug-reporting program) that were used for incident reports during the alpha and beta tests should be updated for use during the general release. Update the forms after any feedback is received during the beta, and make sure forms include a way for users to request new features. Distribute the new forms with your application, and encourage users to report faults.

Developer's Tip: The time-honored method to encourage feedback from users is to give them some sort of reward for reporting bugs or requesting new features. If a user requests a new feature that is included in a later version of your application, give that user a free upgrade. If a user reports a bug first, that user gets some sort of small reward. Common thank-you gifts include T-shirts or other promotional giveaways.

Classifying Reports

You should classify all incident reports according to their priority. These reports are feedback from end users and should be addressed, even though some should receive more attention than others. The number of different priority levels will depend on your application and the amount of detail required in your organization.

Showstopper: In most cases, you should not fix bugs in the order in which they are reported to you. Unless you have one incident report that has not been corrected yet, you should always prioritize your fault-resolution activities so that the most critical problems are addressed first.

After you have prioritized all of your open problems, you should correct them in the order in which you receive them, if possible.

For most applications, there are at least four priorities for incident reports:

- ☐ **Highest.** Most users are affected by this type of fault, which causes severe problems.
- ☐ **Lowest.** Either few users are affected, or minor impact to users when experienced.
- ☐ **Request.** A request for new functionality; the request is not a reported fault.
- ☐ **Duplicate.** A new report of a known fault.

If you have a large staff or a complex operation, you may want to add some priority levels to create more control over scheduling. If you have a simple application and work alone, you may be able to eliminate some of the priorities in the previous list that don't apply to you.

Providing Updates to Users

If you are the only user of the software application that you've written, handling updates is easy. After the number of users grows past this point, things get more complicated. In the best possible case, there will be no updates to distribute. However, unless your application is fairly small, that's not very likely.

Even if you don't need to distribute a series of updates today, you should decide on a distribution method now, so that it is in place when you need it later. Your goal when you release any updates should be to give all of your users the newest released version of your application. Ideally, your update should be widely distributed and easy for users to install.

If the update is difficult to install, or if some users don't know about the update, your support costs will go up, not down, with the new release. Users will still use the old software, complete with bugs solved in the new release. Meanwhile, they'll need support to find or install the update.

> **Note:** Many of these issues apply primarily to updates that fix bugs. Updates that supply new features for your application are covered in the next section.

Planning an update requires almost as much work as a new release, as covered on Day 20. You should run a set of regression tests against the update, and you should probably consider a trial release to a few beta users to make sure the update works as expected. This is not the kind of work you want to repeat constantly, so you should bundle your releases so that several bugs are fixed at the same time, as shown in Figure 21.6.

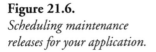
Figure 21.6.
Scheduling maintenance releases for your application.

Occasionally, a fault will be reported that can't wait until the next scheduled update. If an emergency like this happens to you, try to limit the number of users that receive the emergency fix. When the next scheduled update is released, make sure that all of the users with the emergency fix get the official update.

Planning Future Releases

So much for bugs; now take a look at planning future releases of your application. The planning for your next release should, in most cases, be similar to the planning for the current version. Of course, now you have the benefit of experience, so you can plan with more detail and, hopefully, a little more accuracy.

There are several factors that will influence your planning for future releases:

☐ **Your development speed.** The amount of time it takes you to develop new features will have a direct impact on the number of features added to each release.

☐ **Features offered by similar applications.** If you are selling this application as a commercial product or shareware, you need to keep up with applications offered by your competitors. For example, once upon a time Windows applications rarely used three-dimensional user interfaces. Within six months after Microsoft released CTL3D.LIB for easily creating a 3-D look, it seemed as though every application had 3-D effects. Applications that didn't offer 3-D effects looked dated.

☐ **Features requested by end users.** Features requested by end users should be given special attention, because they are already using your application and can identify what needs to be added.

In most cases, it's better to offer smaller, incremental releases with a small number of new features, rather than large releases that require long development cycles. It will be much easier for the end user, and you will find it easier to maintain your high quality level.

Prioritizing New Features

After you have a list of new features that you are considering for the next version of your application, the next step is to prioritize each feature relative to the others. Features that fit well together should be prioritized as a group.

Examine each feature as though it were the only feature to be added to your application, and then weigh it against the others. One good way to determine the relative priority among various features is to place them into three categories: high, medium, and low. If that's not enough detail, you can refine the priorities within those three categories. Figure 21.7 shows different features considered for InfoMan grouped into categories.

Figure 21.7.
Prioritizing new features for future releases.

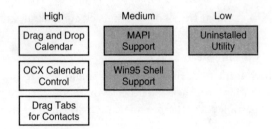

Pay attention to new features that are showing up in other applications. For example, the tabbed dialog boxes in Word for Windows quickly spread to other applications, including InfoMan. If you see new controls or features that help make the user more productive, don't wait for them to be requested; add them as soon as possible.

Scheduling New Releases

When you are scheduling new versions of your application that contain new features, plan the releases so that users will feel comfortable with your release schedule. Of course, this varies between applications, but you should always pace yourself so that the user is neither overwhelmed with a constant flow of new releases nor left wondering when a new version of the application is to be released.

In general, shareware is updated with new versions more often than commercial software. This is due partly to the lower cost of distribution, because most shareware is distributed online. Shareware software is also updated frequently with user-requested features, because the feedback loop between shareware developer and user is much shorter than with commercial applications.

Modification Notes

If you have existing procedures for collecting feedback, you should consider using them. It is much easier to compare feedback between previous releases and your new release if you collect feedback the same way. However, if you aren't happy with the amount or the quality of the feedback you've been getting, give the methods presented today a try.

If you have feedback available from previous releases, you should try to determine in which areas you are improving, and which areas may need more attention during your next project.

Debugging the Process

You might have problems getting feedback from your users for several reasons:

☐ They are happy, but aren't giving you feedback spontaneously for some reason.

☐ They are really unhappy, and don't want to give you feedback.

☐ Your instructions for feedback are unclear, and the users can't figure out how to provide feedback.

Hopefully, if you have this problem it's due to the first reason. Also, the last item should have been ironed out during your alpha and beta testing. In any case, if you aren't receiving the amount of feedback you expect, you should be proactive and survey your users. Feedback is an important part of improving, and if you aren't getting it, go out and look for it.

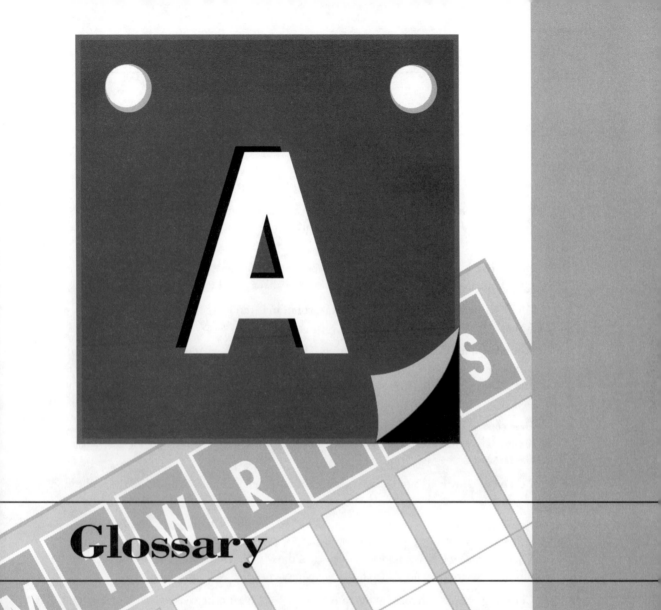

Glossary

Abstract   A general idea or concept. In C++, abstract is often used to refer to classes that are meant to be only base classes. A class that contains a pure virtual function is an abstract class, and no instances of the class may be created.

ACM   See **The Association for Computing Machinery**.

AFX   A prefix used by the team at Microsoft that creates the MFC library. *A* stands for Application, *F* for Framework, and apparently, the *X* doesn't stand for anything (but it looks cool).

Alpha test   The first round of acceptance testing for an application in an unstructured environment. Alpha testing takes place between system-level testing and the beta tests.

ASCII (American Standard Code for Information Interchange)   A standard for exchanging text information between computers. Most "straight text" is ASCII encoded.

Association for Computing Machinery, The (ACM)   The first organization for computing professionals, started in 1947. The ACM sponsors numerous conferences, contests, and awards, and also publishes dozens of newsletters and journals. Members often belong to one of the many Special Interest Groups (SIGS) that specialize in certain areas of computer science.

Base class   A class from which another class inherits some of its functionality. Abstract classes are base classes that are never used to create objects directly. However, not all base classes are abstract.

Beta test   The final round of acceptance testing, which includes shipments of the application to actual customer sites.

Class   The basic unit of programming in a C++ program. Classes in C++ are used to model different parts of the application's domain. For example, the different visual elements of a Windows dialog box are modeled as classes in the MFC class library. There are also classes for threads, file services, and other common components of a Windows application.

Coupling   A measurement of the communication that exists between two or more parts of an application. In general, classes that are tightly coupled have dependencies that reduce their reusability.

Dangling pointer   A pointer to a memory location that is no longer valid. If a block of memory is released when you use free or delete, the pointer should usually be set to zero. It is not possible to determine whether the pointer's value is valid after the memory has been released, so if you fail to reset a pointer, it can be difficult to discover programming errors.

DLGEDIT   An older dialog-box editor supplied with the Win32 SDK. Although DLGEDIT does not have many of the features available in the Visual C++ resource tools, it does support Custom Controls, unlike Visual C++.

DLL   See **Dynamic Link Library**.

DllMain   The library entry point for DLLs in Win32. This procedure is called by the operating system whenever the DLL is loaded or released. It replaces the `LibMain` and `WEP` procedures used in 16-bit Windows applications.

DOC file   A file created and saved in the Word for Windows document file format.

Dynamic Link Library   A binary file, similar to an executable (EXE) file, that can be used by several applications at the same time.

Easter egg   A secret credit screen or information message hidden by the designers of an application. Word for Windows, CorelDRAW!, and Windows 3.1 are examples of programs that had hidden Easter Eggs. The Word for Windows 2.0 Easter egg had a small army attack an evil WordPerfect monster, followed by a credit screen (with fireworks) listing the development team.

Extension DLL   A Dynamic Link Library that contains classes derived from MFC base classes. An Extension DLL can be used to easily pass objects between the EXE and DLL.

Freeware   Software that is provided completely free of charge, although it may still be copyrighted. Shareware is not freeware.

Functional specification   A document that spells out all of the features and functionality that an application is to provide. To really be useful, the functional specification should be completed before the design and coding of the application begins. The design and test planning should be based on the functional specification.

Guideline   A suggestion or preferred method of carrying out a task. A guideline is generally less stringent than a standard. Many coding and programming handbooks are guidelines, because it is difficult to lay down firm rules for every possible situation.

HAS-A   A common description for the relationship between two classes. In a class diagram that shows the relationship between different classes that model an automobile, the wheel and tire classes are in a HAS-A relationship, because each wheel HAS-A tire.

Header   The declarations for each class are usually placed in a header file which is included in every module that uses the interface. This is a characteristic of C that has been carried over into C++. It is generally considered bad form to define anything in a header file.

Inline function   A request to the compiler to insert a function's body wherever it is called, instead of generating a function call. This is useful for small functions, where the overhead for the function call may be a significant part of the entire cost of executing the function. Inline functions also enable C-style macros to be eliminated.

Instance   An individual object. Each object created from a class or other type is a unique instance of that type.

Interface   The class declaration that contains the visible functions and data members. In a C++ class declaration, some of the private and implementation details of the class are also visible. However, strictly speaking, these details are not part of the interface.

IS-A   A common description for a type of relationship that exists between classes. When a class is derived from a base class, the derived class has an IS-A relationship with the base class. For example, assume that there is a base class called CAutomobile. If CSportsCar and CStationWagon are derived from CAutomobile, then they each have an IS-A relationship with CAutomobile; CSportsCar IS-A CAutomobile.

Low-level design   The portion of the design process that is concerned with the design of individual classes and modules that make up an application.

MDI   See **Multiple Document Interface**.

Memory leak   Memory that has been allocated for an application but cannot be reclaimed, usually due to a programming error. Any memory that is dynamically allocated must always keep at least one pointer to the memory block. If the reference to the memory location is lost, the memory cannot be returned to the operating system.

Message map   The method used by MFC applications to route Windows messages to the correct functions.

Multiple Document Interface (MDI)   A standard originally developed by IBM that specifies how applications should handle more than a single document at one time. This standard specifies how child windows should be minimized and maximized, and how they should interact with the main frame window.

Object Linking and Embedding (OLE)   A standard developed by Microsoft, with feedback from other developers, for allowing servers and containers to interact with each other over an open interface. The interface specified by OLE is not language-specific, so it is possible for applications written in Basic, C++, and Pascal to all interact with each other through OLE.

OCX   See **OLE Custom Control**.

OLE   See **Object Linking and Embedding**.

OLE Custom Control   A custom control that uses OLE interfaces to interact with an OLE Custom Control Container. These controls are replacements for the older VBX controls, which could be used only on the 16-bit Windows platform.

Pure virtual function   A virtual function that is declared, but has no definition. A class that contains at least one pure virtual function is an abstract class, and cannot have objects created directly from it.

Regression   Previously unknown or corrected errors that appear in later releases of an application. It is not unusual for fault-correction activities to introduce regressions into an application. When configuration management is not rigidly enforced, previously corrected faults may reappear as regressions.

Regression testing   A test phase that specifically tests for the presence of regressions. A good regression test will retest previously corrected faults, as well as a core part of the application's functionality.

Release candidate   A version of an application that is tested just before the official release of the product. Release candidates are often shipped to a few beta sites to make sure the application is stable and bug-free.

Resource leak   Similar to a memory leak, except that it involves Windows resources. If a resource is allocated but not properly released, under some conditions it may not be possible for the application or the operating system to recover that resource. After a period of time, all available resources may be exhausted by a resource leak.

Rich Text Format (RTF)   A format for document files created by Microsoft. RTF is a type of text mark-up language, which means that the data contains formatting information embedded in the actual document text. RTF files are used as source files when you create a Windows Help program.

RTF   See **Rich Text Format**.

Shareware   Software that is distributed at little or no cost to prospective users. This enables the user to evaluate the software before it is purchased. If the user finds the software useful, he or she can pay a registration fee to the shareware author.

Spiral development   A development method that divides analysis, design, coding, and testing into several iterations that are repeated during the development process. Because the development moves through each development phase several times, this is known as spiral development.

Standard   A set of rules that should be followed. Unlike a guideline, standards are expected to be completely enforced all of the time. See also **Guidelines**.

Subclass   In a Windows application, subclassing means to substitute a new message procedure for the current one used by the window or control. In C++ and other object-oriented languages, a subclass is derived from a base class, and usually provides extra functionality not present in the base class.

System-level design   A design phase that identifies classes to be used in the application, and the relationships between those classes.

Test Basic   The programming language used in MS-Test to write test scripts.

Tuco   In the Sergio Leone spaghetti western *The Good, the Bad, and the Ugly*, Tuco was "the Bad." In addition to being hung by the neck several times and escaping, he also had the memorable line, "There are two kinds of people in this world. Those who use MFC, and those who have to dig." Or something like that.

V and V   See **Verification and Validation**.

Verification and Validation (V and V)   Another name for application testing. Verification tests make sure that the program was constructed properly. Validation tests ensure that the application was built according to the specifications.

Virtual function   A member function usually accessed through a base class pointer that is evaluated at runtime.

Waterfall model   A software development method where analysis, design, coding, and testing are all distinct phases. Each of these phases must be completed before the next one begins. One problem with the waterfall model is that providing feedback to earlier phases can be difficult. See also **Spiral development**.

Win32   The 32-bit programming API that is used for developing Windows applications. The same API, with minor differences, can be used to develop applications for both Windows 95 and Windows NT.

Work-Model
Diagrams

The figures in this appendix show the work-model diagrams used during the InfoMan project.

Basic Development Process

The analysis, design, and coding phases of the development process are iterative, as shown in Figure B.1. In real life, most successful projects have two or more of these activities going on at the same time.

Figure B.1.
Iterative development as used in the InfoMan project.

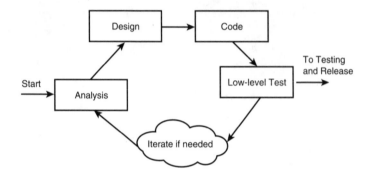

Test Phases in InfoMan

The test phases for InfoMan are split into several distinct phases, each of which has a different role. Regression testing was performed after every test phase.

Figure B.2.
The test phases used in InfoMan.

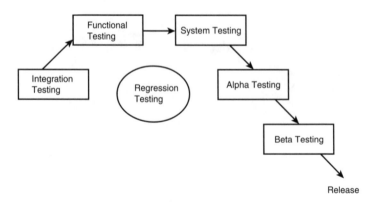

MFC Class
Diagrams

The figures in this appendix show the relationships between the different classes in the Microsoft Foundation Classes. Simple classes that are not involved in inheritance are not shown.

Basic Application Classes

The classes in Figure C.1 help provide the framework for the Document View architecture used by the MFC classes.

Figure C.1.
The basic framework classes derived from CObject *used in the MFC library.*

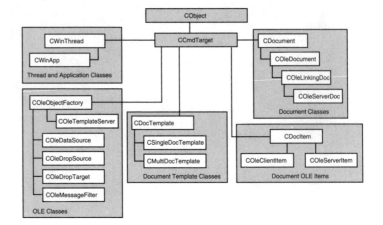

Dialog Boxes and Controls

The classes in Figure C.2 are the dialog boxes and controls provided by MFC. User dialog boxes are generally derived from CDialog.

The classes shown in Figure C.3 are primarily considered "view" classes used in the MFC Document/View model. The CSplitterWnd and CPropertySheet classes are derived directly from CWnd.

Figure C.2.
The dialog and control window classes provided by MFC.

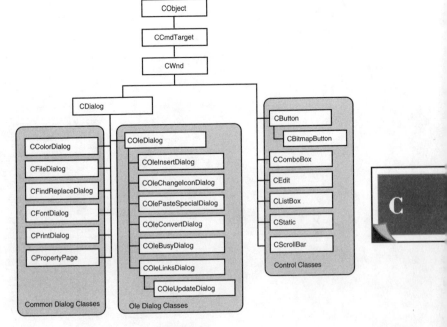

Figure C.3.
The dialog and control window classes provided by MFC.

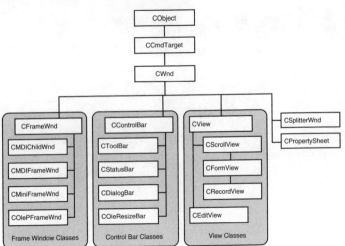

Collections

Collections in MFC are all derived from CObject, as shown in Figure C.4. The CArray, CMap, and CList classes are all template classes.

Figure C.4.
The Collection classes provided by MFC.

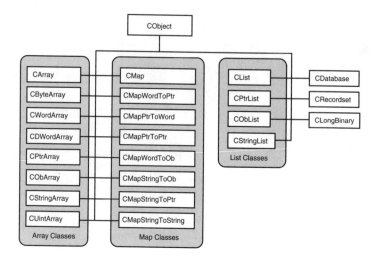

Utility Classes

The utility classes shown in Figure C.5 are all derived directly from CObject.

Figure C.5.
Various MFC utility classes derived directly from CObject.

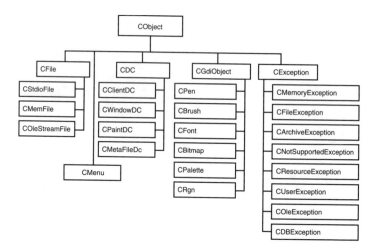

Developer's Resources

Every developer can use a little help now and then. There are times when no matter how many books you've read or how much experience you have, you still need help to solve that last problem. The resources listed in this appendix can not only help you solve those problems that pop up at the worst possible time, they can also help you become a much better developer overall.

The Microsoft Developer Network

No listing of resources for Windows developers would be complete without a reference to the Microsoft Developer Network (MSDN). Four times a year, MSDN members receive a CD that contains all sorts of information that isn't available through any other channels. Tips, white papers, product documentation—it's all here and searchable on CD-ROM.

The MSDN level 2 membership also provides access to all of the SDKs, DDKs, and toolkits offered by Microsoft for desktop development. This package is available for a fraction of the price of the individual components.

Usenet

If you have access to the Internet, CompuServe, Prodigy, or most other online services, you have access to Usenet news.

Using Usenet News

It's a good idea to read the current articles in a newsgroup before posting articles of your own.

All newsgroups have a list of Frequently Asked Questions (FAQ). It's considered poor manners to ask a question that's included in the FAQ. If you are new to Usenet, you should read the articles posted in the newsgroups first. The two newsgroups listed here carry useful information for new users.

`news.announce.newusers` This is a moderated group, which means that postings to the newsgroup are controlled by a group moderator. This group always has a number of articles that are useful to new users. You should read this group before you post an article.

`news.newusers.questions` This group is a good location for you to post questions about Usenet in general. It's intended for new users, so you aren't expected to be a Usenet guru.

Interesting Usenet Groups
for Visual C++ Developers

Although many of the Usenet programming groups are UNIX-related, there are a number of newsgroups that contain interesting articles for Visual C++ programmers. Currently, eleven groups are used for discussing Windows programming. Because new groups can be created on Usenet at any time, look for new groups in the comp.os.ms-windows hierarchy.

comp.os.ms-windows.programmer.misc   This is the "general purpose" newsgroup for Windows programming. If your question or topic doesn't fit in one of the other newsgroups, post it here.

comp.os.ms-windows.programmer.controls   A newsgroup dedicated to discussing controls used in Windows programming. Writing custom controls, using class libraries, and user-interface issues are good topics for this group.

comp.os.ms-windows.programmer.drivers   This group is used for discussing the development of device drivers for Windows. It is not the place to post questions if you are looking for an unusual driver, even if you are a programmer. Remember, the naming tree works backward; this group is for "driver programmers."

comp.os.ms-windows.programmer.graphics   This group is used for all sorts of Windows graphics questions.

comp.os.ms-windows.programmer.memory   If you are having a problem handling memory storage or allocation, this is the place to go for information.

comp.os.ms-windows.programmer.multimedia   Discussions about multimedia programming in Windows. Includes Video for Windows, WinG, WinToon, and third-party libraries.

comp.os.ms-windows.programmer.networks   A group for discussing all sorts of network programming issues in Windows.

comp.os.ms-windows.programmer.ole   This group primarily talks about OLE 2.0, though there is also discussion about DDE, OLE 1.0, and OLE controls.

comp.os.ms-windows.programmer.tools   If you have a question about the Visual C++ environment or MFC class library, this is the group for you. Any questions about the tools and compilers used to develop Windows programs should be asked here.

comp.os.ms-windows.programmer.win32   This is a general-purpose group for discussing Win32 programming issues. If you can't find a more appropriate group, post your question here.

D

`comp.os.ms-windows.programmer.winhelp`   This newsgroup discusses how to program Windows Help. Several authors of tools for creating Windows help files are frequent contributors here.

> **Note:** The hierarchy used in the `comp.os.ms-windows.programmer` newsgroups leaves something to be desired. Sometimes it can be difficult to determine the proper group in which to post.
>
> If your article can be narrowly defined to fit in to one of the specific newsgroups, you should post there first. For example, if you're programming in Windows NT, and you have a question on `BitBlt`, you should try posting in the graphics newsgroup. If your question involves multithreading or the security API, then post to the Win32 group. If your question involves the subset of the GDI system that exists only in Windows NT, you should post first to the graphics group, and if you don't get results, try the more general newsgroup.

Newsgroups for Professional Organizations

The two largest organizations for computing professionals, the ACM and IEEE, have newsgroups on Usenet. These groups are open to everyone—you don't need to be a member of either organization. However, discussion in these groups is generally of interest only if you are already a member, or are considering joining.

Articles in these groups usually consist of information about upcoming conferences and membership questions, although occasionally a political issue will generate a great deal of discussion for a few weeks. The newsgroups that carry ACM and IEEE articles are listed here:

- [ ] `comp.org.acm`
- [ ] `comp.org.ieee`

General Programming Newsgroups

The groups listed next are not specifically used for Windows programming questions or discussion. However, if you have a question about object-oriented design, or a question about overloading operators in C++, one of these groups will be a better location to post your article.

`comp.lang.c++`   Includes questions and discussions about the C++ language. This group has a great deal of traffic and can be difficult to follow, so it's a good idea to post elsewhere if you can. It's also considered bad etiquette to post questions that are best answered in another group, such as Windows programming questions.

`comp.object`   Includes discussions about object-oriented computing, including object-oriented design.

`comp.software-eng`   This group follows all aspects of software engineering. If you have questions about testing or planning, ask them here. If you need advice about a particular design method or tool, this group is a good place to get it.

`comp.software.config-mgmt`   This newsgroup talks about configuration management and tools.

`comp.software.testing`   A newsgroup that focuses on software testing. Tools and methods for different types of testing are often the subject of articles in this group.

Professional Organizations

There are a few professional organizations that can be helpful for software developers. By joining one of the following organizations, you can get information about conferences and events that can help you grow and become a better developer. Most of these organizations also publish a newsletter or magazine for their members. The ACM and IEEE also publish a large number of peer-reviewed journals that are available at a discount to members.

The Association for Computing Machinery

P.O. Box 12114
Church Street Station
New York, NY 10249
+1 (212) 626-0500
E-mail: `info@acm.org`

The Institute of Electrical and Electronic Engineers Computer Society

10662 Los Vaquitos Circle
Los Alamitos, CA 90720

American Society for Quality Control

161 West Wisconsin Avenue
Milwaukee, WI 53203

Association for Shareware Professionals

545 Grover Road
Muskegon, MI 49442-9427

Index

designing

Sams
Learning
Center

SAMS
PUBLISHING

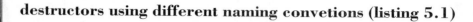

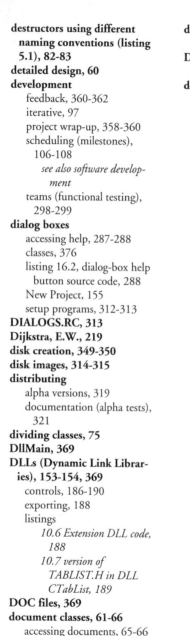

Add to Your Sams Library Today with the Best Books for Programming, Operating Systems, and New Technologies

The easiest way to order is to pick up the phone and call
1-800-428-5331
between 9:00 a.m. and 5:00 p.m. EST.
For faster service please have your credit card available.

ISBN	Quantity	Description of Item	Unit Cost	Total Cost
0-672-30532-1		Master Visual C++ 2, 2nd Edition	$49.99	
0-672-30284-5		Secrets of the Visual C++ Masters	$34.95	
0-672-30487-2		Teach Yourself Object-Oriented Programming with Visual C++ 1.5 in 21 Days	$29.95	
0-672-30535-6		Teach Yourself Turbo C++ Visual Edition for Windows in 21 Days	$29.99	
0-672-30534-8		Teach Yourself Visual C++ 2 in 21 Days, Third Edition	$29.99	
0-672-30370-1		Visual C++ Developer's Guide	$49.95	
0-672-30493-7		What Every Visual C++ 2 Programmer Should Know	$29.99	
0-672-30364-7		Win32 API Desktop Reference	$49.95	
0-672-30695-6		Developing PowerBuilder 4 Applications, Third Edition	$45.00	
0-672-30562-3		Teach Yourself Game Programming in 21 Days	$39.99	
0-672-30715-4		Teach Yourself Visual Basic in 21 Days, Bestseller Edition	$35.00	
❏ 3 ½" Disk		Shipping and Handling: See information below.		
❏ 5 ¼" Disk		TOTAL		

Shipping and Handling: $4.00 for the first book, and $1.75 for each additional book. Floppy disk: add $1.75 for shipping and handling. If you need to have it NOW, we can ship product to you in 24 hours for an additional charge of approximately $18.00, and you will receive your item overnight or in two days. Overseas shipping and handling adds $2.00 per book and $8.00 for up to three disks. Prices subject to change. Call for availability and pricing information on latest editions.

201 W. 103rd Street, Indianapolis, Indiana 46290

1-800-428-5331 — Orders   1-800-835-3202 — FAX   1-800-858-7674 — Customer Service

PLUG YOURSELF INTO...

MACMILLAN INFORMATION SUPERLIBRARY™

que · SAMS PUBLISHING · Hayden Books · que COLLEGE

NRP · alpha books · Brady · ADOBE PRESS

THE MACMILLAN INFORMATION SUPERLIBRARY™

Free information and vast computer resources from the world's leading computer book publisher—online!

FIND THE BOOKS THAT ARE RIGHT FOR YOU!

A complete online catalog, plus sample chapters and tables of contents give you an in-depth look at *all* of our books, including hard-to-find titles. It's the best way to find the books you need!

- **STAY INFORMED** with the latest computer industry news through our online newsletter, press releases, and customized Information SuperLibrary Reports.

- **GET FAST ANSWERS** to your questions about MCP books and software.

- **VISIT** our online bookstore for the latest information and editions!

- **COMMUNICATE** with our expert authors through e-mail and conferences.

- **DOWNLOAD SOFTWARE** from the immense MCP library:
    - Source code and files from MCP books
    - The best shareware, freeware, and demos

- **DISCOVER HOT SPOTS** on other parts of the Internet.

- **WIN BOOKS** in ongoing contests and giveaways!

TO PLUG INTO MCP: → **WORLD WIDE WEB: http://www.mcp.com**

GOPHER: gopher.mcp.com

FTP: ftp.mcp.com

Home Page · What's New · Bookstore · Reference Desk · Software Library · Macmillan Overview · Talk to Us

What's on the CD

The companion CD contains applications and code from the book.

During the installation, you may choose which files you would like to have copied to your hard drive.

Software Installation Instructions

1. Insert the CD into your CD-ROM drive.

2. From File Manager or Program Manager, choose Run from the File menu.

3. Type <*drive*>INSTALL and press Enter, where <*drive*> corresponds to the drive letter of your CD-ROM drive. For example, if your CD-ROM is drive D:, type D:INSTALL and press Enter.

4. Follow the on-screen instructions in the installation program. Files will be installed to a directory named \DVC unless you choose a different directory during installation.